Charles Darwin

Other Titles in the
People Who Made History Series

Adolf Hitler
John F. Kennedy
Martin Luther King Jr.

People Who Made History

Charles Darwin

Don Nardo, *Book Editor*

David L. Bender, *Publisher*
Bruno Leone, *Executive Editor*
Bonnie Szumski, *Editorial Director*
David M. Haugen, *Managing Editor*
Scott Barbour, *Series Editor*

Greenhaven Press, San Diego, CA

Library of Congress Cataloging-in-Publication Data

Charles Darwin / Don Nardo, book editor.
    p.   cm. — (People who made history)
    Includes bibliographical references and index.
    ISBN 0-7377-0081-5 (lib. bdg. : alk. paper). —
ISBN 0-7377-0080-7 (pbk. : alk. paper)
    1. Evolution (Biology) 2. Darwin, Charles, 1809–1882.
I. Nardo, Don, 1947– . II. Series.
QH366.2.C458   2000
576.8'2—dc21   99-19093
                                                   CIP

Every effort has been made to trace the owners of copyrighted material. The articles in this volume may have been edited for content, length, and/or reading level. The titles have been changed to enhance the editorial purpose of the Opposing Viewpoints® concept. Those interested in locating the original source will find the complete citation on the first page of each article.

Cover photo: Popperfoto/Archive Photos

Copyright ©2000 by Greenhaven Press, Inc.
PO Box 289009
San Diego, CA 92198-9009
Printed in the U.S.A.

CONTENTS

Chapter 1: Pre-Darwinian Theories for Life's Origins

Before Darwin published his *Origin of Species* in 1859, only a handful of people had given any thought to the origins of life beyond the traditional Biblical explanation. Most, including Darwin himself in his youth, accepted without question that plant and animal species were the result of God's conscious design.

Charles Darwin did not invent the idea of plant and animal species changing and evolving over time. His grandfather, Erasmus, was one of several scientific theorists who proposed evolutionary ideas of their own, notions that Darwin later built on and/or refuted in his own work.

Few people are aware that almost a century before Charles Darwin presented his widely debated theory of evolution by natural selection, a French scientist named Pierre Maupertuis advocated an evolutionary thesis that in several ways foreshadowed the work of later biologists and geneticists.

The ideas of French naturalist Jean Baptiste Lamarck constitute one of the most important precursors of Darwin's evolutionary theory. Although Lamarck was on the right track, much of his work was ultimately invalidated because he accepted certain ideas that were later proven false, including the notion of spontaneous generation.

Chapter 2: Darwin Develops and Publishes His Theory of Evolution

of the central core of his evolutionary theory—the "struggle for existence," in which plants and animals compete to survive.

Chapter 3: The Immediate Impact of Darwin's *Origin of Species*

Chapter 4: Modern Reevaluations of and Objections to Darwin's Ideas

logical and geological evidence. A noted scientist tells why
he and the vast majority of his colleagues have not accepted other alternatives, such as creationism.

FOREWORD

In the vast and colorful pageant of human history, a handful of individuals stand out. They are the men and women who have come variously to be called "great," "leading," "brilliant," "pivotal," or "infamous" because they and their deeds forever changed their own society or the world as a whole. Some were political or military leaders–kings, queens, presidents, generals, and the like–whose policies, conquests, or innovations reshaped the maps and futures of countries and entire continents. Among those falling into this category were the formidable Roman statesman/general Julius Caesar, who extended Rome's power into Gaul (what is now France); Caesar's lover and ally, the notorious Egyptian queen Cleopatra, who challenged the strongest male rulers of her day; and England's stalwart Queen Elizabeth I, whose defeat of the mighty Spanish Armada saved England from subjugation.

Some of history's other movers and shakers were scientists or other thinkers whose ideas and discoveries altered the way people conduct their everyday lives or view themselves and their place in nature. The electric light and other remarkable inventions of Thomas Edison, for example, revolutionized almost every aspect of home-life and the workplace; and the theories of naturalist Charles Darwin lit the way for biologists and other scientists in their ongoing efforts to understand the origins of living things, including human beings.

Still other people who made history were religious leaders and social reformers. The struggles of the Arabic prophet Muhammad more than a thousand years ago led to the establishment of one of the world's great religions–Islam; and the efforts and personal sacrifices of an American reverend named Martin Luther King Jr. brought about major improvements in race relations and the justice system in the United States.

Each anthology in the People Who Made History series begins with an introductory essay that provides a general overview of the individual's life, times, and contributions. The group of essays that follow are chosen for their accessibility to a young adult audience and carefully edited in consideration of the reading and comprehension levels of that audience. Some of the essays are by noted historians, professors, and other experts. Others are excerpts from contemporary writings by or about the pivotal individual in question. To aid the reader in choosing the material of immediate interest or need, an annotated table of contents summarizes the article's main themes and insights.

Each volume also contains extensive research tools, including a collection of excerpts from primary source documents pertaining to the individual under discussion. The volumes are rounded out with an extensive bibliography and a comprehensive index.

Plutarch, the renowned first-century Greek biographer and moralist, crystallized the idea behind Greenhaven's People Who Made History when he said, "To be ignorant of the lives of the most celebrated men of past ages is to continue in a state of childhood all our days." Indeed, since it is people who make history, every modern nation, organization, institution, invention, artifact, and idea is the result of the diligent efforts of one or more individuals, living or dead; and it is therefore impossible to understand how the world we live in came to be without examining the contributions of these individuals.

INTRODUCTION

CHARLES DARWIN AND THE
THEORY THAT CHANGED THE WORLD

Charles Robert Darwin, who would grow up to be the most famous and controversial naturalist in human history, was born on February 12, 1809, in Shrewsbury, an English market town located near the country's border with Wales. He was the fifth of the six children born to Robert Darwin, the most respected doctor in the region, and his wife Susannah. From the very beginning, young Charles regarded his father, a large, imposing man (who stood six-foot-two and weighed 330 pounds), with respect, even with awe. "His recollection of everything that was connected with him was peculiarly distinct," Charles' son Francis wrote many years later,

> and he spoke of him [Robert Darwin] frequently, generally prefacing an anecdote with some such phrase as "My father, who was the wisest man I ever knew," etc. It was astonishing how clearly he remembered his father's opinions, so that he was able to quote some maxim or hint of his in many cases of illness. As a rule, he put small faith in doctors, and thus his unlimited belief in Dr. Darwin's medical instinct and methods of treatment was all the more striking.[1]

It was to prove a vital underpinning of Charles Darwin's character and life's work that his parents passed on to him a family tradition of the highest respect for knowledge and learning. Robert Darwin was the son of Erasmus Darwin, a noted scholar who had written a number of widely-read volumes about nature and had had the audacity to turn down an offer to be King George III's personal physician. Susannah Darwin's father was Josiah Wedgwood, the renowned maker of fine pottery. Wedgwood was also a philanthropist who contributed a great deal of money to educational causes and instilled a love of learning in his children. Young Charles was clearly fortunate to be part of a family in which the adults on both sides were well-to-do and well-educated.

Unlike most of the other children in Shrewsbury and neighboring towns, who came from poorer families, he and his siblings each had their own room; the Darwins had servants to do most of the chores, so there was ample time for the children to read and learn outside of school; and the latest and best books were always readily available to them.

FAR FROM AN AVID STUDENT

From this strong family emphasis on learning and education, it would seem to follow that young Charles would be an avid and remarkable student. But this was not the case. In 1818, Robert Darwin enrolled the boy, then nine, in Shrewsbury School, situated about a mile from the Darwins' residence. The headmaster was an Anglican minister named Dr. Samuel Butler, who enforced strict discipline among his students, yet allowed them to work out their differences "honorably" in supervised fistfights. As for the quality of the education Butler offered, Darwin himself later wrote:

> Nothing could have been worse for the development of the mind than Dr. Butler's school, as it [the curriculum it offered] was strictly classical [i.e., consisted of works written by or about the ancient Greeks and Romans], nothing else being taught, except a little ancient geography and history. The school as a means of education to me was simply a blank. During my whole life I have been singularly incapable of mastering any language. Especial attention was made [in the school] to verse-making, and this I could never do well. . . . Much attention was paid to learning by heart the lessons of the previous day; this I could effect with great facility [ease], learning forty or fifty lines of [the Roman poet] Virgil or [the Greek poet] Homer, whilst I was in morning chapel; but this exercise was utterly useless, for every verse was forgotten in forty-eight hours.[2]

Darwin much preferred scientific topics, especially those relating to nature, to memorizing Latin and Greek verses. However, during his childhood science was not yet systematically taught in secondary schools, the common wisdom being that scientific notions were nearly useless knowledge for young upper-class gentlemen and ladies. Attempting to make up for this educational oversight, the boy often took long walks in the forests and fields, observing nature and hunting. "I do not believe," he later recalled, "that anyone could have shown more zeal for the most holy cause than I did for shooting birds."[3] Yet while involved in this very act of killing birds, the young Darwin found himself drawn to studying them. "I took much pleasure in watching the habits of birds, and even made notes on the subject. In my simplicity, I remember wondering why every gentleman did not become an ornithologist [bird expert]."[4] The boy also began collecting and studying insects: (Although at first he collected only dead ones, his sister having convinced him that killing them for study was wrong.)

As Darwin himself later told it, Dr. Butler did not approve of the boy "wasting" his time on such "useless" pursuits. Moreover, the elder Darwin, whose opinions mattered a good deal more to Charles than Butler's did, agreed.

> To my deep mortification, my father once said to me, "You care for nothing but shooting, dogs, and rat-catching, and you will be a disgrace to yourself and all your family." But my father, who was the kindest man I ever knew, and whose memory I love with all my heart, must have been angry and somewhat unjust when he used such words.[5]

THE YEARS AT EDINBURGH AND CAMBRIDGE

Angry and unjust or not, Robert Darwin hoped to set his son straight, and in 1825 removed Charles, then sixteen, from Dr. Butler's school and enrolled him in Edinburgh University. There, the young man was forced to study medicine, in the expectation that he would become a respectable doctor like his father and grandfather before him. But this was not to be. Darwin was bored by his medical studies and found the act of dissecting animals repulsive. Even worse was the spectacle of surgery on a human being. One day he had to attend an operation performed on a child, who was held down during the procedure, as was the custom, because anesthesia had not yet been introduced into operating rooms. The child's screams were too much for Darwin and he fled, horrified, from the room.[6]

After two years, Darwin's father finally saw that the young man would not be a promising doctor. But Robert Darwin's alternative was to force his son to study for the ministry at Cambridge University, where Charles spent the next three years, as unmotivated as ever with his studies. Actually, it was mainly his theology classes that bored the younger Darwin; for while at Cambridge he met and began studying informally with John Stevens Henslow, a widely respected botanist. According to Darwin's own recollection:

> Before coming up to Cambridge, I had heard of him from my

brother as a man who knew every branch of science, and I was accordingly prepared to reverence him. He kept open house once every week when all undergraduates and some older members of the University, who were attached to science, used to meet in the evening. I soon. . . went there regularly. Before long I became well acquainted with Henslow, and during the latter half of my time at Cambridge took long walks with him on most days; so that I was called by some . . . "the man who walks with Henslow.". . . His knowledge was great in botany, entomology [the study of insects], chemistry, mineralogy, and geology.[7]

After obtaining his bachelor's degree in theology in January 1831, Darwin also met and studied with the renowned geologist and clergyman Adam Sedgwick, whom the young man considered a brilliant teacher. Darwin became close with Sedgwick, as well as with some of Henslow's friends, all of whom were a good deal older than he. "Looking back," Darwin later wrote,

I infer that there must have been something in me a little superior to the common run of youths, otherwise, the above-mentioned men, so much older than me and higher in academical position, would never have allowed me to associate with them.[8]

A ONCE IN A LIFETIME OPPORTUNITY

Indeed, far from the "common run of youths," Darwin was really a brilliant, restless young man whose enormous talents and potential had still hardly become apparent, even to Henslow and Sedgwick. It was during his studies with Sedgwick that Darwin stumbled into a new direction, one that would finally allow him to unlock his hidden potential. The initial key was his reading of *A Personal Narrative of Travels to the Equinoctial Regions of America During the Years 1790–1804* by the most famous scientific explorer of the era, Baron Alexander von Humboldt. The young man became completely fascinated by Humboldt's descriptions of his adventures in the Canary islands, South America, Mexico, and the United States. At that time, much of these lands remained unexplored and unnamed and sometimes the members of Humboldt's party were the first Europeans to see them. Darwin longed to be a part of such a voyage of discovery, to break new scientific ground and see such wonders for himself.[9]

To Darwin's surprise and delight, just such a once in a lifetime opportunity soon materialized for him. Henslow wrote to him, saying that the *Beagle,* a vessel piloted by Captain Robert FitzRoy, was about to leave on a five-year trip to explore foreign lands and gather scientific data. FitzRoy needed a naturalist to go on the voyage, and Henslow had personally recommended Darwin for the position. At first, the elder Darwin objected, fearing that such an endeavor would delay his son's plans to join the clergy. But these were, after all, really Robert Darwin's plans, not Charles'; and after Josiah Wedgwood wrote a long, impassioned letter on the young man's behalf, Robert relented and gave his consent.

The HMS *Beagle* set sail on December 27, 1831. Darwin shared a tiny, cramped cabin with the expedition's surveyor and slept on an uncomfortable hammock that hung above the other man's charts. But the young man was more than willing to suffer such discomforts. He could now say with great pride that he was, officially, what he had long dreamed of becoming—a naturalist; and he kept himself constantly busy. When not collecting and studying plant and animal specimens, he read voraciously and wrote many letters home. Typical was the enthusiasm, maturity, and attention to detail of his May 18, 1832, letter to Henslow, in which he said in part:

> One great source of perplexity to me is an utter ignorance whether I note the right facts, and whether they are of sufficient importance to interest others. . . . On the coast [of South America, near Rio de Janeiro] I collected many marine animals. . . . I took several specimens of an octopus which possessed a most marvelous power of changing colors, equaling any chameleon. . . . Yellowish, green, dark brown, and red, were the prevailing colors. . . . Geology and the invertebrate animals [those without backbones] will be my chief object of pursuit through the whole voyage. . . . I [have] never experienced such intense delight. I formerly admired Humboldt, [and] I now almost adore him; he alone gives any notion of the feelings which are raised in the mind on first entering the tropics.[10]

"THE MOST IMPORTANT EVENT IN MY LIFE"

Before returning to England on October 2, 1836, the *Beagle* sailed around the world. And Darwin was able to explore, often in detail, the plants and animals of many diverse regions. Many years later, as an old man, he summed up the crucial nature of the experience in shaping his later life and work:

> The voyage of the *Beagle* has been by far the most important event in my life, and has determined my whole career. . . . I have always felt that I owe to the voyage the first real training

or education of my mind; I was led to attend closely to several branches of natural history, and thus my powers of observation were improved. . . . I had brought with me the first volume of [noted geologist Charles] Lyell's *Principles of Geology,* which I studied attentively; and the book was of the highest service to me in many ways. The very first place which I examined. . . showed me clearly the wonderful superiority of Lyell's manner of treating geology, compared with that of any other author whose works I had with me or ever afterwards read. . . . Everything about which I thought or read was made to bear directly on what I had seen or was likely to see; and this habit of mind was continued during the five years of the voyage. I feel sure that it was this training which has enabled me to do whatever I have done in science.[11]

On returning to England in 1836, Darwin discovered to his surprise that in his absence he had become a well-known and respected figure in upper-class society. This was the result of Henslow's diligent efforts. The older scientist had frequently sent Darwin's detailed letters describing the voyage and its discoveries to scientists and other scholars; and some of these, and/or commentaries on them, had made their way into various newspapers.

After moving into a small London apartment, Darwin wrote a 200,000-word account of the voyage and in 1837 published it as *The Journal of Researches into the Geology and Natural History of the Various Countries Visited by H.M.S. "Beagle," under the Command of Captain FitzRoy, R.N., from 1832 to 1836.* The *Journal* was both a financial and scholarly success for Darwin. A worthy successor to Humboldt's *Personal Narrative,* it captured the imagination of the reading public and inspired the careers of younger naturalists, including Joseph Dalton Hooker, who would become a world-renowned botanist and one of Darwin's closest friends. The tireless Darwin soon followed up this volume with others, including *Coral Reefs* (1842), *Geological Observations of the Volcanic Islands* (1844), and *Geological Observations of South America* (1846).

CONCEPTION OF THE PRINCIPLE OF NATURAL SELECTION

It was during this period of the late 1830s and early 1840s that Darwin became obsessed with transmutation. This was the idea that plant and animal species are not immutable, or fixed forever in their present forms, but tend to change over time, in the process evolving into new forms. Much of the data he had collected on the *Beagle*'s voyage, especially his studies of finches and other creatures off the coast of South America, seemed to show that such evolution was indeed taking place. In and of itself, evolution was far from a new idea. Some ancient Greek scholars had seriously discussed it, as had several eighteenth- and nineteenth-century European scientists, including Darwin's own grandfather, Erasmus. What all of Darwin's predecessors in the area had failed to do, however, was to propose a convincing explanation for exactly *how* evolutionary change takes place.

Darwin attacked the problem repeatedly. But though he had basically the right idea, he still had trouble expressing it in clear, logical, and believable terms. "I soon perceived," he later recalled,

> that selection [of one species over another] was the keystone of man's success in making useful races of animals and plants. But how selection could be applied to organisms living in a state of nature remained for some time a mystery to me.

Then, in October 1838, a shining ray of light illuminated Darwin's darkness.

> I happened to read for amusement [the essay by economist Thomas] Malthus on *Population* [which proposes that as human populations grow, more people must compete for the same amount of food], and being well prepared to appreciate the struggle for existence which everywhere goes on from long-continued observation of the habits of animals and plants, it at once struck me that under these circumstances favorable variations would tend to be preserved and unfavorable ones to be destroyed. The result of this would be the formation of a new species.[12]

Darwin referred to the concept as natural selection, which, he came to see as the driving force behind the process of evolution. In his view, physical characteristics, such as size, strength, shape of body parts, and quality of vision and hearing, regularly pass from parents to offspring. This process is random, however, and always results in tiny variations from one generation to another. Also, he explained, life consists of a fierce struggle for existence in which all species compete for the same limited supplies of food, water, and territory. Darwin reasoned that this struggle would be most severe among the individuals of the same species, for they frequent the same districts, need the same foods, and are faced with the same dangers.

Following from these facts, Darwin's essential thesis was

that nature tends to "select," or allow the survival of, those individuals whose variations are favored over those of others; that is, plants and animals that manage to adapt to changing environmental conditions will survive and pass on their favorable characteristics to their offspring. These new, favored kinds of living things will, over time, become increasingly different from their parents, and after the passage of thousands of generations they will have become so different as to constitute a new species.

At the same time, Darwin advocated, species with favored characteristics tend to crowd out those that cannot adapt as quickly or as well. These less successful living things inevitably become extinct. Thus, he said, although evolution occurs much too slowly to be directly detectable, its workings can be seen in the fossil record, which reveals the rise and fall of countless species over the eons. Darwin's thesis neatly explained why the most ancient fossils least resemble modern ones. Succeeding generations of offspring become increasingly less like an original set of parents, and the longer evolution proceeds the less the older forms resemble the new ones.

THE TWO DEFINING DECADES

It was one thing to conceive such a theory, Darwin realized, and quite another to provide strong and convincing evidence for it. So between 1838 and 1859, which proved to be the two defining decades of his life, he worked on amassing that evidence. During these years he also married his cousin, Emma Wedgwood, moved to Down House, a lovely home in the countryside about sixteen miles southeast of London, and began raising a family. He and Emma had ten children in all, but three of these did not survive infancy.

From the late 1830s on, Darwin was also frequently ill. At first, he assumed he had something ordinary like the flu, but weeks and then months passed, and he only felt worse. In the grip of the mysterious illness, which plagued him nearly the rest of his life, Darwin suffered from headaches, stomach cramps, sleepless nights, and periodic episodes of extreme fatigue. The doctors who examined him over the years could not identify the problem, and none could supply a cure. Modern doctors have tried to diagnose the problem, based on the symptoms described by him and his own physicians. Although it will probably never be confirmed, most modern researchers think that Darwin suffered from Chagas's disease, an infection found mainly in tropical regions. If so, he could easily have contracted the affliction during his field work in South America.[13]

During these same years, Darwin met and became close to Charles Lyell, the renowned geologist whose book he had read while on the *Beagle*. Lyell subsequently introduced Darwin to Joseph Hooker, who supplied Darwin with a great deal of information on plants. Darwin gratefully used this data as he painstakingly continued to piece together the evidence for his theory of evolution. In 1844, Darwin showed Hooker a 230-page outline of the theory. The botanist agreed with many of the conclusions his friend had drawn but still had reservations about the idea of one species actually changing into another; nevertheless, Hooker correctly suspected that Darwin was on to something momentous and urged him to keep working on the project.

PUBLICATION AND CONTROVERSY

Encouraged by Lyell and Hooker, as well as by other close associates, including the brilliant biologist Thomas Henry Huxley, in 1856 Darwin began writing a book with the tentative title of *Natural Selection*. The work was finally completed in March 1859 and published in November/December of that year as *On the Origin of Species by Means of Natural Selection, or the Preservation of Favored Races in the Struggle for Life*.

The reception to this massive collection of scientific evidence supporting the theory of evolution was, as Darwin had expected, loud and mixed. Some scientists and also some educated nonscientists, including a few religious leaders, thought the book fascinating and were willing at least to consider what he had to say. But most people were unwilling to accept any idea or claim that contradicted the biblical explanation for the creation of life. They, like nearly everyone before them, assumed that God had created all species miraculously in a single stroke and that the forms of these plants and animals were immutable. The idea that all of the earth's life forms have been and remain locked in an eternal, violent struggle in which the strong survive and the weak die out disturbed them; and because they could not see this alleged process of evolution happening before their eyes, they criticized Darwin and rejected his theory.

But despite the numerous assaults on his work and character, some of them quite vicious, Darwin prevailed. This was because the evidence he presented for the workings of the evolutionary process was overwhelming. In page after page, chapter after chapter, he had relentlessly constructed a powerfully convincing case for natural selection. Also, he had fully anticipated the strong objections of many religious people (like himself, for he remained, as he had always been, a devout believer in God); and in the book's conclusion he appealed to the common sense and fairness of religious leaders and scientists alike, saying:

I see no good reason why the views given in this volume should shock the religious feelings of any one. It is satisfactory, as showing how transient [temporary] such impressions are, to remember that the greatest discovery ever made by man, namely, the law of the attraction of gravity [by English scientist Isaac Newton], was also attacked. . . "as subversive of natural, and. . . revealed, religion." A celebrated author. . . has written to me that "he has gradually learnt to see that it is just as noble a conception of the Deity [God] to believe that He created a few original forms capable of self-development into other and needful forms, as to believe that He required a fresh act of creation to supply the voids caused by the action of His laws." Why, it may be asked, until recently did nearly all the most eminent living naturalists and geologists disbelieve in the mutability [capacity for change] of species? . . . The belief that species were immutable productions was almost unavoidable as long as the history of the world was thought to be of short duration; and now that we have acquired some idea of the lapse of time, we are too apt to assume, without proof, that the geological record is so perfect that it would have afforded us plain evidence of the mutation of species, if they had undergone mutation. But the chief cause of our natural unwillingness to admit that one species has given birth to clear and distinct species, is that we are always slow in admitting great changes of which we do not see the steps. . . . The mind cannot possibly grasp the full meaning of the term of even a million years; it cannot add up and perceive the full effects of many slight variations, accumulated during an almost infinite number of generations. Although I am fully convinced of the truth of the views given in this volume. . . I by no means expect to convince experienced naturalists whose. . . [views are] directly opposite to mine. . . . A few naturalists, endowed with much flexibility of mind, and who have already begun to doubt the immutability of species, may be influenced by this volume; but I look with confidence to the future,—to young and rising naturalists, who will be able to view both sides of the question with impartiality. . . for thus only can the load of prejudice by which this subject is over-whelmed be removed.[14]

Darwin also stated that no false theory could possibly explain so much so well. Indeed, as modern scholar Tom McGowen explains:

> It is a common happening in science that any theory based on incorrectly understood evidence or faulty reasoning eventually gets demolished by the work of other scientists, whereas a theory based fully on fact gains strength as new evidence comes to light, as was the case with [Polish astronomer Nicolaus] Copernicus' theory that the earth revolved around the sun. And even as the arguments about evolution were going on, new evidence was accumulating to back up Darwin's theory. . . . The discovery in 1856 of fossil skeletons of an apparently different human species [the Neanderthals]. . . showed that there had indeed been a more primitive kind of human. And the discovery of the fossil remains of a prehistoric creature that was clearly a combination of both reptile and bird [the *Archaeopteryx*]. . . was a titanic piece of proof for Darwin's claim that birds had evolved from reptiles.[15]

THE RECLUSE OF DOWN HOUSE

In fact, Darwin's book seemed to explain so much, so well about plants and animals that it quickly won the acceptance and strong support of several of the world's most renowned scientists. Among the first of these giants to champion Darwin were his friends, Lyell, Hooker, and Huxley. In 1860, not long after the publication of *Origin*, Huxley and Hooker successfully defended Darwin, his book, and his theory at a raucous public debate held at the prestigious Oxford University. And subsequently, as the book sold out in printing after printing, increasing numbers of scholars and other educated people found Darwin's arguments compelling and inescapable. So powerful were these arguments, that by the end of 1863 nearly every important scientist in the world had accepted either some or all of them. In that year, Darwin's friend, the Reverend Charles Kingsley, wrote to a colleague, "Darwin is conquering everywhere and rushing in like a flood, by the mere force of truth and fact."[16]

Whether one accepted Darwin's ideas or not, considered him harmless or dangerous, loved him or hated him, there was no denying that he was now a world-renowned figure. Important public people and newspapers regularly discussed, quoted, defended, or criticized him; and for the rest of his days a long line of distinguished scientists, theologians, and other scholars made pilgrimages to Down House in Kent. This was the only way they could meet and converse with him in person, for he had become almost literally a recluse. In large part because of his continued ill health, but also because he was shy and retiring by nature, he left Huxley and others to travel the world defending his ideas and rarely ventured from the peaceful and secure atmosphere of his home. Moreover, he became thin, bald, and grew a long white beard, all of which made him appear much older than he actually was.

Yet Darwin still remained busy, sometimes puttering in the garden, other times conducting new plant experiments, and year after year managing to maintain an impressive output of books and articles. In 1867, for instance, he began work on *The Descent of Man.* Ironically, much of the fuss attending the publication of *Origin* had been based on Darwin's supposed suggestion that human beings had descended from beasts, which to many people seemed degrading. Yet the reality was that *Origin* had not dealt directly with human evolution. It had instead focused most of its attention on natural selection and other natural processes and presented facts about plants and animals as evidence.

In *Descent,* published in 1871, Darwin finally plunged headlong into the subject of human evolution, his main purpose being to show that it was possible for an organ as complex as the human brain to evolve via natural selection. He did not suggest, as is still commonly assumed by those who have not actually read his works, that humans had descended from apes. In Darwin's view, both apes and humans had evolved from some common, less-complex ancestor. Anticipating some of the same cries of outrage that had greeted *Origin,* he included this powerful defensive statement in *Descent's* conclusion:

> The main conclusion arrived at in this work, namely, that man is descended from some lowly organized form, will, I regret to think, be highly distasteful to many. But there can hardly be a doubt that we are descended from barbarians. The astonishment which I felt on first seeing a party of Fuegians [the primitive people then inhabiting the tip of South America] on a wild and broken shore will never be forgotten by me, for the reflection at once rushed into my mind—such were our ancestors. These men were absolutely naked... and their expression was wild, startled, and distrustful. They possessed hardly any arts, and like wild animals lived on what

they could catch. . . . He who has seen a savage in his native land will not feel much shame to acknowledge that the blood of some more humble creature flows in his veins. For my own part, I would as soon be descended from that heroic little monkey, who braved his dreaded enemy in order to save the life of his keeper. . . as from a savage who delights to torture his enemies, offers up bloody sacrifices, practices infanticide without remorse, [and] treats his wives like slaves. . . . We are not here concerned with hopes or fears; only with the truth as far as our reason permits us to discover it; and I have given the evidence to the best of my ability.[17]

LYING BESIDE NEWTON

Much to Darwin's surprise, however, the storm of protest he had expected *Descent* to incite never materialized. There were a few unkind jabs at his character and the usual journalistic lampoons, to be sure. The English magazine *Hornet*, for example, printed a cartoon showing his bearded head atop a gorilla's torso. But for the most part, critical reviews were as tame as the one in the *Contemporary Review*, which said of the book, "There is very little that is absolutely new."[18] The outspoken Huxley commented that the "mixture of ignorance and insolence" that had characterized many of the reviews of *Origin* were "no longer the sad distinction of anti-Darwinian criticism."[19]

Reactions to Darwin's later works were even milder, mainly because the subjects he tackled in his last years were very scholarly and of limited interest to all save a handful of biologists, botanists, and horticulturists. These included *The Expressions of the Emotions of Man and Animals* (1872), *Insectivorous Plants* and *The Movements and Habits of Climbing Plants* (1875), *The Various Contrivances by which Orchids are Fertilized by Insects* (1877), and *The Formation of Vegetable Mold, through the Action of Worms, with Observations on Their Habits* (1881).

While working on these volumes, Darwin remained always at Down House, leaving its walls only to take walks through the nearby fields. He was often accompanied by visitors, for the pilgrimages of his fans continued unabated. One young researcher was so anxious about meeting his hero that when he finally did so he found himself physically unable to speak and finally burst into tears. The modest and unassuming Darwin never ceased to be mystified by such adoration.

Darwin was equally mystified when, in the late 1870s, the

strange, unidentified illness that had plagued him for three decades suddenly and inexplicably disappeared. Unfortunately, though, his by now frail body had already sustained too much damage to allow a restoration of his health. In December 1881 and again a few months later, he suffered heart seizures; and on April 19, 1882, he died at the age of seventy-three at Down House. A week later, in a solemn ceremony, his coffin was carried into London's Westminster Abbey and placed near the final resting place of his own hero, Isaac Newton, another man whose ideas had changed the world. The faithful Huxley further linked these two giants of science in the following words, which can stand as a fitting epitaph to Darwin:

> The name of Charles Darwin stands alongside [that] of Isaac Newton. . . [and] calls up the grand ideal of a searcher after truth and interpreter of Nature. . . . [He was] a rare combination of genius, industry, and unswerving veracity [truthfulness], who earned his place among the most famous men of the age by sheer native power. . . . And with respect to that theory of the origin of forms of life. . . with which Darwin's name is bound up as closely as that of Newton with the theory of gravitation. . ., "the struggle for existence" and "natural selection" have become household words and everyday conceptions. . . . No one doubts their vast and far-reaching significance. Wherever the biological sciences are studied, *The Origin of Species* lights the paths of the investigator; wherever they are taught, it permeates the course of instruction.[20]

This volume for Greenhaven's People Who Made History series is designed to "light the path" for investigators of Darwin himself and the historical importance of his ideas. It does so by focusing principally on how *The Origin of Species* and the concepts it expounds changed human thinking. To that end, the book examines how scientists and other thinkers before Darwin viewed the origins of life; how Darwin conceived of his evolutionary ideas and wrote *Origin;* and the reception the publication of these controversial ideas received.

This anthology also explores Darwinian evolution's acceptance and constant reevaluation by modern scientists and its continued rejection by creationists and others. It must be noted that the inclusion of this material is not meant to be part of a balanced presentation of the debate between Darwin's supporters and opponents; rather, literature critical of Darwin and his theory is included to show that some people continue to resist the sweeping scientific, intellectual, and educational changes the theory has wrought in the past century and a half.

Some of the authors of the essays in these chapters were major players in the Darwinian drama. Included, for instance, are selections from Darwin's own letters and scientific works, as well as the writings of some of his contemporaries and original reviews of *Origin*. The more contemporary authors are or were (until their deaths) noted scientists, professors at leading colleges and universities, or representatives of widely known informational organizations.

Among this volume's several special features: Each of the essays explains or discusses in detail a specific, narrowly focused topic; the introduction to each essay previews the main points; and inserts interspersed within the essays serve as examples of ideas expressed by the authors, offer supplementary information, and/or add authenticity and color. These inserts come from the works and letters of Darwin and his contemporaries or from modern popular and scholarly works about evolution and Darwin's impact. The list of study questions aids the reader in picking out and evaluating the most important and thought-provoking themes and ideas in each chapter. And the bibliography, which includes works covering the whole spectrum of Darwin's work and impact, is conveniently divided into subsections for easy access and reference.

Though fulsome for a book designed for young adults, the bibliography constitutes only a brief introductory to the vast literature about Darwin and his ideas. That so much has been and will no doubt continue to be written about him is only fitting, for he was indeed one of the preeminent examples of a single person affecting the course of human history. "Darwin is arguably the best-known scientist in history," remark his biographers Adrian Desmond and James Moore. "More than any modern thinker. . . this affable old-world naturalist. . . has transformed the way we see ourselves on the planet."[21]

NOTES

1. *The Autobiography of Charles Darwin and Selected Letters.* Ed., Francis Darwin. New York: Dover Publications, 1958, pp. 2–3.

2. *Autobiography,* in *Autobiography of Charles Darwin and Selected Letters,* p. 9.

3. *Autobiography,* in *Autobiography of Charles Darwin and Selected Letters,* p. 10.

4. *Autobiography,* in *Autobiography of Charles Darwin and Selected Letters,* p. 11.

5. *Autobiography,* in *Autobiography of Charles Darwin and Selected Letters,* p. 9.

6. The second half of this paragraph quoted from Don Nardo, *Charles Darwin.* New York: Chelsea House, 1993, p. 27.

7. *Autobiography,* in *Autobiography of Charles Darwin and Selected Letters,* p. 22.

8. *Autobiography,* in *Autobiography of Charles Darwin and Selected Letters,* p. 24.

9. The second half of this paragraph quoted from Nardo, *Charles Darwin,* p. 31.

10. Quoted in Francis Darwin, ed., *The Life and Letters of Charles Darwin.* 2 vols. New York: Basic Books, 1959, vol. 1, pp. 208–10.

11. *Autobiography,* in *Autobiography of Charles Darwin and Selected Letters,* pp. 28–29.

12. *Autobiography,* in *Autobiography of Charles Darwin and Selected Letters,* pp. 42–43.

13. Most of this paragraph quoted from Nardo, *Charles Darwin,* pp. 66–67.

14. *The Origin of Species.* New York: New American Library, 1958, pp. 443–44.

15. *The Great Monkey Trial: Science vs. Fundamentalism in America.* New York: Franklin Watts, 1990, pp. 21–22.

16. Quoted in *Autobiography of Charles Darwin and Selected Letters,* p. 267.

17. *The Descent of Man.* New York: Random House, n.d., pp. 919–20. Darwin's mention of the monkey and its keeper was a reference to a true story cited earlier in the work; a small monkey had displayed the intelligent traits of affection and loyalty by fighting a much larger and stronger baboon that had attacked its master.

18. Quoted in William Irvine, *Apes, Angels, & Victorians: The Story of Darwin, Huxley, and Evolution.* New York: McGraw-Hill, 1955, p. 241.

19. Quoted in Irvine, *Apes, Angels, & Victorians,* p. 240.

20. "On the Reception of *The Origin of the Species,*" in *The Life and Letters of Charles Darwin,* vol. 1, pp. 533–34.

21. *Darwin.* New York: Warner Books, 1992, p. xxi.

CHAPTER 1

Pre-Darwinian Theories for Life's Origins

The Traditional View: Creation by Conscious Design

Richard Dawkins

In this excerpt from his widely read and critically acclaimed book *The Blind Watchmaker*, Richard Dawkins, a professor of zoology at Oxford University, introduces the fundamental question of biology: How did living things get here? According to Dawkins, there can be only two basic answers to the question. Plant and animal species were either created by some purposeful being or force; or they came into existence through nonpurposeful, natural means. Using the analogy of a watch and its maker, he explains that the most prevalent view before Darwin's day was the "argument from design," the idea that God consciously constructed living things. As an example, Dawkins cites the eighteenth-century theologian William Paley, the first writer to make the watchmaker analogy. Before Darwin's time, the vast majority of people accepted without question Paley's thesis of divine creation—a thesis that Dawkins rejects.

We animals are the most complicated things in the known universe. The universe that we know, of course, is a tiny fragment of the actual universe. There may be yet more complicated objects than us on other planets, and some of them may already know about us. But this doesn't alter the point that I want to make. Complicated things, everywhere, deserve a very special kind of explanation. We want to know how they came into existence and why they are so complicated. The explanation, as I shall argue, is likely to be broadly the same for complicated things everywhere in the universe; the same for us, for chimpanzees, worms, oak trees and monsters from outer space. On the other hand, it will not be the same for what I shall call 'simple' things, such as rocks, clouds, rivers, galaxies and quarks. These are the stuff of physics. Chimps and dogs and bats and cockroaches and people and worms and dandelions and bacteria and galactic aliens are the stuff of biology.

The difference is one of complexity of design. Biology is the study of complicated things that give the appearance of having been designed for a purpose. Physics is the study of simple things that do not tempt us to invoke design. At first sight, man-made artefacts like computers and cars will seem to provide exceptions. They are complicated and obviously designed for a purpose, yet they are not alive, and they are made of metal and plastic rather than of flesh and blood. . . .

I said that physics is the study of simple things. . . . Physics appears to be a complicated subject, because the ideas of physics are difficult for us to understand. Our brains were designed to understand hunting and gathering, mating and child-rearing: a world of medium-sized objects moving in three dimensions at moderate speeds. . . . We think that physics is complicated because it is hard for us to understand, and because physics books are full of difficult mathematics. . . .

Physics *books* may be complicated, but physics books, like cars and computers, are the product of biological objects— human brains. The objects and phenomena that a physics book describes are simpler than a single cell in the body of its author. And the author consists of trillions of those cells, many of them different from each other, organized with intricate architecture and precision-engineering into a working machine capable of writing a book. . . . Our brains are no better equipped to handle extremes of complexity than extremes of size and the other difficult extremes of physics. Nobody has yet invented the mathematics for describing the total structure and behaviour of such an object as a physicist, or even of one of his cells. What we can do is understand some of the general principles of how living things work, and why they exist at all.

Why Do We Exist?

This was where we came in. We wanted to know why we, and all other complicated things, exist. And we can now answer that question in general terms, even without being able to comprehend the details of the complexity itself. To take an analogy, most of us don't understand in detail how an airliner works. Probably its builders don't comprehend it fully either: engine specialists don't in detail understand wings, and wing specialists understand engines only vaguely. Wing specialists don't even understand wings with full mathematical precision: they can predict how a wing will behave in turbulent conditions, only by examining a model in a wind tunnel or a computer simulation—the sort of thing a biologist might do to understand an animal. But however incompletely we understand how an airliner works, we all understand by what general process it came into existence. It was designed by humans on drawing boards. Then other humans made the bits from the drawings, then lots more humans (with the aid of other machines designed by humans) screwed, riveted, welded or glued the bits together, each in its right place. The process by which an airliner came into existence is not fundamentally mysterious to us, because humans built it. The systematic putting together of parts to a purposeful design is something we know and understand, for we have experienced it at first hand, even if only with our childhood Meccano or Erector set.

What about our own bodies? Each one of us is a machine, like an airliner only much more complicated. Were we designed on a drawing board too, and were our parts assembled by a skilled engineer? The answer is no. It is a surprising answer, and we have known and understood it for only a century or so. When Charles Darwin first explained the matter, many people either wouldn't or couldn't grasp it. I myself flatly refused to believe Darwin's theory when I first heard about it as a child. Almost everybody throughout history, up to the second half of the nineteenth century, has firmly believed in the opposite—the Conscious Designer theory. Many people still do, perhaps because the true, Darwinian explanation of our own existence is still, remarkably, not a routine part of the curriculum of a general education. It is certainly very widely misunderstood.

PALEY'S WATCHMAKER

The watchmaker of my title is borrowed from a famous treatise by the eighteenth-century theologian William Paley. His *Natural Theology—or Evidences of the Existence and Attributes of the Deity Collected from the Appearances of Nature*, published in 1802, is the best-known exposition of the 'Argument from Design', always the most influential of the arguments for the existence of a God. It is a book that I greatly admire, for in his own time its author succeeded in doing what I am struggling to do now. He had a point to make, he passionately believed in it, and he spared no effort to ram it home clearly. He had a proper reverence for the complexity of the living world, and he saw that it demands a very special kind of explanation. The only thing he got wrong—admittedly quite a big thing!—was the explanation itself. He gave the traditional religious answer to the riddle, but he articulated it more clearly and convincingly than anybody had before. The true explanation is utterly different, and it had to wait for one of the most revolutionary thinkers of all time, Charles Darwin.

Paley begins *Natural Theology* with a famous Passage:

> In crossing a heath, suppose I pitched my foot against a *stone*, and were asked how the stone came to be there; I might possibly answer, that, for anything I knew to the contrary, it had lain there for ever: nor would it perhaps be very easy to show the absurdity of this answer. But suppose I had found a *watch* upon the ground, and it should be inquired how the watch happened to be in that place; I should hardly think of the answer which I had before given, that for anything I knew, the watch might have always been there.

Paley here appreciates the difference between natural physical objects like stones, and designed and manufactured objects like watches. He goes on to expound the precision with which the cogs and springs of a watch are fashioned, and the intricacy with which they are put together. If we found an object such as a watch upon a heath, even if we didn't know how it had come into existence, its own precision and intricacy of design would force us to conclude

> that the watch must have had a maker: that there must have existed, at some time, and at some place or other, an artificer or artificers, who formed it for the purpose which we find it actually to answer; who comprehended its construction, and designed its use.

Nobody could reasonably dissent from this conclusion, Paley insists, yet that is just what the atheist, in effect, does when he contemplates the works of nature, for:

> every indication of contrivance, every manifestation of design, which existed in the watch, exists in the works of nature; with the difference, on the side of nature, of being greater or more, and that in a degree which exceeds all computation.

Paley drives his point home with beautiful and reverent descriptions of the dissected machinery of life, beginning with the human eye, a favourite example which Darwin was later to use. . . . Paley compares the eye with a designed instrument such as a telescope, and concludes that 'there is precisely the same proof that the eye was made for vision, as there is that the telescope was made for assisting it'. The eye must have had a designer, just as the telescope had.

A BLIND, AUTOMATIC PROCESS

Paley's argument is made with passionate sincerity and is informed by the best biological scholarship of his day, but it is wrong, gloriously and utterly wrong. The analogy between telescope and eye, between watch and living organism, is false. All appearances to the contrary, the only watchmaker in nature is the blind forces of physics, albeit deployed in a very special way. A true watchmaker has foresight: he designs his cogs and springs, and plans their interconnections, with a future purpose in his mind's eye. Natural selection, the blind, unconscious, automatic process which Darwin discovered, and which we now know is the explanation for the existence and apparently purposeful form of all life, has no purpose in mind. It has no mind and no mind's eye. It does not plan for the future. It has no vision, no foresight, no sight at all. If it can be said to play the role of watchmaker in nature, it is the *blind* watchmaker.

Evolutionary Theory Before Charles Darwin

Desmond King-Hele

Charles Darwin was not the first person to suspect that plant and animal species change over time. Noted English biographer Desmond King-Hele ably summarizes the contributions of the key naturalists and thinkers who preceded Charles Darwin and the publication of the landmark *Origin of Species* in 1859. As King-Hele explains, these included a number of ancient Greeks, as well as Darwin's grandfather, Erasmus Darwin.

Since the word evolution has, down the centuries, acquired so many meanings, we must begin by defining it. In this chapter *evolution* refers to the development of organic types from earlier distinct yet related types; but it should be remembered that neither Erasmus nor Charles Darwin used the word in this sense when propounding their theories of what we now call evolution, since before 1860 the prime meaning of the word was quite different. Historically, the theory of evolution, with its claim that species are variable, stood opposed to the theory of special creation, according to which species remain unchanged in form and any new ones arise as an 'act of God'. Yet this antithesis, despite the bitter controversy it once aroused, always had a touch of unreality about it, since no one has ever defined a species exactly.

THE ANCIENT GREEKS

The theory of evolution has a long history. . . . The concept of evolution stems from the ancient Greeks, who, with their usual acumen, foretold in speculative form many aspects of the modern theory. The belief that life originated in water goes back to Thales, about 600 B.C.; and Anaximander (611–547 B.C.) thought that men developed, by gradual stages, from fish. Anaximenes (588–524 B.C.) was one of the first to suggest that life began spontaneously in primordial slime, an idea accepted by many later Greeks, such as Parmenides, Democritus and Anaxagoras. Speculations like these, and the influential view of Heraclitus that everything is in a state of flux, provided fertile ground for the growth of evolutionary ideas. The theory was first properly outlined by Empedocles (495–435 B.C.), who held that life developed gradually, plants preceded animals, and more perfect forms replaced the imperfect, which died out. His views were summed up as follows by Aristotle: 'Where chance brought about the sort of combination that might have been arranged on purpose, the creatures, having been suitably formed by chance, survived; but those which were not so formed perished, and still perish'. Aristotle makes this summary only with the aim of refuting it: 'but it is impossible that this should be the way of it', he says. For, although among the greatest of biologists, he opposed the evolutionary theories of his predecessors. Nevertheless, he did define a concept which now seems like a step on the road to evolution, his 'Ladder of Nature'. Man is at the top of the ladder, the other mammals next, then the cetaceans, reptiles and fish, cephalopods, crustaceans, and so on, down through plants to inanimate matter. Aristotle stresses the small differences between these classes: for example, it is difficult to tell whether certain sea-dwellers are animal or vegetable. But he fails to draw the conclusion that the plant and animal kingdoms have similar ancestors. . . .

LITERAL INTERPRETATION OF GENESIS

As the influence of the Greeks declined, so did the open-minded approach to Nature. In the 1,500 years after Aristotle, when Christian teaching became dominant in Europe, basic questions about life were answered by an appeal to authority rather than by speculation. The Book of Genesis, taken literally, supported the special-creation theory; but Augustine preferred a roundabout interpretation of Genesis, which brought him near to an evolutionary view, and Aquinas followed, more or less, in his footsteps. So, in the Middle Ages, a belief in evolution was not odiously heretical [against established beliefs]. Indeed, two Biblical episodes might seem to require it. First, there was the delicate problem of Adam, whose progeny must have suffered at least some change of colour if he was the ancestor of white, yellow and black races: this conclusion could only be avoided by making either the unpleasant assumption that only the whites were descended from him, or the unsupported speculation that Adam was white and Eve black. . . . The second relevant Biblical story was that of Noah. . . . Species must formerly have been much fewer, if Noah really did take two of each in his ark. Despite the dissension aroused by Adam and Noah, literal interpretation of Genesis won the day, and from 1600 until after 1850 special creation was the orthodox Christian teaching.

EARLY NATURALISTS

The idea of evolution did not lapse when the Christians turned away from it, for the renaissance of the spirit of inquiry into nature brought new advocates of evolution. . . . The question was only of academic interest, however, until in 1735 and after, [Swedish botanist Carolus] Linnaeus proposed his binomial classification of plants and animals, which seemed to imply the fixity of species.

'Are species fixed or variable?' remained perhaps not a burning question, but at least a smouldering one, during the rest of the eighteenth century. Linnaeus himself, combining piety with a natural desire not to undermine his own system, usually tended to regard species as fixed: there are, he said, as many species as issued in pairs from the hands of the Creator. The second famous naturalist of the century, [Frenchman Georges L.L. de] Buffon, whose 44-volume *Natural History* had an immense vogue, often discussed the question and mentioned most of the factors later seized on as important, but expressed such a bewildering variety of opinions that he must be regarded not as an advocate of either view but as a stimulator of discussion. . . .

More important than any of these was [French natural philosopher Pierre L.M. de] Maupertuis (1698–1759), whose discoveries in various branches of science seem never to have received the credit they deserve. . . . His contributions to evolution and genetics occur in three books published between 1745 and 1751. The species we now see, he said, 'are but a small part of all those that a blind destiny has produced'; for only those animals which were well adapted to their environment would survive. He developed a theory of heredity in terms of elementary particles derived from both mother and father, and worked out the mathematical probabilities. . . . His remarks on the variation of species sound like a modern geneticist talking about chromosomes:

> [Variations in species] could have owed their first origination only to certain fortuitous productions, in which the elementary particles failed to retain the order they possessed in the father and mother animals; each degree of error would have produced a new species; and by reason of repeated deviations would have arrived at the infinite diversity of animals that we see to-day. . . .

Despite these speculative insights, Maupertuis offered no real-life evidence of evolution in action.

ERASMUS DARWIN

In the late eighteenth century the theory of evolution, if it was to make any headway, needed a strong advocate who would specify a mechanism for the process, would show how it operated in nature and would not be afraid to outrage conventional opinion and the Church. Buffon was well-placed to fill this role, but either did not believe in the theory or, if he did, was unwilling to defy convention: the Church asked him to say he opposed evolution, and he complied. The credit for first propounding a well-rounded theory of evolution, with examples in support, belongs instead to Erasmus Darwin. . . .

Erasmus Darwin first explained the processes of evolution in section 39 of *Zoonomia*, entitled 'Of generation', though he had believed in evolution for many years, probably since 1771. He begins perversely by putting forward the view (which would have sabotaged his evolutionary theory) that in the foetus the male provided the active nucleus and the female merely the food on which it grows. But fortunately he modifies this view when, after pondering over the mule, he admits that the female contributes almost equally to the make-up of the progeny. He rejects the theory of preformation, then widely held—the theory that the embryo is, as it were, a scaled-down version of an adult—and suggests that the embryo consists of a living filament having no structural resemblance to a man, which gradually acquires new parts as it grows.

Then Darwin draws attention to the great changes which occur in animals. First, there are the changes during the life of an individual animal 'as in the production of the butterfly with painted wings from the crawling caterpillar; or of the respiring frog from the subnatant tadpole. . . .' Secondly, like

BUFFON DEFINES THE CONCEPT OF SPECIES

In these excerpts from his 1749 work Natural History, *French naturalist Georges Buffon offers a definition for distinct species and suggests how a member of a species develops in the embryo.*

We should regard two animals as belonging to the same species if, by means of copulation, they can perpetuate themselves and preserve the likeness of the species; and we should regard them as belonging to different species if they are incapable of producing progeny by the same means. Thus the fox will be known to be a different species from the dog, if it proves to be a fact that from the mating of a male and a female of these two kinds of animals no offspring is born; and even if there should result a hybrid offspring, a sort of mule, this would suffice to prove that fox and dog are not of the same species—inasmuch as this mule would be sterile (*ne produirait rien*). For we have assumed that, in order that a species might be constituted, there was necessary a continuous, perpetual and unvarying reproduction (*une production continue, pérpituelle, invariable*)—similar, in a word, to that of the other animals. . . .

There exists . . . a living matter, universally distributed through all animal and vegetal substances, which serves alike for their nutrition, their growth and their reproduction. . . . Reproduction takes place only through the same matter's becoming superabundant in the body of the animal or plant. Each part of the body then sends off (*renvoie*) the organic molecules which it can not admit. Each of these particles is absolutely analogous to the part by which it is thrown off, since it was destined for the nourishment of that part. Then, when all the molecules sent off by all the parts of the body unite, they necessarily form a small body similar to the first, since each molecule is similar to the part from which it comes. It is in this way that reproduction takes place in all species. . . . There are, therefore, no preexisting germs, no germs contained within one another *ad infinitum*; but there is an organic matter, always active, always ready to be shaped and assimilated and to produce beings similar to those which receive it. Animal or vegetable species, therefore, can never, of themselves, disappear (*s'épuiser*). So long as any individuals belonging to it subsist, the species will always remain wholly new. It is as much so today as it was three thousand years ago.

Quoted in Bentley Glass et al., eds., *Forerunners of Darwin: 1745–1859.* Baltimore: Johns Hopkins University Press, 1968, pp. 93–94.

his grandson in the *Origin of Species,* he specially emphasizes the great changes which have, down the centuries,
been produced in animals 'by artificial or accidental cultivation, as in horses, which we have exercised for the different
purposes of strength or swiftness, in carrying burthens or in
running races'; or in the various breeds of dog, the bulldog
for strength and courage, the greyhound for speed; and so
on, with many further detailed examples, including cattle,
pigeons, sheep and camels. . . . Thirdly, he discusses mon-
strous births, and notes the crucial point that the monstrosities, or mutations as we should now say, may be inherited:
'Many of these enormities of shape are propagated, and continued as a variety at least, if not as a new species of animal.
I have seen a breed of cats with an additional claw on every
foot; of poultry also with an additional claw, and with wings
to their feet. . . . Mr. Buffon mentions a breed of dogs without tails'. All these undeniable examples of anatomical
changes and the similar structure of the warm-blooded animals lead him

> to conclude that they have alike been produced from a simi-
> lar living filament. In some this filament in its advance to
> maturity has acquired hands and fingers, with a fine sense of
> touch, as in mankind. In others it has acquired claws or
> talons, as in tygers and eagles. In others, toes with an inter-
> vening web, or membrane, as in seals and geese. . . .

With these many examples to back him up, he feels justi-
fied in asserting that 'all animals undergo perpetual transformations, which are in part produced by their own exertions' and in part by their environment. He believes that
'many of these acquired forms or propensities are transmitted to their posterity'. This statement is important because it
seems to be the first recognition that some variations must
be inherited if evolution is to come about. . . .

Darwin concludes:

> Would it be too bold to imagine, that in the great length of
> time since the earth began to exist, perhaps millions of ages
> before the commencement of the history of mankind, would
> it be too bold to imagine, that all warm-blooded animals have
> arisen from one living filament, which THE GREAT FIRST
> CAUSE endued with animality, with the power of acquiring
> new parts, attended with new propensities, directed by irrita-
> tions, sensations, volitions, and associations; and thus pos-
> sessing the faculty of continuing to improve by its own inher-
> ent activity, and of delivering down those improvements by
> generation to its posterity, world without end! . . .

Darwin (1) gave plenty of evidence to show that species do suffer change, (2) specified many of the factors which increase the chances of survival, such as special organs or protective adaptation, and (3) appreciated the process of natural selection. One question he does not answer: are the changes on which natural selection operates caused by the creature's own exertions or by chance mutations? Erasmus, like his grandson, assumed that both processes contributed, though orthodox modern theory allows only the second. It would be very unfair to expect Erasmus to have been more specific, however, for even now the question has not been finally answered, in that the word *chance* is a cloak for ignorance.

HUTTON, MALTHUS, AND LAMARCK

After 1794, statements of the principle of natural selection and theories of evolution come fairly thick and fast. It is not easy to say how many of them derived from *Zoonomia*; but a book popular enough to go through three editions in seven years is not likely to have been entirely unknown to subsequent theorizers on the same subject.

The first of the statements comes from the great geologist James Hutton (who was an acquaintance of Darwin). In his book *Principles of Agriculture,* which was left incomplete on his death in 1797 and not examined until 1947, Hutton wrote:

> In the infinite variation of the breed, that form best adapted to the exercise of those instinctive arts by which the species is to live, will be the most certainly continued in the propagation of this animal, and will be always tending more and more to perfect itself by the natural variation which is continually taking place.

The next year, 1798, saw the publication of [British economist Thomas] Malthus's *Essay on Population,* which has to be mentioned because Charles Darwin and [his contemporary evolutionist Alfred Russel] Wallace both said it gave them the idea of the struggle for existence. Malthus propounded the view that human populations tend to grow in a geometric progression, whereas the means of subsistence, he thought, increase in an arithmetic progression. Since a geometric progression always overtakes an arithmetic one, population would always outgrow the means of subsistence. . . .

Between 1800 and 1820 the French biologist [Jean Baptiste] Lamarck propounded his theory of evolution, primarily in the *Philosophie zoologique* (1809). He uses so many of the same arguments as Erasmus Darwin that he has often been suspected of plagiarism. . . . But the suspicion remains unproved. The chief difference between them is that for the mechanism of evolution Lamarck depends entirely on the wishes and needs of the animals rather than upon chance variations winnowed by natural selection, whereas Darwin propounded a judicious mixture of the two, as did his grandson Charles. To put the difference at its crudest, Lamarck imagined the proto-giraffe adding an inch to his own stature by stretching up to eat high leaves, and then, as a result, having taller progeny. According to orthodox modern theory, based on natural selection, those proto-giraffes which happen to be taller than average because of small differences in their genes, will have a better chance of surviving, and their progeny will form a larger proportion of the next generation. . . .

The main point of interest here is that Lamarck developed the theory of evolution in more detail than Erasmus Darwin, but in doing so, set it on a wrong path which took many years to correct. To-day, we can see that Lamarck's evolutionary theory, though somewhat fallacious in its emphasis, should have served as a valuable step forward. Unfortunately, however, Lamarck's speculations in other subjects also incurred great odium in the biological world of the early nineteenth century, and he was severely criticized. . . . Lamarck's name was a millstone round the neck of the theory of evolution, and, combined with the Church's opposition to the idea, prevented it breaking surface more than momentarily until Charles Darwin came along with his mass of evidence.

PROPONENTS OF NATURAL SELECTION

Lamarck's theory was further developed, sometimes into fantastic forms, by Geoffroy Saint-Hilaire (1772–1844). His work, too, merely brought evolution into further disrepute.

Between 1810 and 1830 Lamarck's mistakes were combated by several British authors, who all denied that acquired characters could be transmitted: in the usual phrase, they believed heredity was hard, not soft, and they relied on the other of Erasmus Darwin's mechanisms, natural selection, rather than purposive or directive evolution.

The best known of these British expositors of natural selection, whose contribution was almost contemporary with Lamarck's, was the physician W.C. Wells (1757–1817). His paper on the subject was read before the Royal Society in April 1813, and published in 1818 in a new edition of his famous *Essay on Dew*. After remarking that negroes, and to a lesser extent mulattoes, remain immune from tropical diseases which are often fatal to whites, Wells points out that animals vary in some degree, and that these variations are exploited artificially by breeders. 'What is here done by art, seems to be done, with equal efficacy, though more slowly, by nature.' Of the accidental varieties of early man in Africa, 'one would be better fitted than the others to bear the diseases of the country. This race would consequently multiply' at the expense of its neighbours, until in the end the best-fitted race, which evidently happened to be black-skinned, would form the vast majority of the population. As Charles Darwin acknowledged, this account clearly describes the essentials of natural selection.

Evolutionary views were also propounded in 1813 by J.C. Prichard (1786–1848) in his *Researches into the Physical History of Mankind*, but in later editions of the book he became more cautious.

A much more complete exposition . . . came in 1819 from W. Lawrence (1783–1867) in his book *Lectures on Physiology, Zoology and the Natural History of Man*. Lawrence made a grave tactical error, however: he applied his conclusions to man, and explained the degenerative effects of inbreeding in royal families and aristocracies. . . . Lawrence was attacked and repudiated with vigour by his medical seniors, the Church and the Government. . . . To save his livelihood, Lawrence suppressed the book and channelled his talents into the strait and narrow path thereafter, ending as . . . Sergeant-Surgeon to Queen Victoria.

The next proponent of natural selection, who persuaded Charles Darwin to admit his priority, was Patrick Mathew (1790?–1874). He expounded the principle in his book *On Naval Timber and Arboriculture* of 1831. Mathew, who was something of a curmudgeon [an ill-tempered person] in his later years, used to put on the title-pages of his books 'Discoverer of the principle of Natural Selection'. Mathew pointed out that Nature produced far more offspring than were needed 'to fill up the vacancies caused by senile decay'. Only the hardier individuals, or those better suited to their circumstances, 'struggle forward to maturity'; the weaker perish. 'This principle is in constant action, it regulates the colour, the figure, the capacities and instincts.' Mathew, like Wells, knew and profited from the work of Erasmus Darwin.

ROBERT CHAMBERS'S *VESTIGES*

After Mathew, the next notable evolutionist was Robert Chambers, whose *Vestiges of the Natural History of Creation* was published anonymously in 1844. The book was condemned by almost every professional biologist (including [British biologist Thomas H.] Huxley and Charles Darwin) because of its factual errors, but these did not vitiate the book's lengthy account of evolution, which now seems perceptive and mostly correct. And, whatever his deficiencies in knowledge, Chambers had an intuitive grasp of evolution in action, acquired perhaps through being born six-fingered and six-toed. Despite its rough handling by the reviewers, the book went through ten editions in nine years, partly because its author was rumoured to be Prince Albert. So it had a wide influence. . . .

Even if the lay public took notice of *Vestiges of Creation,* the scientists didn't: evolution was no nearer acceptance in the 1850s than when Erasmus Darwin expounded it so completely.

Maupertuis: The First Modern Evolutionist

Bentley Glass

Long before Charles Darwin, Jean Baptiste Lamarck, or even Erasmus Darwin presented their theories, the eighteenth-century French scientist-philosopher Pierre Maupertuis conceived what was, especially for its day, a brilliant theory of the evolution of plants and animals. Like Charles Darwin did later, Maupertuis noticed that domestic plant and animal breeders generated new kinds of animals and plants, suggesting that under certain conditions the forms of species were not fixed, but could change. He also observed the phenomenon that later came to be called mutation, and correctly noted its importance in the generation of new plant and animal forms. Maupertuis and his ideas were largely forgotten at least in part because he lacked what Charles Darwin provided later—a mass of observational data collected over several decades to back up the revolutionary tenets of his theory.

The mid-eighteenth century was a period almost unexampled in the vigor and advancement of science. Newton's physics had finished remaking the Heaven and the Earth. In biology, the new classification of plants and animals, introduced in 1735 by Linnaeus and developed into the binomial system in 1753, gave a vast stimulus to the discovery and description of new species. Louis Leclerc, Comte de Buffon, was beginning his tremendous *Natural History,* which ran to 36 volumes, yet was a best-seller to be found in the library of every European with any pretension to culture. . . .

MAUPERTUIS'S EARLY ACHIEVEMENTS

Preeminent among natural philosophers of the time was Pierre Louis Moreau de Maupertuis, President of Frederick

Excerpted from *Forerunners of Darwin, 1745–1859,* edited by Bentley Glass, Owsei Temkin, and William L. Straus Jr., pages 51–53, 59–60, 72–77. Copyright ©1959, 1968, by The Johns Hopkins Press. Reprinted by permission of the publisher.

the Great's Academy of Sciences in Berlin. As a young man, Maupertuis was the first person on the Continent to understand and appreciate Newton's laws of gravitation; and indeed, it was through Maupertuis that [the renowned French writer Francois-Marie] Voltaire first became convinced of their truth. When thirty years of age, in 1728, Maupertuis had visited London. It was the year of Newton's death. Here Maupertuis became a member of the Royal Society and a disciple of Newton. Upon his return to France, at a time when Newton's theory of gravitation was still violently opposed [by a majority of scientists] . . . Maupertuis became the open defender and expounder of the new scientific doctrines, just as [Thomas] Huxley over a century later sprang to the defense of Darwinism. . . . In that same year Voltaire, more and more interested in scientific pursuits . . . wrote to Maupertuis, asking him in flattering terms for his judgment upon Newton's theory. Voltaire's conversion followed, and later, his own work on the subject, which was by far his most serious scientific production.

Four years later, in 1736, Maupertuis headed one of two expeditions sent out to test the flattening of the earth toward the poles, by accurately measuring a degree along a meridian of longitude in two places, in the one instance at the equator, and in the other, just as far to the north as feasible. Maupertuis directed the expedition into Lapland, [French soldier and geographer Charles Marie de] La Condamine the expedition to Peru; and between them they provided the first convincing proof to the world that Newton was correct, just as the expeditions to measure the gravitational deflection of light rays around the sun during an eclipse were in a later day and age to confirm the relativity theory of [physicist Albert] Einstein. There was no Nobel prize in those days, or surely Maupertuis would have earned one, at the age of 38.

Upon his return from Lapland, Maupertuis was addressed by Voltaire in these flattering words (letter of 19th Jan., 1741): "You are marquis of the arctic circle, and you have won for yourself one degree of the meridian in France and one in Lapland. Your name covers a good part of the globe. I find you really a very great seigneur. Remember me in your glory." It was, in fact, on Voltaire's recommendation that, in 1740, Maupertuis was invited by Frederick the Great to come to Berlin as head of the reorganized Academy of Sciences.

Maupertuis, however, came to consider that his work as a

champion of Newton on the Continent afforded him no great personal glory, and therefore in later years he laid great weight on his discovery in 1746 of the Principle of Least Action, which is all too commonly credited to one of the three great mathematicians, Euler, Lagrange, and Hamilton, who further developed it. This Principle is indeed one of the greatest generalizations in all physical science, although not fully appreciated until the advent of quantum mechanics in the [twentieth] century. . . .

AN EARLY THEORY OF GENETICS

Eminent as were these contributions to physical science and to philosophy, it is in his biological ideas that Maupertuis was most clearly gifted with prevision. Here he must be reckoned as fully a century or a century and a half before his time. His biological ideas may be considered under the three heads of the formation of the individual, the nature of heredity, and the evolution of species, although obviously these are so closely interrelated that the division is largely artificial.

He began with an interest in the formation of the embryo, and quickly put his finger on the soundest argument against the preformationists, who believed the embryo to be fully preformed before conception, and present either in the sperm or the egg. This argument led him to a study of heredity, and he may be justly claimed as the first person to record and interpret the inheritance of a human trait through several generations. He was also the first to apply the laws of probability to the study of heredity. He was led by the facts he had uncovered to develop a theory of heredity that astonishingly forecast the theory of the genes. He believed that heredity must be due to particles derived both from the mother and from the father, that similar particles have an affinity for each other that makes them pair, and that for each such pair either the particle from the mother or the one from the father may dominate over the other, so that a trait may seemingly be inherited from distant ancestors by passing through parents who are unaffected. From an accidental deficiency of certain particles there might arise embryos with certain parts missing, and from an excess of certain particles could come embryos with extra parts, like the six-fingered persons or the giant with an extra lumbar vertebra whom Maupertuis studied. There might even be complete alterations of particles—what today we would call "mutations"—and these fortuitous changes might be the beginning of new species, if acted upon by a survival of the fittest and if geographically isolated so as to prevent their intermingling with the original forms. In short, virtually every idea of the Mendelian [relating to Gregor Mendel, the Austrian botanist who founded the study of genetics] mechanism of heredity and the classical Darwinian reasoning from natural selection and geographic isolation is here combined, together with [Dutch botanist Hugo] De Vries' theory of mutations as the origin of species, in a synthesis of such genius that it is not surprising that no contemporary of its author had a true appreciation of it. . . .

His House a Menagerie

But Maupertuis was not content to make only this analysis. He undertook actual breeding experiments with animals to test out his theories, although of the results of these he has unfortunately left us only the account of a single one. It is related that he "adored animals and lived surrounded by them." "You are more pleased with Mme. d'Aiguillon than with me," wrote Mme. du Deffand to him one day, "she sends you cats." And Frederick wrote, too: "I know that at Paris just as at Berlin you are enjoying the delights of good company. . . . I am only afraid that Mme. la duchesse d'Aiguillon is spoiling you. She loves parrots and cats, which is a prodigious merit in your eyes . . ." Maupertuis had established himself in the outskirts of Berlin, in a spacious house adjacent to the royal park, near the present Tiergarten; and this house he had converted into a virtual Noah's ark. Samuel Formey, permanent secretary of the Berlin Academy, has left us the following description: "The house of M. de Maupertuis was a veritable menagerie, filled with animals of every species, who failed to maintain the proprieties. In the living-rooms troops of dogs and cats, parrots and parakeets, etc. In the fore-court all sorts of strange birds. He once had sent from Hamburg a shipment of rare hens with a cock. It was sometimes dangerous to pass by the run of these animals, by whom some had been attacked. I was especially afraid of the Iceland dogs. M. de Maupertuis amused himself above all by creating new species by mating different races together; and he showed with complaisance the products of these matings, who partook of the qualities of the males and of the females who had engendered them.

I loved better to see the birds, and especially the parakeets, which were charming. . . ."

A Dog's Toes

It was of the Iceland dogs that Maupertuis has left us the account of his breeding experiment: "Chance led me to meet with a very singular bitch, of that breed (*espèce*) that is called in Berlin the Iceland Dogs: she had her whole body the color of slate, and her head entirely yellow; a singularity which those who observe the manner in which the colors are distributed in this sort (*genre*) of animals will find perhaps rarer than that of supernumerary digits. I wished to perpetuate it; and after three litters of dogs by different fathers which did not yield anything of the sort, at the fourth litter she gave birth to one who possessed it. The mother died; and from that dog, after several matings with different bitches, there was born another who was exactly like him. I actually have them both." His breeding of dogs led him to wonder particularly about the supernumerary fifth digit which is not uncommon on the hind foot: "There are no animals at all upon whom supernumerary digits appear more frequently than upon dogs. It is a remarkable thing that they ordinarily have one digit less on the hind feet than on those in front, where they have five. However, it is not at all rare to find dogs who have a fifth digit on the hind feet, although most often detached from the bone and without articulation. Is this fifth digit of the hind feet then a supernumerary? or is it, in the regular course, only a digit lost from breed (*race*) to breed throughout the entire species, and which tends from time to time to reappear? For mutilations can become hereditary just as much as superfluities." Were all dogs, in other words, once five-toed on both front and back feet? Have we here a remnant, a vestige of a once functional structure? These observations might well have been made by Charles Darwin.

Two Heads Are Always on the Neck

Maupertuis' studies thus led him to evolution. Here with certainty he must be ranked above all the precursors of Darwin. To begin with, he was faced with the problem of accounting for supernumerary digits, albinism [lack of normal skin pigmentation], and other hereditary anomalies on the basis of his theory of generation. This he solved ingeniously. "If each particle is united to those that are to be its neighbors, and only to those, the child is born perfect. If some particles are too distant, or of a form too little suitable, or too weak in affinity to unite with those with which they should be united, there is born a monster with deficiency (*monstre par défaut*). But if it happens that superfluous particles nevertheless find their place, and unite with the particles whose union was already sufficient, there is a monster with extra parts (*monstre par exces*)." Even Mendel did not foresee that deficiencies and duplications of the hereditary material might constitute a basis of abnormal development, a sort of mutation! Maupertuis comments on the remarkable fact that in monsters with extra parts, these are always to be found in the same locations as the corresponding normal parts: two heads are always on the neck, extra fingers are always on the hand, extra toes on the foot. This is very difficult to explain on the basis of the theory that monsters come from the union of two foetuses or eggs, which was the explanation forced upon the preformationists by the nature of their views; but it was not at all difficult to explain on the basis of Maupertuis' concepts. He described the skeleton of a giant man, preserved in the Hall of Anatomy of the Academy in Berlin, with an extra vertebra in the lumbar region, inserted in a regular fashion between the ordinary vertebrae. How could this be the remains of a second foetus fused with the first? he asked.

But on Maupertuis' particulate theory, "chance, or the scarcity of family traits, will sometimes make rarer assemblages; and one will see born of black parents a white child, or perhaps even a black of white parents . . . ." ". . . there are elements so susceptible of arrangement, or in which recollection is so confused, that they become arranged with the greatest facility . . . ;" elements which represent the condition in an ancestor rather than that in the immediate parent may enter into union in forming the embryo, producing resemblance to the ancestor rather than to the parent, but also "a total forgetfulness of the previous situation" may occur.

CHANCE "BRINGS OUT" MUTATIONS

Maupertuis thus came to the conclusion that hereditary variants are sudden, accidental products—mutations, to use the modern term. Moreover, since negroes could by mutation produce "whites" (i.e., albinos), it was clear that racial, or species, differences—the distinction was not too clear in the eighteenth century—are produced by mutations. To Maupertuis, exactly as to Hugo de Vries a century and a half later, a species was merely a mutant form that had become established in nature. The evidence for this was clear from the artificial breeds of domestic animals. As in the case of Charles Darwin a century later, it was in particular the pigeons that clinched the argument. "Nature contains the basis of all these variations: but chance or art brings them out. It is thus that those whose industry is applied to satisfying the taste of the curious are, so to say, creators of new species. We see appearing races of dogs, pigeons, canaries, which did not at all exist in Nature before. These were to begin with only fortuitous individuals; art and the repeated generations have made species of them. The famous Lyonnés [Lyonnet] every year created some new species, and destroyed that which was no longer in fashion. He corrects the forms and varies the colors: he has invented the species of the harlequin, the mopse, etc."...

If the ingenuity of man can produce species, why not nature, either by "fortuitous combinations of the particles of the seminal fluids, or effects of combining powers too potent or too weak among the particles" or by the action of the environment, such as the effect of climate or nutrition, on the hereditary particles. It is worth emphasizing, for it has been misunderstood, that Maupertuis raises the latter possibility only as one worthy of investigation; but clearly at this point he anticipated both Erasmus Darwin and [Jean Baptiste] Lamarck in suggesting the possibility of evolution through an inheritance of environmentally modified characters. Even so, it is the direct mutational action of heat or other factors on the hereditary material itself that Maupertuis seems most to have had in mind. "For the rest," he says, "although I suppose here that the basis of all these variations is to be found in the seminal fluids themselves, I do not exclude the influence that climate and foods might have. It seems that the heat of the torrid zone is more likely to foment the particles which render the skin black, than those which render it white: and I do not know to what point this influence of climate or of foods might extend, after long centuries of time."

THE INFINITE DIVERSITY OF ANIMALS

It is likewise clear that Maupertuis understood that most mutant forms are deleterious [abnormal or harmful] and at a disadvantage in comparison with the normal or wild types. "What is certain is that all the varieties which can characterize new species of animals and plants, tend to become extinguished: they are the deviations of Nature, in which she perseveres only through art or system. Her *works* always tend to resume the upper hand."

How, then, account for the distribution of different races and species? The "thousands" of human varieties are insuperable difficulties for the preformationist; but by mutation, migration, and isolation they are readily accounted for by Maupertuis. Perhaps, he suggested, in the tropics all the peoples are dark of skin in spite of the interruptions caused by the sea, because of the heat of the torrid zone over a long period of time. The geographical isolation of Nature's deviations must play a part here, for "in travelling away from the equator, the color of the people grows lighter by shades. It is still very brown just outside the tropics; and one does not find complete whiteness until one has reached the temperate zone. It is at the limits of this zone that one finds the whitest peoples." Well, "men of excessive stature, and others of excessive littleness, are species of monsters; but monsters which can become peoples, were one to apply himself to multiplying them." Are there not races of giants and dwarfs? These "have become established, either by the suitability of climates, or rather because, in the time when they commenced to appear, they would have been chased into these regions by other men, who would have been afraid of the Colossi, or disdain the Pygmies.

"However many giants, however many dwarfs, however many blacks, may have been born among other men; pride or fear would have armed against them the greater part of mankind; and the more numerous species would have relegated these deformed races to the least habitable climates of the Earth. The Dwarfs will have retired toward the arctic pole: the Giants will have inhabited the Magellanic lands: the Blacks will have peopled the torrid zone." However naïve these anthropological conceptions may be—and they were an easy target for the sharp gibes of Voltaire—there is nevertheless a groping here for a truth that was only to be captured fully by Charles Darwin and Alfred Russel Wallace in a later day.

There is no naïvety, only pure genius, in these final words: "Could one not explain by that means [mutation] how from two individuals alone the multiplication of the most dissimilar species could have followed? They could have owed their first origination only to certain fortuitous productions, in which the elementary particles failed to retain the order they possessed in the father and mother animals; each degree of error would have produced a new species; and by reason of repeated deviations would have arrived at the infinite diversity of animals that we see today; which will perhaps still increase with time, but to which perhaps the passage of centuries will bring only imperceptible increases."

Lamarck's Theory of Transformism

L.J. Jordanova

French naturalist Jean Baptiste Lamarck's evolutionary theory, usually referred to as transformism, was
an important precursor of Charles Darwin's work
on evolution. Although seemingly logical in its own
time, Lamarck's version was based on certain notions later shown to be false. L.J. Jordanova, a lec-
turer in history at the University of Essex, points out
in this essay, for example, that Lamarck accepted the
doctrine of spontaneous generation. This theory held
that living things could spring almost magically from
nonliving things (as maggots appeared to spring
from rotten meat before people realized that the
maggots grew from eggs that flies laid in the meat).
According to Jordanova, Lamarck also believed that
physical changes that occurred in one generation
could be inherited by the next. But apparently he did
not, as is often supposed, accept teleology, the idea
that nature has an underlying purpose.

Lamarck arrived at his theory of the transformation of organic forms in 1799–1800 in the context of heated debates on
extinction and fossils. In 1800, the opening lecture of his
course at the Muséum [French National Museum of Natural
History] revealed his new-found belief in the mutability of
living nature. The undoubted novelty of his ideas and the
controversies they provoked should not distract us from the
equally important point that the roots of transformism went
back to his earliest scientific work.

His theory rested on the following propositions: nothing in
nature is constant; organic forms develop gradually from
each other, and were not created all at once in their present
form; all the natural sciences must recognise that nature has

Reprinted from *Lamarck*, by L.J. Jordanova (1984) by permission of Oxford University
Press. Copyright © L.J. Jordanova 1984.

a history; and the laws governing living things have produced increasingly complex forms over immense periods of time.

Lamarck drew on numerous instances of transformations in both the inorganic and organic realms: the tides, chemical and geological mutations, spontaneous generation, processes of learning and development, ageing and adaptation. By 1800, the belief that 'nothing in nature is immutable' was a basic axiom in his natural philosophy. Despite their distinctive organic characteristics, the historical changes plants and animals underwent were only one aspect of the flux of nature.

'THE POWER OF LIFE'

The most complete and best-known formulation of Lamarck's transformism was the *Zoological Philosophy* of 1809, which placed transformism in a broad biological context. The work must be seen as an ensemble, and an appreciation of its overall structure illuminates Lamarck's ideas of organic change. The *Zoological Philosophy* brought together classification, an analysis of the nature of life, especially in simple animals, and an account of the complex behavioural capacities of higher animals. . . . His mind was, by 1809, firmly fixed on two projects: a natural history of invertebrates, and a study of man with particular reference to the nervous system and ethics. This twin focus, on the simplest and the most complex parts of the animal kingdom—central to transformism—was everywhere manifest in the *Zoological Philosophy.*

It was divided into three parts, each dealing with a distinct aspect of Lamarck's theories of living things: the natural history of animals, the physical causes of life, and the physical causes of what he called *sentiment.* Although this is best translated as 'feeling' or 'sentience', it is crucial to recognise that it was the biological capacity to receive sensations which concerned Lamarck, and not conscious acts.

The first part reassessed the classification of animals. From his botanical work, Lamarck was aware of the problem of imposing a system of classification on the natural world and then treating it as if it derived from nature itself. While other naturalists might have been content merely to acknowledge the artificiality of their systems, Lamarck was not. He strove to develop a way of coherently ordering animals while following nature's own plan. The project took on new significance with his transformism which offered a strong underpinning for a more natural classification because of its capacity to determine the actual order in which organisms were produced. For Lamarck, classificatory schemes ought to express the real relationships between living objects. Transformism and taxonomy [the classification of plants and animals according to natural relationships] were not mutually exclusive; although species were mutable they should still be named and their relationships with other forms specified. Before classifying, it helped if one had a theory to account for both the differences and the similarities between animals. Lamarck attributed the differences largely to the accidental effect of environmental factors. The similarities derived from 'the power of life', a law of nature which produced higher animals out of lower ones. Nature's use of basic templates to generate organic series of increasing complexity explained the observed relationships between forms.

SEARCHING FOR NATURE'S LAWS

Before Lamarck, it had been customary to begin classificatory schemes with the most complex animals, gradually descending towards the more simple ones, as, indeed, he himself had done in early writings. Following the pattern he had established in the *System of Invertebrate Animals* (1800) and the *Researches on the Organisation of Living Bodies* (1802), Lamarck devoted a lengthy chapter to the 'degradation and simplification in organisation from one end to the other of the animal chain, going from the most complex towards the most simple'. The concept of degradation was not a new one and would have been familiar to many of Lamarck's readers from [Georges] Buffon's *Natural History.* Lamarck used it to suggest that, taken as a whole, the animal series displayed a striking gradation between complex and simple, from those with many faculties, a skeleton and vertebral column, to those entirely lacking these features. Having established the idea of a linkage between the main groups of animals, the 'principal masses' (Lamarck was careful to say that he was not concerned here with *species*), he reversed the direction of the series, making a chain of decreasing complexity into one of increasing complexity, starting with the most simple animals. The *real* history of the animal kingdom was conveyed by this new sequence. Natural history was now truly the history of nature.

Lamarck's ultimate goal was to understand the plan nature had followed and thereby to discover uniform, constant natural laws. He implied in early sections of the *Zoological Philosophy* that it was a law of nature to produce ever more complex living things which displayed regular, fine relationships between them. He was aware, of course, that the animal kingdom was not like that, and that the discrepancy was increasingly apparent the more one examined families and genera, rather than classes and 'principal masses'. Whereas nature's laws were responsible for the gradations among living things, the action of the environment accounted for specialised adaptations. . . . For Lamarck the environment was a major part of nature; it operated according to natural laws, yet it was also in some sense the antithesis of life. 'Life' was the special power of nature to produce ever more elaborate, integrated and active organic beings. The inorganic matter which made up the physical environment, left to itself, would decompose into its simplest constituents. Hence the natural world was composed of two forces constantly interacting in a dialectical manner; for an accurate classificatory system to be arrived at, they had to be unscrambled.

The influence of the environment was more evident in some cases than in others. Families of genera and species were groups with only fine gradations of organisation between members, there having been no extreme environmental changes to cause greater differences. Indeed, this seemed to act as a definition of 'family' as a taxonomic grouping. Had it acted without impediment, the 'power of life' would have produced a succession of regularly graduated forms starting with simple ones. Hence, if one looked at the general series of animals as a whole, the impact of the environment was clear in any deviation from this pattern.

CAUSE AND EFFECT

Having argued in the first part of the book that species were not fixed, that animals could be arranged on a scale of increasing complexity which used human beings as the standard, and that classification should follow the chronological order of nature and hence be as 'natural' as possible, Lamarck set the scene for the analysis of the most important concept of the book, that of life.

The purpose of the second part of the book was to show that life was a purely physical phenomenon and to sketch out some of its basic properties. It therefore set out the first principles of biology with particular reference to zoology. The analysis of life was of considerable explanatory importance, for transformism rested on a number of presuppositions about the properties of the organic world, and 'the power of life' was itself a mechanism of transformation. Lamarck outlined his technique of finding out 'what life really is' by looking at simple animals with no special organs.

Between excited and communicated motion Lamarck drew a distinction the importance of which cannot be exaggerated:

LAMARCK PROPOSES AN ANCIENT EARTH

One idea that Lamarck got right was the great age of the earth. In these two brief comments, the first from his 1802 work Hydrogéologie *and the second from an 1805 memoir, he summarizes the importance of this observation and points out, to his regret, that most people cannot grasp it and so will not accept much of his work.*

Oh! how great is the antiquity of the terrestrial globe! and how little the ideas of those who attribute to the globe an existence of six thousand and a few hundred years duration from its origin to the present!

The natural philosopher and the geologist see things much differently in this respect; because, if they consider ever so little, first, the nature of fossils spread in such great numbers in all parts of the exposed globe, either at heights, or at considerable depths; second, the number and disposition of the beds, as well as the nature and order of the materials composing the external crust of the globe, studied in a great part of its thickness and in the mass of the mountains, how many occasions they have to be convinced that the antiquity of this same globe is so great that it is absolutely outside the power of man to appreciate it in any manner! ...

These considerations, I know, having never been presented elsewhere than in my *Hydrogéologie,* and not having obtained the serious examination that I believe they deserve, can only appear extraordinary even to the most enlightened persons.

Indeed, man, who judges the greatness of duration only relative to himself and not to nature, will undoubtedly never really find the slow mutations which I have just presented and consequently he will believe it necessary to reject without examination my opinion on these great subjects.

Quoted in Bentley Glass et al., eds., *Forerunners of Darwin: 1745–1859.* Baltimore: Johns Hopkins University Press, 1968, pp. 249, 250.

vital motion acted by excitation, motion in inert bodies was by communication. The definitions expressed his belief that although life could be analysed in physical terms, different physical principles should be invoked to explain inert matter. When motion was transmitted from one physical object to another, it was quite permissible to speak in terms of cause and effect for these could in fact be clearly separated. This was not the case in the living world, where cause and effect were inextricably intertwined as the nature and speed of the operations of the vertebrate nervous system illustrated. It should be emphasised that Lamarck did not thereby abdicate his responsibility as a scientist to find a physical explanation; he was merely asserting that the inorganic and organic worlds worked in different ways. Lamarck's sense that cause and effect could not be neatly separated in the organic realm was consistent with his emphasis on the dialectical relationship between organism and environment, and between different parts of the organism itself.

NERVOUS AND MENTAL PHENOMENA

Locating the *source* of vital stimulation was Lamarck's next step. He thought that in simple animals it was the imponderable, invisible fluids in the environment, while in the most perfect animals, the excitatory cause of life was within each individual. Lamarck, following eighteenth-century medical and physiological traditions, located it principally in the nervous system. The environment as a source of vitality was exemplified by the spontaneous generation of rudimentary organisms. Lamarck stressed the role of fluids as mediators between organism and environment, as agents of all vital actions and as the mechanism whereby the number of organs and their associated functions increased. The superior vital energy of higher animals was manifested in their fluids, especially in nervous fluid, which acted on their passive parts (what Lamarck called 'containing' parts), the cellular tissue. All these remarks laid the foundations for the hierarchical distinctions Lamarck wished to make, for example between animals and plants and between vertebrates and invertebrates. . . .

Lamarck was struck by the capacity of higher animals to change and adapt their behaviour through a highly complex nervous system. In human beings, it was the extraordinary capabilities of the brain and nervous system which characterised the species. Man—the masterpiece of nature—served as a vivid illustration of how the most intricate vital processes function. Lamarck therefore devoted the third part of the *Zoological Philosophy* to 'the physical causes of sentience', a section close to three hundred pages long in which, starting with first principles, he set out his approach to the analysis of nervous phenomena, including the operations of the human mind. His most important premises [were] the rejection of innate ideas, the belief that all experience comes from the senses, and the assertion that structure and function are indissolubly linked. This part of Lamarck's masterpiece sometimes embarrassed subsequent generations because its emphasis on mental phenomena appeared to give weight to the commonly held view that Lamarck had illegitimately attributed consciousness and will to all animals, and hence had been guilty of psychologising biological phenomena. . . .

Lamarck's earliest work in botany had embodied the idea that identifying degrees of complexity was an essential step in developing an adequate classificatory system. This was achieved by establishing which were the most and the least complex forms, and then by filling in the space between them through assessing whole plants, not just isolated parts. He subsequently applied the method to zoology: 'if the lower end of this scale displays the minimum of animality, the other end necessarily displays the maximum'. The levels of complexity in plants were less striking to Lamarck than in animals; plant activity and life was relatively impoverished. The most vivid example of structural levels of complexity was provided by the animal nervous system. Lamarck did not say that one nervous system developed directly out of a previous one, but he pointed out that anatomical parts were added on in more complex animals, giving rise to more elaborate capacities. Anatomical, physiological and taxonomic levels were identical. . . .

ACQUIRED CHARACTERISTICS

When it came to mechanisms for transformism, Lamarck quite unselfconsciously assumed the inheritance of acquired characters, in the sense in which he understood it, to be so obvious and unexceptionable as to require very little comment. Since antiquity it had been believed that adaptations to changes which had taken place during the lifetime of an individual would be passed on to their offspring. Scientists continued to employ the idea, and the closely related one of habit, long after Lamarck's death. In addition to the inheritance of acquired characters, he simply postulated that nature was constantly in change and that life, by its very nature, became more complex with time. The environment certainly played a role as an agent of change. These ideas had been set out in his *Researches on the Organisation of Living Bodies* in 1802 and they remained the foundation of his later writings. It should be noted that for Lamarck transformism was a logical consequence of his views on the nature of the organic world; it was arrived at by deduction from the fundamental axioms governing all living things rather than by induction from a large number of empirical examples. This is not to say, of course, that Lamarck did not have a deep fund of natural historical knowledge on which to draw, for clearly he did. It was rather that since he regarded transformism as proven, he did not feel obliged to go and search for instances of it.

Adaptation was an empirical phenomenon which was important for Lamarck's arguments, and he understood it to be built into the nature of organisms. Biological need, grounded in the interaction of life and environmental forces, was a stimulus for action in animals without any 'effort' or 'will' being involved. The straightforward absence of the organ systems necessary for consciousness meant that most animals reacted to prevailing conditions by instinct rather than intelligence—a faculty which, according to Lamarck, nature had distributed with exceptional parsimony. The drive to adapt was so strong that animals responded automatically to stimuli from the outside world, and from inside their own bodies, like thirst or hunger. The emphasis on adaptation gave a teleological cast to Lamarck's arguments in that much stress was laid on the purposiveness of living things. His repeated personification further heightened the sense of nature having goals. Not only did it seem as if there was a pre-ordained purpose in nature, but Lamarck's language also implied that nature worked, even laboured, in the service of specific ends. This impression was an unfortunate product of Lamarck's rhetoric. In fact he thought there was no purpose outside nature, and human beings were merely one species among the many nature had produced. What commentators have construed as teleology, Lamarck saw as adaptation and progress generated by the interaction of physical forces.

The real achievement of the *Zoological Philosophy* was its fusion of a number of hitherto distinct areas—natural history, classification, physiology and psychology. It was the direct product of Lamarck's project for a treatise on biology, in that life and its unique characteristics were at its centre. At the same time, the mutability of organic forms was simply one example of uniform, natural laws which governed change in all bodies. The distinction between life and non-life notwithstanding, Lamarck saw nature as a single system of natural laws.

An Anonymous Book Keeps Interest in Evolution Alive

Gerhard Wichler

In the early 1840s, Darwin was quietly communicating on a regular basis with Charles Lyell, Joseph Hooker, and other close colleagues, discussing with them some of his ideas about physical variations in plant and animal species. It had been a few decades since Jean Baptiste Lamarck's work had appeared, and evolution was not presently a major topic of public interest or debate. Then, Scottish publisher Robert Chambers anonymously introduced a book about evolution titled *Vestiges of the Natural History of Creation,* which was similar in some ways to Lamarck's works. As the late and noted German scholar and university professor Gerhard Wichler explains here, the *Vestiges* was a thoughtful but thinly documented study that caught the attention of professional scientists and laymen alike. It was also the last important pre-Darwinian attempt to explain the descent of plant and animal species.

In 1844 a book by an unknown author appeared in England; the title of the book was: *Vestiges of the Natural History of Creation.* The author contended therein the descent of all living organisms from the lowest forms up to man; this view had not been upheld since Lamarck (1809). On publication, this book aroused so much interest even far beyond the circle of natural scientists, that four editions were published within one year (ten editions appeared up to 1859). The zoologist Karl Vogt published a German translation (1847, after the 6th English edition, a second edition of this translation appeared in 1858). Only four years after the publication of the *Vestiges* people took for granted that Robert Chambers was the author

Excerpted from Gerhard Wichler, *Charles Darwin: The Founder of the Theory of Evolution and Natural Selection* (New York: Pergamon Press, 1961).

of this book; this was subsequently confirmed.

The author of the most well-known theory of descent before Darwin (except Lamarck) was not a biologist but a very well-known publisher in Edinburgh. Apart from his book on biology, the *Vestiges*, Chambers was already famous for his many historical works on the history of Scotland and for his biographies of [Walter] Scott and [Robert] Burns. Later on it became known that Robert Chambers had retired from business for two years in order to be able to work undisturbed on a completely different type of book, the *Vestiges*. He did not take anyone into his confidence and concealed the fact that he was the author of this book because—being a religious man—he wanted to avoid all controversies which could have arisen with the Church. As far as his occupation allowed him, Chambers had worked on problems connected with natural history for many years.

SOME CREATURES EVOLVED, OTHERS WERE CREATED?

Chambers' teachings were essentially the same as those of Lamarck: the complete descent of all animals in "an infinitely long time". He discussed two already known principally different evolution factors which he named the "tendency for grade improvement" and "modification by the surroundings". Similarly, as in Lamarck's case, known arguments for descent are quoted and again attempts to follow up counter-arguments are absent.

Chambers considered "appetencies" [strong natural attractions or desires] as a modifying factor; his examples are as unconvincing as those of Lamarck, e.g. "the hermit crab is a striking illustration of what I regard as the true history of species". On superficial consideration it can be assumed that the hermit crab was made by the Creator himself. However, "according to the development theory the peculiarities of hermit crabs are simply . . . modifications from the parent form brought about in the course of generations in consequence of an appetency which had led these creatures to seek a kind of shelter in turbinate shells". Both Lamarck and Chambers rejected the theory of catastrophes, both supported the principle of *Natura non facit saltum* [nature does not make leaps]. However, soon after they both accepted, in contradiction of these principles, the occurrence of great gaps which were due to the tendency for evolution. They attempted later on to mask this contradiction. Chambers, for instance, wrote of a startlingly rapid "grade improvement" and added: "We may deem this as a leap which in reality is none."

At the beginning Chambers, as Lamarck, was familiar with a linear series of evolution and only later . . . recognized a ramification of this series, i.e. a phylogenetic [evolutionary] tree. Similarly, Lamarck at first taught that there was one series for the total evolution but rejected this information later on.

Finally, both authors retracted at the end of their respective books certain statements which they had maintained throughout the book. . . . Chambers on page 152 [of *Vestiges*] no longer upheld the genetic inter-relation of all animals, but only recognized the evolution within large classes. In another instance he even rejected descent for certain classes of animals in favour of creation. As he was unable to define the class of spiders in the system of animals he suddenly posed the question: "Can it be possible that the *arachnida* (spiders) have sprung wholly at once from inorganic elements under the proper electric influences?" Chambers seemed to answer the question in the affirmative as he added: "We know that the acarus, a lonely member of the *arachnida*, is often produced from certain solutions, where ova were rigidly excluded." The next section in *Animal Geography* is also very unsatisfactory; often the facts are not explained in correlation with Chambers' theories, but earlier views are suddenly incorporated and used as *ad hoc* explanations. According to the theory of descent, for instance, it can be accepted that the fauna of the Galapagos Islands could be explained by immigration and subsequent modification. Instead, Chambers assumed (as Erasmus Darwin did in 1794) that a special evolution of animals occurred in these islands which originated at a later date than the development of the rest of the world and, therefore, the animals had only advanced to the stage of reptiles. In another example the similarity of the fauna of North America and Europe are explained by the fact that both are descended from the same maritime form which originally lived in the Atlantic Ocean. . . .

CHAMBERS' BOOK IS WELL ORGANIZED

The last chapter of the *Vestiges* and the appendix of [Lamarck's] *Zoological Philosophy* prove that neither of the two scientists succeeded in clarifying any of the problems of the theory of descent.

So far, a great similarity of the works of Lamarck and Chambers has been emphasized. Why then were the *Vestiges* read far more diligently than the *Zoological Philosophy?*

The two main reasons are, firstly, the clarity with which Chambers arranged his ideas, and secondly the fact that his theories are based to a larger degree on natural science, whilst Lamarck based his work more on natural philosophy.

Arrangement. Nowadays, any discussion of the theory of descent is required to give a clear separation of the proofs of evolution, the factors that led to evolution and of the phylogenetic trees. No such division can be discovered in Lamarck's work; his arrangement is very confused. Chambers, however, carried out this division for the first time. The reader is always grateful for a clear arrangement, especially in a subject as confusing as the problem of the species. Chambers was not able entirely to avoid confusion when discussing the problems of the phylogenetic trees and of the distribution of species, but Darwin's verdict on the first part of the book still applies: "the writing and arrangement are certainly admirable" (1844).

The basis of natural science. It must be remembered that philosophical trends of thought led Lamarck to believe in the theory of descent. Therefore, a large part of his book was devoted to developing philosophical ideas. Chambers, however, abandoned the belief in the constancy of the species by considering scientific facts, mainly the conception of geological progression. Furthermore, Chambers was able to communicate his own impressions to other people very clearly. Proofs of the theory of descent, as presented by him, became very stimulating and interesting.

A THOUGHTFUL HYPOTHESIS

The annotations of Karl Vogt in the German translation of the *Vestiges* contained derogatory remarks: "thoughtlessness" in the assertions "which are hardly understandable", "contradictions", a large number of "errors", "mistakes" which were accepted without criticism, etc. [Thomas] Huxley expressed an equally unfavourable opinion: "As for the *Vestiges*, I confess that the book simply irritated me by the prodigious ignorance manifested by the writer". Darwin also noted a lack of scientific attitude: "His geology strikes me as bad, and his zoology far worse" (1844). This criticism is certainly correct. Chambers was only an amateur as far as natural sciences were concerned: it is understandable that his knowledge did not approach professional standards and that his arguments did not influence scientists such as [Louis] Agassiz, Asa Gray, [Joseph] Hooker and [Adam] Sedgwick.

Nevertheless, the book appeared in six editions within three years and was widely discussed by scientists and non-scientists. A.R. Wallace, for instance, wrote . . . , "Chambers is dealing with a subject which is of interest to every natural scientist. I consider his book not as a hasty generalization but as a thoughtful hypothesis; but naturally, many more facts have to be taken into account in order to prove it." It can be seen that in spite of all inadequacies the *Vestiges* were very stimulating, especially at that time when everyone felt that the problem of descent was of paramount importance.

Two aspects contributed to the fact that this book "has made more talk than any work of late": the manner of presentation by Chambers and the special interest of the public in the subject itself.

It can be concluded that Chambers' ideas and proofs did not further the problem of descent, but his book kept interest in the theory of descent alive during the years 1844–1859. This agrees with Darwin's view: "I must think that such a book, if it does no other good, spreads the taste for Natural Science."

CHAPTER 2

Darwin Develops and Publishes His Theory of Evolution

Darwin's Evolutionary Theories Are Born on the Voyage of the *Beagle*

Carl Sagan and Ann Druyan

In this excerpt from their book *Shadows of Forgotten Ancestors,* the highly popular scientists Carl Sagan and Ann Druyan tell about the now famous 1831 exploratory voyage of the *Beagle.* They begin with a synopsis of how young Charles Darwin managed (with the help of his maternal grandfather, the influential Josiah Wedgwood) to convince his conservative father to let him go on the trip. They then show how the voyage, the one and only great adventure of Darwin's life, gave Darwin valuable life experiences. More importantly, the readings and observations he made on the trip sparked the beginnings of the evolutionary theory that would, some three decades later, change the world.

The scene is not hard to imagine: The twenty-two-year-old races home from college breathless with excitement. He squirms in his chair while Father, an intimidating man in the best of circumstances, harangues him with a litany of past indulgences and harebrained schemes. First, doctor, then, clergyman, now, this? Afterwards, what congregation will want you? They must have first offered it to others and been turned down. . . . Doubtless something is seriously wrong with the vessel . . . Or the expedition . . .

And then, after much discussion: "If you can find any man of common sense, who advises you to go, I will give my consent." The chastened son regards the situation as hopeless. . . .

The next day he rides over to the Wedgwoods' for a visit. Uncle Josiah—named after Charles' grandfather's boon companion—sees the voyage as a once-in-a-lifetime opportunity. He drops what he's doing to write Charles' father a

Excerpted from Carl Sagan and Ann Druyan, *Shadows of Forgotten Ancestors: A Search for Who We Are* (New York: Random House). Copyright 1992 by Carl Sagan and Ann Druyan. Reprinted by permission of Janklow & Nesbit Associates, as agents for the authors. (Endnotes in the original have been omitted in this reprint.)

point-by-point refutation of his objections. Later that same day, Josiah worries that a personal appearance might accomplish what a note might not. He grabs Charles and gallops over to the Darwin household to try to convince the young man's father to let him go. Robert keeps his word and agrees. Touched by his father's generosity and feeling a little guilty over past extravagances, Charles seeks to reconcile him, saying, "I should be deuced clever to spend more than my allowance whilst on board the *Beagle.*"

"But they tell me you are very clever," his father answers with a smile.

CAPTAIN FITZROY'S EARLIER VOYAGE

Robert Darwin had given his blessing, but some obstacles still remained. Captain Robert FitzRoy was having second thoughts about sharing such close quarters for such an extended period of time. A relation of his had known the young Darwin at Cambridge. He said he wasn't a bad sort, but did FitzRoy, the high Tory, know that he'd be rooming for two years with a Whig? And then there was the pesky problem of Darwin's nose. FitzRoy was, as were many of his contemporaries, a believer in phrenology, which held that the shape of the skull was indicative of intelligence and character, or their absence. Some adherents expanded this doctrine to include noses. To FitzRoy, Darwin's nose proclaimed at a glance grave deficiencies in energy and determination. After the two men had spent a little time together, though, FitzRoy, despite his reservations, decided to take a chance on the young naturalist. Darwin wrote, "I think he was afterwards well satisfied that my nose had spoken falsely."

The *Beagle*'s earlier survey mission to South America had been such an unpleasant experience, the weather so consistently rotten, that her Captain had committed suicide before it was over. The British admiralty office in Rio de Janeiro turned to the twenty-three-year-old Robert FitzRoy to assume command. By all accounts he did brilliantly. He was at the helm when the *Beagle* resumed her survey of Tierra del Fuego and the islands nearby. After the theft of one of the *Beagle*'s whale boats, FitzRoy kidnapped five of the local people, who were called Fuegians by the British. When he gave up hope of recovering the boat and humanely released his hostages, one of them, a little girl they called Fuegia Basket, didn't want to leave—or so the story goes. FitzRoy had been wondering about bringing some Fuegians back to England so they might learn its language, mores, and religion. Upon returning home, FitzRoy imagined, they would provide a liaison with other Fuegians and become loyal protectors of British interests at the strategic southern tip of South America. The Lords Commissioners of the Admiralty granted FitzRoy permission to bring the Fuegians to England. Although they were vaccinated, one died of smallpox. Fuegia Basket, a teenaged boy they called Jemmy Button, and a young man they called York Minster survived to study English and Christianity with a clergyman in Wandsworth, and to be presented by FitzRoy to the King and Queen.

Now it was time for the Fuegians—whose real names no one in England had bothered to learn—to go back; and for the *Beagle* to resume her survey of South America and [as John Bowlby puts it in his biography of Darwin] "to determine more accurately . . . the longitude of a large number of oceanic islands as well as of the continents." This assignment was expanded to include "observations of longitude right round the world." She would sail down the east coast of South America, up the west coast, cross the Pacific, and circumnavigate the planet before returning home to England. Once the *Beagle* had been re-commissioned under Captain FitzRoy's command, he took measures to insure that this new expedition would be very different from the previous one. Largely at his own expense, he had the 90-foot square-rigger completely re-fit. He resurfaced her hull, raised her deck, and festooned her bowsprit and her three tall masts with state-of-the-art lightning conductors. He tried to learn everything he could about weather and became one of the founders of modern meteorology in the process. On December 27, 1831, the *Beagle* was finally ready to sail.

DARWIN'S READING MATERIAL

On the eve of her departure, Darwin had suffered an anxiety attack and heart palpitations. There would be episodes of these symptoms, gastrointestinal distress, and profound bouts of exhaustion and depression throughout his life. Much speculation has been offered on the cause of these spells. They've been attributed to a psychosomatic reaction to the traumatic loss of his mother at so tender an age; to anxieties about the reactions his life's work might elicit from God and the public; to an unconscious tendency to hyperventilate [wheeze from taking in too much oxygen]; and, strangely, although the symptoms pre-date his marriage by many years, to the pleasure he took in his beloved wife's genius for nursing the sick. The sequence of events also makes implausible the contention that his illness was due to a

---

"THE MOST IMPORTANT EVENT OF MY LIFE"

This reminiscence of the voyage and its impact on Darwin's young mind is taken from Darwin's autobiography, penned many years later.

The voyage of the *Beagle* has been by far the most important event in my life, and has determined my whole career; yet it depended on so small a circumstance as my uncle offering to drive me thirty miles to Shrewsbury, which few uncles would have done, and on such a trifle as the shape of my nose. I have always felt that I owe to the voyage the first real training or education of my mind; I was led to attend closely to several branches of natural history, and thus my powers of observation were improved, though they were always fairly developed.

The investigation of the geology of all the places visited was far more important, as reasoning here comes into play.

On first examining a new district, nothing can appear more hopeless than the chaos of rocks; but by recording the stratification and nature of the rocks and fossils at many points, always reasoning and predicting what will be found elsewhere, light soon begins to dawn on the district, and the structure of the whole becomes more or less intelligible. I had brought with me the first volume of [Charles] Lyell's *Principles of Geology*, which I studied attentively; and the book was of the highest service to me in many ways. The very first place which I examined, namely, St. Jago, in the Cape de Verde islands, showed me clearly the wonderful superiority of Lyell's manner of treating geology, compared with that of any other author whose works I had with me or ever afterwards read. . . .

The various special studies were, however, of no importance compared with the habit of energetic industry and of concentrated attention to whatever I was engaged in, which I then acquired. Everything about which I thought or read was made to bear directly on what I had seen or was likely to see; and this habit of mind was continued during the five years of the voyage. I feel sure that it was this training which has enabled me to do whatever I have done in science.

Quoted from *Autobiography and Selected Letters*. Ed., Francis Darwin. New York: Dover Publications, 1958, pp. 28–29.

South American parasite acquired during the *Beagle*'s voyage. We simply do not know. His symptoms caused this explorer to be mainly housebound for the last third of his life.

Darwin's personal library on the journey included two books, each a *bon voyage* gift. One was an English translation of Humboldt's *Travels* that [his friend] Henslow had given him. Before Darwin left Cambridge he had read [naturalist Alexander von] Humboldt's *Personal Narrative* and [astronomer John] Herschel's *Introduction to the Study of Natural Philosophy*, which together evoked in Darwin "a burning zeal to add even the most humble contribution to the noble structure of Natural Science." The other gift was from the Captain. It was Volume I of Charles Lyell's *Principles of Geology*, and FitzRoy would live to regret bitterly his choice of going-away present.

The scientific revelations of the European Enlightenment had posed disturbing challenges to the biblical account of the Earth's origin and history. There were those who tried to reconcile the new data and new insights with their faith. They held that Noah's flood was the primary agent responsible for the present configuration of the Earth's crust. A big enough flood, they thought, could transform the Earth's geology in just forty days and forty nights, consistent with an Earth only a few thousand years old. With a little spin control on a literal reading of the Book of Genesis, they felt they had managed to pull it off.

Lyell had been a lawyer for as long as he could stand it. When he was thirty years old, he abandoned the law for geology, his true passion. He wrote *Principles of Geology* to advance the "Uniformitarian" view that the Earth has been shaped by the same gradual processes that we observe today, but operating not merely over a few weeks, or a few thousand years, but ages. There were distinguished geologists who held that floods and other catastrophes might explain the Earth's landforms, but the Noachic flood wasn't enough. I would take *many* floods, *many* catastrophes. These scientific Catastrophists were comfortable with Lyell's long time scales. But for the biblical literalists Lyell posed an awkward problem. If Lyell was right, the rocks were saying that the Bible's six days of Creation, and the age of the Earth deduced by adding up the "begats," were somehow in error. It was through this apparent hole in *Genesis* that the *Beagle* would sail into history.

His Sense of Justice

Hired mainly as FitzRoy's companion and sounding board, Darwin was obliged to bear with equanimity the Captain's politically conservative, racist, and fundamentalist harangues. For most of the voyage, the two men managed to maintain a truce with regard to their philosophical and political differences. However, Darwin was simply unable to let FitzRoy's opinion on one particular issue go unchallenged:

> [A]t Bahia, in Brazil, he defended and praised slavery, which I abominated, and told me that he had just visited a great slave-owner, who had called up many of his slaves and asked them whether they wished to be free, and all answered "No." I then asked him, perhaps with a sneer, whether he thought that the answers of slaves in the presence of their master was worth anything? This made him excessively angry, and he said that as I doubted his word we could not live any longer together.

Darwin fully expected to be kicked off the ship. But when the gunroom officers heard of the row, they vied with each other for the privilege of sharing their quarters with him. FitzRoy calmed down and actually apologized to Darwin, rescinding the eviction. Possibly, Darwin's evolutionary views emerged, in part, out of his exasperation with FitzRoy's inflexible conventionalism, and the necessity of the young man to suppress for five years the counterarguments that were welling up inside him.

Perhaps it was the legacy of his grandfathers that enabled Darwin to detect the inconsistencies and injustices that other members of his social class would not see. At the very beginning of his book, *The Voyage of the Beagle*, he tells of a place not far from Rio de Janeiro:

> This spot is notorious from having been, for a long time, the residence of some runaway slaves, who, by cultivating a little ground near the top, contrived to eke out a subsistence. At length they were discovered, and a party of soldiers being sent, the whole were seized with the exception of one old woman, who, sooner than again be led into slavery, dashed herself to pieces from the summit of the mountain. In a Roman matron this would have been called the noble love of freedom: in a poor negress it is mere brutal obstinacy.

Darwin had been lured to South America by the prospect of discovering new birds and new beetles, but he couldn't help noticing the carnage the Europeans were inflicting. Colonial arrogance, the institution of slavery, the extirpation of countless species for the enrichment and entertainment of the invaders, the first depredations of the tropical rain forest—in short, many of the crimes and stupidities that haunt us today—troubled Darwin at a time when Europe was confident that colonialism was an unalloyed benefit for the uncivilized, that the forests were inexhaustible, and that there would always be enough egret feathers for every millinery shop until the Day of Judgment. In part because of these sensitivities, in part because Darwin always wrote as clearly and directly as he could—striving to communicate to the greatest number of people—*The Voyage of the Beagle* is still a stirring and accessible adventure story.

THE VOYAGE'S SCIENTIFIC FRUITS

However, this book has watershed status because it was during the course of the expedition it recounts that Darwin began to amass the great body of evidence—not intuition, but data—that makes the case for evolution by natural selection. "At last gleams of light have come," he was later to write, "and I am almost convinced that species are not (it is like confessing a murder) immutable."

The Galapagos is an archipelago of thirteen good-sized islands and many smaller ones lying off the coast of Ecuador. If all the species on Earth were immutable, then why did the beaks of the otherwise very similar finches on islands separated by no more than fifty or sixty miles of ocean vary so dramatically? Why narrow, tiny, pointy beaks on the finches of one island and larger, parrot-like curved beaks on the finches of the next? "Seeing this gradation and diversity of structure in one, small intimately related group of birds," he later wrote in *The Voyage*, "one might really fancy that, from an original paucity of birds in this archipelago, one species had been taken and modified for different ends." (These volcanic islands, we now know, are less than 5 million years old.) And it wasn't just the finches that raised such problems, but the giant tortoises and the mockingbirds, too.

Back in England, Henslow and [Adam] Sedgwick [Darwin's old teacher] had been reading Darwin's letters aloud at meetings of scientific societies. When Darwin returned home in October 1836, he found he had acquired something of a reputation as an explorer and naturalist. His father was now well pleased with him, and all talk of a parsonage ceased. The same month he met the geologist, Lyell, for the first time. Though not without its rough spots, it was to be a lifelong friendship.

Darwin made important contributions to geology. His interpretation of coral reefs—that they mark the locations of slowly subsiding seamounts that had once been islands—was substantiated on the *Beagle* and corresponds to the modern understanding. In 1838 he published a paper arguing that earthquakes, volcanoes, and the thrusting up of islands are all caused by slow, intermittent, but irresistible global motions in the semi-liquid interior of the Earth. This . . . thesis, as far as it goes, is part and parcel of modern geophysics. In his 1838 Presidential Address to the Geological Society, William Whewell mentioned Darwin's name (in the context of this work) more than twice as often as any other geologist, living or dead. In geology, following Lyell, as in biology, Darwin championed the idea that profound changes are worked little by little over vast intervals of time.

How Darwin Conceived of Natural Selection, the Kernel of His Theory

Daniel C. Dennett

This essay is by Daniel C. Dennett, arts and sciences professor and director of the Center for Cognitive Studies at Tufts University. As he explains, Darwin's great idea was not evolution itself, since several other researchers, including his own grandfather, had proposed that species change and evolve over time. Darwin's main contribution was an explanation of the specific physical process driving evolution, a process he came to call natural selection. Dennett tells how Darwin got the inspiration for the idea from reading Thomas Malthus's famous essay on population.

Darwin's project in *Origin of Species* can be divided in two: to prove *that* modern species were revised descendants of earlier species—species had evolved—and to show *how* this process of "descent with modification" had occurred. If Darwin hadn't had a vision of a mechanism, natural selection, by which this well-nigh-inconceivable historical transformation could have been accomplished, he would probably not have had the motivation to assemble all the circumstantial evidence that it had actually occurred. Today we can readily enough imagine proving Darwin's first case—the brute historic fact of descent with modification—quite independently of any consideration of natural selection or indeed any other mechanism for bringing these brute events about, but for Darwin the idea of the mechanism was both the hunting license he needed, and an unwavering guide to the right questions to ask.

The idea of natural selection was not itself a miraculously novel creation of Darwin's but, rather, the offspring of earlier ideas that had been vigorously discussed for years and even generations. Chief among these parent ideas was an insight Darwin gained from reflection on the 1798 *Essay on the Principle of Population* by Thomas Malthus, which argued that population explosion and famine were inevitable, given the excess fertility of human beings, unless drastic measures were taken. The grim Malthusian vision of the social and political forces that could act to check human overpopulation may have strongly flavored Darwin's thinking (and undoubtedly has flavored the shallow political attacks of many an anti-Darwinian), but the idea Darwin needed from Malthus is purely logical. It has nothing at all to do with political ideology, and can be expressed in very abstract and general terms.

CRUNCH TIME

Suppose a world in which organisms have many offspring. Since the offspring themselves will have many offspring, the population will grow and grow ("geometrically") until inevitably, sooner or later—surprisingly soon, in fact—it must grow too large for the available resources (of food, of space, of whatever the organisms need to survive long enough to reproduce). At that point, whenever it happens, not all organisms will have offspring. Many will die childless. It was Malthus who pointed out the mathematical inevitability of such a crunch in *any* population of long-term reproducers—people, animals, plants (or, for that matter, Martian clone-machines, not that such fanciful possibilities were discussed by Malthus). Those populations that reproduce at less than the replacement rate are headed for extinction unless they reverse the trend. Populations that maintain a stable population over long periods of time will do so by settling on a rate of overproduction of offspring that is balanced by the vicissitudes encountered. This is obvious, perhaps, for houseflies and other prodigious breeders, but Darwin drove the point home with a calculation of his own: "The elephant is reckoned to be the slowest breeder of all known animals, and I have taken some pains to estimate its probable minimum rate of natural increase: . . . at the end of the fifth century there would be alive fifteen million elephants, descended from the first pair" (*Origin*, p. 64). Since elephants have been around for millions of years, we can be sure that only a fraction of the elephants born in any period have progeny of their own.

So the normal state of affairs for any sort of reproducers is one in which more offspring are produced in any one generation than will in turn reproduce in the next. In other words, it is almost always crunch time. At such a crunch, which prospective parents will "win"? Will it be a fair lottery, in which

---

THE MECHANISM FOR PASSING ON NEW TRAITS

Scientists Robert M. Hazen and James Trefil here explain how later researchers filled in a missing piece from Darwin's theory, namely DNA, the genetic code that is literally life's blueprint. The discovery of genes, DNA, and how they can change over time, leading to physical variations in plants and animals, helped to confirm Darwin's theory of natural selection.

The great gap in Darwin's thesis, and an obvious target for his critics, was the absence of any known mechanism to introduce and pass on new traits and variation. Gregor Mendel and subsequent geneticists learned part of the story, but not until the structure and function of DNA were determined did the way variations are produced become clear. No matter how reliable the duplication of DNA might be, mistakes do happen. Damage from X rays, ultraviolet radiation, heat, or certain chemicals increases the rate of errors. Over time many small changes, called mutations, creep into a gene. Some errors are unimportant and get passed on to offspring without any discernible effect. Some errors are disastrous and destroy any chance for viable offspring. Some errors lead to genetic diseases, by which some small but critical part of the body's chemical machinery fails to operate properly. And once in a very great while a chance error results in a new, desirable trait that confers an advantage on offspring, and natural selection takes over to spread that trait through subsequent generations. Over the span of millions of years such small changes accumulate to become major differences.

One of Darwin's most profound insights is that life evolves because it is so competitive. Random variations and chance mutations occasionally lead to advantages, which are preserved as *nonrandom* evolution. Giraffes did not evolve long necks by stretching to reach the highest branches. Rather, natural selection favored the animals that by chance happen to be slightly taller. Individual traits vary at random, but nature selects traits by circumstance.

Robert M. Hazen and James Trefil, *Science Matters: Achieving Scientific Literacy.* New York: Doubleday, 1991, p. 250.

every organism has an equal chance of being among the few that reproduce? In a political context, this is where invidious themes enter, about power, privilege, injustice, treachery, class warfare, and the like, but we can elevate the observation from its political birthplace and consider in the abstract, as Darwin did, what would—must—happen in nature. Darwin added two further logical points to the insight he had found in Malthus: the first was that at crunch time, if there was significant variation among the contestants, then any advantages enjoyed by any of the contestants would inevitably bias the sample that reproduced. However tiny the advantage in question, if it was actually an advantage (and thus not absolutely invisible to nature), it would tip the scales in favor of those who held it. The second was that *if* there was a "strong principle of inheritance"—if offspring tended to be more like their parents than like their parents' contemporaries—the biases created by advantages, however small, would become amplified over time, creating trends that could grow indefinitely. "More individuals are born than can possibly survive. A grain in the balance will determine which individual shall live and which shall die,—which variety or species shall increase in number, and which shall decrease, or finally become extinct" (*Origin,* p. 467).

IN THE STRUGGLE FOR LIFE

What Darwin saw was that if one merely supposed these few general conditions to apply at crunch time—conditions for which he could supply ample evidence—the resulting process would *necessarily* lead in the direction of individuals in future generations who tended to be better equipped to deal with the problems of resource limitation that had been faced by the individuals of their parents' generation. This fundamental idea—Darwin's dangerous idea, the idea that generates so much insight, turmoil, confusion, anxiety—is thus actually quite simple. Darwin summarizes it in two long sentences at the end of chapter 4 of *Origin:*

> If during the long course of ages and under varying conditions of life, organic beings vary at all in the several parts of their organization, and I think this cannot be disputed; if there be, owing to the high geometric powers of increase of each species, at some age, season, or year, a severe struggle for life, and this certainly cannot be disputed; then, considering the infinite complexity of the relations of all organic beings to each other and to their conditions of existence, caus-

ing an infinite diversity in structure, constitution, and habits, to be advantageous to them, I think it would be a most extraordinary fact if no variation ever had occurred useful to each being's own welfare, in the same way as so many variations have occurred useful to man. But if variations useful to any organic being do occur, assuredly individuals thus characterized will have the best chance of being preserved in the struggle for life; and from the strong principle of inheritance they will tend to produce offspring similarly characterized. This principle of preservation, I have called, for the sake of brevity, Natural Selection. [*Origin*, p. 127]

This was Darwin's great idea, not the idea of evolution, but the idea of evolution *by natural selection*, an idea he himself could never formulate with sufficient rigor and detail to prove, though he presented a brilliant case for it.

The Progress of Darwin's Research as Revealed in His Letters to Hooker

Charles Darwin (edited by his son, Francis)

Darwin wrote the following letters to his close colleague and friend, botanist J.D. Hooker between 1844 and 1856. Along with other similar letters, they reveal some of the many ideas and researches that Darwin concerned himself with during these busy and productive years. Note the contrast between his tentative statement in the January 11, 1844, letter: "I am almost convinced . . . that species are not . . . immutable [unchangeable]," and the more assertive one of July 18, 1855: "The way in which I intend treating the subject, is to show . . . the facts and arguments for and against the common descent of species."

C. Darwin to J.D. Hooker.
[January 11th, 1844.]

Besides a general interest about the southern lands, I have been now ever since my return engaged in a very presumptuous work, and I know no one individual who would not say a very foolish one. I was so struck with the distribution of the Galapagos organisms, &c. &c., and with the character of the American fossil mammifers, &c. &c., that I determined to collect blindly every sort of fact, which could bear any way on what are species. I have read heaps of agricultural and horticultural books, and have never ceased collecting facts. At last gleams of light have come, and I am almost convinced (quite contrary to the opinion I started with) that species are not (it is like confessing a murder) immutable. Heaven forfend me from [Jean Baptiste] Lamarck nonsense of a "tendency to progression," "adaptations from the slow

Reprinted from Charles Darwin's letters to J.D. Hooker between 1844 and 1856, in *The Life and Letters of Charles Darwin*, edited by Francis Darwin, vol. 1 (New York: Basic Books, 1959).

willing of animals," &c.! But the conclusions I am led to are not widely different from his; though the means of change are wholly so. I think I have found out (here's presumption!) the simple way by which species become exquisitely adapted to various ends. You will now groan, and think to yourself, "on what a man have I been wasting my time writing to." I should, five years ago, have thought so. . . .

[February 23, 1844.]

DEAR HOOKER,—I hope you will excuse the freedom of my address, but I feel that as co-circum-wanderers and as fellow labourers (though myself a very weak one) we may throw aside some of the old-world formality. . . . I have just finished a little volume on the volcanic islands which we visited. I do not know how far you care for dry simple geology, but I hope you will let me send you a copy. I suppose I can send it from London by common coach conveyance.

. . . I am going to ask you some *more* questions, though I daresay, without asking them, I shall see answers in your work, when published, which will be quite time enough for my purposes. First for the Galapagos, you will see in my journal, that the Birds, though peculiar species, have a most obvious S. [South] American aspect: I have just ascertained the same thing holds good with the sea-shells. It is so with those plants which are peculiar to this archipelago; you state that their numerical proportions are continental (is not this a very curious fact?) but are they related in forms to S. America. Do you know of any other case of an archipelago, with the separate islands possessing distinct representative species? I have always intended (but have not yet done so) to examine [the work of researchers] Webb and Berthelot on the Canary Islands for this object. Talking with [the noted botanist] Mr. [George] Bentham, he told me that the separate islands of the Sandwich Archipelago possessed distinct representative species of the same genera of Labiatae: would not this be worth your enquiry? How is it with the Azores; to be sure the heavy western gales would tend to diffuse the same species over that group.

I hope you will (I dare say my hope is quite superfluous) attend to this general kind of affinity in isolated islands, though I suppose it is more difficult to perceive this sort of relation in plants, than in birds or quadrupeds, the groups of which are, I fancy, rather more confined. Can St. Helena [a volcanic island in the southern Atlantic] be classed, though remotely, either with Africa or S. America? From some facts, which I have collected, I have been led to conclude that the fauna of mountains are *either* remarkably similar (some-times in the presence of the same species and at other times of same genera), *or* that they are remarkably dissimilar; and it has occurred to me that possibly part of this peculiarity of the St. Helena and Galapagos floras may be attributed to a great part of these two Floras being mountain Floras. I fear my notes will hardly serve to distinguish much of the habi-tats of the Galapagos plants, but they may in some cases; most, if not all, of the green, leafy plants come from the sum-mits of the islands, and the thin brown leafless plants come from the lower arid parts: would you be so kind as to bear this remark in mind, when examining my collection.

I will trouble you with only one other question. In discus-sion with [the noted ornithologist] Mr. [John] Gould, I found that in most of the genera of birds which range over the whole or greater part of the world, the individual species have wider ranges, thus the Owl is mundane, and many of the species have very wide ranges. So I believe it is with land and fresh-water shells—and I might adduce other cases. Is it not so with Cryptogamic plants; have not most of the species wide ranges, in those genera which are mundane? I do not suppose that the converse holds, viz.—that when a species has a wide range, its genus also ranges wide. Will you so far oblige me by occasionally thinking over this? It would cost me vast trouble to get a list of mundane phanerogamic gen-era and then search how far the species of these genera are apt to range wide in their several countries; but you might occasionally, in the course of your pursuits, just bear this in mind, though perhaps the point may long since have oc-curred to you or other Botanists. Geology is bringing to light interesting facts, concerning the ranges of shells; I think it is pretty well established, that according as the geographical range of a species is wide, so is its persistence and duration in time. I hope you will try to grudge as little as you can the trouble of my letters, and pray believe me very truly yours,

C. DARWIN.

P.S. I should feel extremely obliged for your kind offer sketch of [the well-known German naturalist Alexander von] Humboldt; I venerate him, and after having had the pleasure of conversing with him in London, I shall still more like to have any portrait of him. . . .

C. Darwin to J.D. Hooker.

Down [1844].

. . . The conclusion, which I have come at is, that those areas, in which species are most numerous, have oftenest been divided and isolated from other areas, united and again divided; a process implying antiquity and some changes in the external conditions. This will justly sound very hypothetical. I cannot give my reasons in detail; but the most general conclusion, which the geographical distribution of all organic beings, appears to me to indicate, is that isolation is the chief concomitant or cause of the appearance of *new* forms (I well know there are some staring exceptions). Secondly, from seeing how often the plants and animals swarm in a country, when introduced into it, and from seeing what a vast number of plants will live, for instance in England, if kept *free from weeds, and native plants,* I have been led to consider that the spreading and number of the organic beings of any country depend less on its external features, than on the number of forms, which have been there originally created or produced. I much doubt whether you will find it possible to explain the number of forms by proportional differences of exposure; and I cannot doubt if half the species in any country were destroyed or had not been created, yet that country would appear to us fully peopled. With respect to original creation or production of new forms, I have said that isolation appears the chief element. Hence, with respect to terrestrial productions, a tract of country, which had oftenest within the late geological periods subsided and been converted into islands, and reunited, I should expect to contain most forms.

But such speculations are amusing only to one self, and in this case useless, as they do not show any direct line of observation: if I had seen how hypothetical [is] the little, which I have unclearly written, I would not have troubled you with the reading of it. Believe me,—at last not hypothetically,

Yours very sincerely,

C. Darwin.

C. Darwin to J.D. Hooker.

Down, 1844.

. . . I forget my last letter, but it must have been a very silly

one, as it seems I gave my notion of the number of species being in great degree governed by the degree to which the area
had been often isolated and divided; I must have been cracked
to have written it, for I have no evidence, without a person be
willing to admit all my views, and then it does follow; but in
my most sanguine moments, all I expect, is that I shall be able
to show even to sound Naturalists, that there are two sides to
the question of the immutability of species;—that facts can be
viewed and grouped under the notion of allied species having
descended from common stocks. With respect to books on this
subject, I do not know of any systematical ones, except
Lamarck's, which is veritable rubbish; but there are plenty, as
[Charles] Lyell, Pritchard, &c., on the view of the immutability. . . . Is it not strange that the author, of such a book as the
'Animaux sans Vertèbres,' [Jean Baptiste Lamarck] should
have written that insects, which never see their eggs, should
will (and plants, their seeds) to be of particular forms, so as to
become attached to particular objects. The other, common
(specially Germanic) notion is hardly less absurd, viz. that climate, food, &c., should make a Pediculus formed to climb
hair, or wood-pecker, to climb trees. I believe all these absurd
views arise, from no one having, as far as I know, approached
the subject on the side of variation under domestication, and
having studied all that is known about domestication. I was
very glad to hear your criticism on island-floras and on non-
diffusion of plants: the subject is too long for a letter: I could
defend myself to some considerable extent, but I doubt
whether successfully in your eyes, or indeed in my own. . . .

C. Darwin to J.D. Hooker.
Down, 18th [July, 1855].

. . . I think I am getting a *mild* case about Charlock seed;
but just as about salting, ill luck to it, I cannot remember
how many years you would allow that Charlock seed might
live in the ground. Next time you write, show a bold face,
and say in how many years, you think, Charlock seed would
probably all be dead. A man told me the other day of, as I
thought, a splendid instance,—and *splendid* it was, for according to his evidence the seed came up alive out of the
lower part of the London Clay!!! I disgusted him by telling
him that Palms ought to have come up.

You ask how far I go in attributing organisms to a common descent; I answer I know not; the way in which I intend

treating the subject, is to show (*as far as I can*) the facts and arguments for and against the common descent of the species of the same genus; and then show how far the same arguments tell for or against forms, more and more widely different: and when we come to forms of different orders and classes, there remain only some such arguments as those which can perhaps be deduced from similar rudimentary structures, and very soon not an argument is left. . . .

C. Darwin to J.D. Hooker.

May 9th, [1856].

. . . I very much want advice and *truthful* consolation if you can give it. I had a good talk with Lyell about my species work, and he urges me strongly to publish something. I am fixed against any periodical or journal, as I positively will *not* expose myself to an Editor or a Council, allowing a publication for which they might be abused. If I publish anything it must be a *very thin* and little volume, giving a sketch of my views and difficulties; but it is really dreadfully unphilosophical to give a *resumé* without exact references of an unpublished work. But Lyell seemed to think I might do this, at the suggestion of friends, and on the ground, which I might state, that I had been at work for eighteen years, and yet could not publish for several years, and especially as I could point out difficulties which seemed to me to require especial investigation. Now what think you? I should be really grateful for advice. I thought of giving up a couple of months and writing such a sketch, and trying to keep my judgment open whether or no to publish it when completed. It will be simply impossible for me to give exact references; anything important I should state on the authority of the author generally; and instead of giving all the facts on which I ground my opinion, I could give by memory only one or two. In the Preface I would state that the work could not be considered strictly scientific, but a mere sketch or outline of a future work in which full references, &c., should be given. Eheu, eheu, I believe I should sneer at any one else doing this, and my only comfort is, that I *truly* never dreamed of it, till Lyell suggested it, and seems deliberately to think it advisable.

I am in a peck of troubles and do pray forgive me for troubling you.

Yours affectionately,
C. Darwin.

Wallace's Theory of Evolution

Alfred Russel Wallace (with a synopsis by John L. Brooks)

One of the major factors affecting the latter stages of Darwin's writing of his masterwork, *The Origin of Species,* was the unexpected discovery that a colleague, Alfred Russel Wallace, was independently working along extremely similar lines. Because of the fear of losing priority (credit for being the first to discover the idea), Darwin speeded up his work on *Origin.* Following is a slightly edited version of the essay Wallace sent to Darwin, unaware that the older naturalist had already come to similar conclusions (and had even adopted similar terminology, such as the "struggle for existence") and accumulated a vast amount of evidence to substantiate it. To aid the general reader, the essay is preceded by an eight-point synopsis of the main points, as provided by John L. Brooks, Division Director of Biotic Systems and Resources at the National Science Foundation in Washington, D.C.

1. Varieties can be expected to differ in organization and habits from each other and from the "parent species," and hence in their ability to gather food.
2. Even slight differences will make a variety "inferior" or "superior" to the parent species *under a given set of conditions.*
3. The size of any population is the reflection of its food-gathering ability, not of its reproductive capacities.
4. Suppose, then, that a "parent species" is represented in different geographical areas by an "inferior" and a "superior" variety. If the general circumstances should worsen, as in a prolonged drought, making basic food scarce, the

Excerpted from *Just Before the Origin*, by Alfred Russel Wallace. Copyright ©1984 by Columbia University Press. Reprinted with the permission of the publisher.

populations of all three will dwindle.

5. But the variety "inferior" in its food-gathering abilities
   and the consequent size of its population will be the first
   to dwindle to extinction, followed by the parent species. At
   that point only the "superior" variety, initially most numerous, will survive.

6. If conditions ameliorate, the basic food (plants) will again
   become abundant, and the population of the only surviving population, the "superior" variety, will increase its
   numbers and extend its range, alone attaining the size
   and range of the three former populations.

7. Thus the "superior" variety has replaced the parent
   species, becoming what must be called a new species and
   in time becoming a "parent," geographical representatives of which may become new varieties.

8. Repetition of the process results in progressive development (progression of types) and continued divergence
   from the original type.

On the Tendency of Varieties to Depart Indefinitely from the Original Type
By Alfred Russel Wallace

One of the strongest arguments which have been adduced
to prove the original and permanent distinctness of species is,
that *varieties* produced in a state of domesticity are more or
less unstable, and often have a tendency, if left to themselves,
to return to the normal form of the parent species; and this
instability is considered to be a distinctive peculiarity of all
varieties, even of these occurring among wild animals in a
state of nature, and to constitute a provision for preserving
unchanged the originally created distinct species.

In the absence or scarcity of facts and observations as to
varieties occurring among wild animals, this argument has
had great weight with naturalists, and has led to a very general and somewhat prejudiced belief in the stability of
species. Equally general, however, is the belief in what are
called "permanent or true varieties,"—races of animals
which continually propagate their like, but which differ so
slightly (although constantly) from some other race, that the
one is considered to be a *variety* of the other. Which is the *variety* and which the original *species*, there is generally no
means of determining, except in those rare cases in which
the one race has been known to produce an offspring unlike

itself and resembling the other. This, however, would seem quite incompatible with the "permanent invariability of species," but the difficulty is overcome by assuming that such varieties have strict limits, and can never again vary further from the original type, although they may return to it, which, from the analogy of the domesticated animals, is considered to be highly probable, if not certainly proved.

It will be observed that this argument rests entirely on the assumption, that *varieties* occurring in a state of nature are in all respects analogous to or even identical with those of domestic animals, and are governed by the same laws as regards their permanence or further variation. But it is the object of the present paper to show that this assumption is altogether false, that there is a general principle in nature which will cause many *varieties* to survive the parent species, and to give rise to successive variations departing further and further from the original type, and which also produces, in domesticated animals, the tendency of varieties to return to the parent form.

ABUNDANCY AND SCARCITY

The life of wild animals is a struggle for existence. The full exertion of all their faculties and all their energies is required to preserve their own existence and provide for that of their infant offspring. The possibility of procuring food during the least favourable seasons, and of escaping the attacks of their most dangerous enemies, are the primary conditions which determine the existence both of individuals and of entire species. These conditions will also determine the population of a species; and by a careful consideration of all the circumstances we may be enabled to comprehend, and in some degree to explain, what at first sight appears to be inexplicable—the excessive abundance of some species, while others closely allied to them are very rare.

The general proportion that must obtain between certain groups of animals is readily seen. Large animals cannot be so abundant as small ones; the carnivora [meat eaters] must be less numerous than the herbivora [plant eaters]; eagles and lions can never be so plentiful as pigeons and antelopes; the wild asses of the Tartarian deserts cannot equal in numbers the horses of the more luxuriant prairies and pampas of America. The greater or less fecundity [fertility] of an animal is often considered to be one of the chief causes of its abundance or scarcity; but a consideration of the facts will show us that it really has little or nothing to do with the matter. Even the least prolific of animals would increase rapidly if unchecked, whereas it is evident that the animal population of the globe must be stationary, or perhaps, through the influence of man, decreasing. Fluctuations there may be; but permanent increase, except in restricted localities, is almost impossible. For example, our own observation must convince us that birds do not go on increasing every year in a geometrical ratio, as they would do, were there not some powerful check to their natural increase. Very few birds produce less than two young ones each year, while many have six, eight, or ten; four will certainly be below the average; and if we suppose that each pair produce young only four times in their life, that will also be below the average, supposing them not to die either by violence or want of food. Yet at this rate how tremendous would be the increase in a few years from a single pair! A simple calculation will show that in fifteen years each pair of birds would have increased to nearly ten millions! whereas we have not reason to believe that the number of the birds of any country increases at all in fifteen or in one hundred and fifty years. With such powers of increase the population must have reached its limits, and have become stationary, in a very few years after the origin of each species. It is evident, therefore, that each year an immense number of birds perish—as many in fact as are born; and as on the lowest calculation the progeny are each year twice as numerous as their parents, it follows that, whatever be the average number of individuals existing in any given country, *twice that number must perish annually*—a striking result, but one which seems at least highly probable, and is perhaps under rather than over the truth.

THE WEAKEST ALWAYS SUCCUMB

It would therefore appear that, as far as the continuance of the species and the keeping up the average numbers of individuals are concerned, large broods are superfluous. On the average all above *one* become food for hawks and kites, wild cats and weasels, or perish of cold and hunger as winter comes on. This is strikingly proved by the case of particular species; for we find that their abundance in individuals bears no relation whatever to their fertility in producing offspring. Perhaps the most remarkable instance of an immense bird population is that of the passenger pigeon of the United States, which lays only one, or at most two eggs, and is said to rear generally but one young one. Why is this bird so extraordinarily abundant, while others producing two or three times as many young are much less plentiful? The explanation is not difficult. The food most congenial to this species, and on which it thrives best, is abundantly distributed over a very extensive region, offering such differences of soil and climate, that in one part or another of the area the supply never fails. The bird is capable of a very rapid and long-continued flight, so that it can pass without fatigue over the whole of the district it inhabits, and as soon as the supply of food begins to fail in one place is able to discover a fresh feeding ground. This example strikingly shows us that the procuring a constant supply of wholesome food is almost the sole condition requisite for ensuring the rapid increase of a given species, since neither the limited fecundity, nor the unrestrained attacks of birds of prey and of man are here sufficient to check it. In no other birds are these peculiar circumstances so strikingly combined. Either their food is more liable to failure, or they have not sufficient power of wing to search for it over an extensive area, or during some season of the year it becomes very scarce, and less wholesome substitutes have to be found; and thus, though more fertile in offspring, they can never increase beyond the supply of food in the least favourable seasons. . . . This is probably the reason why woodpeckers are scarce with us, while in the tropics they are among the most abundant of solitary birds. Thus the house sparrow is more abundant than the redbreast, because its food is more constant and plentiful,— seeds of grasses being preserved during the winter, and our farm-yards and stubble-fields furnishing an almost inexhaustible supply. Why, as a general rule, are aquatic, and especially sea birds, very numerous in individuals? Not because they are more prolific than others, generally the contrary; but because their food never fails, the sea-shores and river-banks daily swarming with a fresh supply of small mollusca and crustacea. Exactly the same laws will apply to mammals. Wild cats are prolific and have few enemies; why then are they never as abundant as rabbits? The only intelligible answer is, that their supply of food is more precarious. It appears evident, therefore, that so long as a country remains physically unchanged, the numbers of its animal population cannot materially increase. If one species does so, some other requiring the same kind of food must diminish in proportion. The numbers that die annually must be immense; and as the individual existence of each animal depends upon itself, those that die must be the weakest—the very young, the aged, and the diseased,—while those that prolong their existence can only be the most perfect in health and vigour—those who are best able to obtain food regularly, and avoid their numerous enemies. It is, as we commenced by remarking, "a struggle for existence," in which the weakest and least perfectly organized must always succumb.

Effects of Variations

Now it is clear that what takes place among the individuals of a species must also occur among the several allied species of a group,—viz. that those which are best adapted to obtain a regular supply of food, and to defend themselves against the attacks of their enemies and the vicissitudes of the seasons, must necessarily obtain and preserve a superiority in population; while those species which from some defect of power or organization are the least capable of counteracting the vicissitudes of food, supply, &c., must diminish in numbers, and, in extreme cases, become altogether extinct. Between these extremes the species will present various degrees of capacity for ensuring the means of preserving life; and it is thus we account for the abundance or rarity of species. Our ignorance will generally prevent us from accurately tracing the effects to their causes; but could we become perfectly acquainted with the organization and habits of the various species of animals, and could we measure the capacity of each for performing the different acts necessary to its safety and existence under all the varying circumstances by which it is surrounded, we might be able even to calculate the proportionate abundance of individuals which is the necessary result.

If now we have succeeded in establishing these two points—1st, *that the animal population of a country is generally stationary, being kept down by a periodical deficiency of food and other checks;* and, 2nd, *that the comparative abundance or scarcity of the individuals of the several species is entirely due to their organization and resulting habits, which, rendering it more difficult to procure a regular supply of food and to provide for their personal safety in some cases than in others, can only be balanced by a difference in the population which have to exist in a given area*—we shall be in a condition to proceed to the consideration of *varieties*, to which the preceding remarks have a direct and very important application.

Most or perhaps all the variations from the typical form of a species must have some definite effect, however slight, on the habits or capacities of the individuals. Even a change of colour might, by rendering them more or less distinguishable, affect their safety; a greater or less development of hair might modify their habits. More important changes, such as an increase in the power or dimensions of the limbs or any of the external organs, would more or less affect their mode of procuring food or the range of country which they inhabit. It is also evident that most changes would affect, either favourably or adversely, the powers of prolonging existence. An antelope with shorter or weaker legs must necessarily suffer more from the attacks of the feline carnivora [i.e., lion or other big cat]; the passenger pigeon with less powerful wings would sooner or later be affected in its powers of procuring a regular supply of food; and in both cases the result must necessarily be a diminution of the modified species. If, on the other hand, any species should produce a variety having slightly increased powers of preserving existence, that variety must inevitably in time acquire a superiority in numbers. These results must follow as surely as old age, intemperance, or scarcity of food produce an increased mortality. In both cases there may be many individual exceptions; but on the average the rule will invariably be found to hold good. All varieties will therefore fall into two classes— those which under the same conditions would never reach the population of the parent species, and those which would in time obtain and keep a numerical superiority. Now, let some alteration of physical conditions occur in the district— a long period of drought, a destruction of vegetation by locusts, the irruption of some new carnivorous animal seeking "pastures new" —any change in fact tending to render existence more difficult to the species in question, and tasking its utmost powers to avoid complete extermination; it is evident that, of all the individuals composing the species, those forming the least numerous and most feebly organized variety would suffer first, and, were the pressure severe, must soon become extinct. The same causes continuing in action, the parent species would next suffer, would gradually diminish in numbers, and with a recurrence of similar unfavourable conditions might also become extinct. The superior variety would then alone remain, and on a return to favourable circumstances would rapidly increase in numbers and occupy the place of the extinct species and variety.

CONTINUED DIVERGENCE

The *variety* would now have replaced the *species*, of which it would be a more perfectly developed and more highly organized form. It would be in all respects better adapted to secure its safety, and to prolong its individual existence and that of the race. Such a variety *could not* return to the original form; for that form is an inferior one, and could never compete with it for existence. Granted, therefore, a "tendency" to reproduce the original type of the species, still the variety must ever remain preponderant in numbers, and under adverse physical conditions *again alone survive.* But this new, improved, and populous race might itself, in course of time, give rise to new varieties, exhibiting several diverging modifications of form, any of which, tending to increase the facilities for preserving existence, must, by the same general law, in their turn become predominant. Here, then, we have *progression and continued divergence* deduced from the general laws which regulate the existence of animals in a state of nature, and from the undisputed fact that varieties do frequently occur. It is not, however, contended that this result would be invariable; a change of physical conditions in the district might at times materially modify it, rendering the race which had been the most capable of supporting existence under the former conditions now the least so, and even causing the extinction of the new and, for a time, superior race, while the old parent species and its first inferior varieties continued to flourish. Variations in unimportant parts might also occur, having no perceptible effect on the life-preserving powers; and the varieties so furnished might run a course parallel with the parent species, either giving rise to further variations or returning to the former type. All we argue for is, that certain varieties have a tendency to maintain their existence longer than the original species, and this tendency must make itself felt; for though the doctrine of chances or averages can never be trusted to on a limited scale, yet if applied to high numbers, the results come nearer to what theory demands, and, as we approach to an infinity of examples, become strictly accurate. Now the scale on which nature works is so vast—the numbers of individuals and periods of time with which she deals approach so near to infinity, that any cause, however slight, and however liable to be veiled and counteracted by accidental circumstances, must in the end produce its full legitimate results.

WILD VERSUS DOMESTIC ANIMALS

Let us now turn to domesticated animals, and inquire how varieties produced among them are affected by the principles here enunciated. The essential difference in the condition of wild and domestic animals is this,—that among the former, their well-being and very existence depend upon the full exercise and healthy condition of all their senses and physical powers, whereas among the latter, these are only partially exercised, and in some cases are absolutely unused. A wild animal has to search, and often to labour, for every mouthful of food—to exercise sight, hearing, and smell in seeking it, and in avoiding dangers, in procuring shelter from the inclemency of the seasons, and in providing for the subsistence and safety of its offspring. There is no muscle of its body that is not called into daily and hourly activity; there is no sense or faculty that is not strengthened by continual exercise. The domestic animal, on the other hand, has food provided for it, is sheltered, and often confined, to guard it against the vicissitudes [changes] of the seasons, is carefully secured from the attacks of its natural enemies, and seldom even rears its young without human assistance. Half of its senses and faculties are quite useless; and the other half are but occasionally called into feeble exercise, while even its muscular system is only irregularly called into action.

Now when a variety of such an animal occurs, having increased power or capacity in any organ or sense, such increase is totally useless, is never called into action, and may even exist without the animal ever becoming aware of it. In the wild animal, on the contrary, all its faculties and powers being brought into full action for the necessities of existence, any increase becomes immediately available, is strengthened by exercise, and must even slightly modify the food, the habits, and the whole economy of the race. It creates as it were a new animal, one of superior powers, and which will necessarily increase in numbers and outlive those inferior to it.

Again, in the domesticated animal all varieties have an equal chance of continuance; and those which would decidedly render a wild animal unable to compete with its fellows and continue its existence are no disadvantage whatever in a state of domesticity. Our quickly fattening pigs, short-legged sheep, pouter pigeons, and poodle dogs could never have come into existence in a state of nature, because the very first steps toward such inferior forms would have led to the rapid extinction of the race; still less could they now exist in competition with their wild allies. The great speed but slight endurance of the race horse, the unwieldy strength of the ploughman's team, would both be useless in a state of nature. If turned wild on the pampas, such animals would probably soon become extinct, or under favourable circumstances might each lose those extreme qualities which would never be called into action, and in a few generations would revert to a common type, which must be that in which the various powers and faculties are so proportioned to each other as to be best adapted to procure food and secure safety,—that in which by the full exercise of every part of his organization the animal can alone continue to live. Domestic varieties, when turned wild, *must* return to something near the type of the original wild stock, *or become altogether extinct.* . . .

A BALANCE IN NATURE

The hypothesis of [Jean Baptiste] Lamarck—that progressive changes in species have been produced by the attempts of animals to increase the development of their own organs, and thus modify their structure and habits—has been repeatedly and easily refuted by all writers on the subject of varieties and species, and it seems to have been considered that when this was done the whole question has been finally settled; but the view here developed renders such an hypothesis quite unnecessary, by showing that similar results must be produced by the action of principles constantly at work in nature. The powerful retractile talons of the falcon- and the cat-tribes have not been produced or increased by the volition of those animals: but among the different varieties which occurred in the earlier and less highly organized forms of these groups, *those always survived longest which had the greatest facilities for seizing their prey.* Neither did the giraffe acquire its long neck by desiring to reach the foliage of the more lofty shrubs, and constantly stretching its neck for the purpose, but because any varieties which occurred among its anti-types [ancestral forms] with a longer neck than usual *at once secured a fresh range of pasture over the same ground as their shorter-necked companions, and on the first scarcity of food were thereby enabled to outlive them.* Even the peculiar colours of many animals, especially insects, so closely re-sembling the soil or the leaves of the trunks on which they habitually reside, are explained on the same principle; for though in the course of ages varieties of many tints have oc-curred, *yet those races having colours best adopted to con-cealment from their enemies would inevitably survive the longest.* We have also here an acting cause to account for that balance so often observed in nature,—a deficiency in one set of organs always being compensated by an increased devel-opment of some others—powerful wings accompanying weak feet, or great velocity making up for the absence of de-fensive weapons; for it has been shown that all varieties in which an unbalanced deficiency occurred could not long continue their existence. The action of this principle is ex-actly like that of the centrifugal governor of the steam engine, which checks and corrects any irregularities almost before they become evident; and in like manner no unbalanced de-ficiency in the animal kingdom can ever reach any conspic-uous magnitude, because it would make itself felt at the very first step, by rendering existence difficult and extinction al-most sure soon to follow. . . .

We believe we have now shown that there is a tendency in nature to the continued progression of certain classes of *va-rieties* further and further from the original type—a progres-sion to which there appears no reason to assign any definite limits—and that the same principle which produces this re-sult in a state of nature will also explain why domestic vari-eties have a tendency to revert to the original type. This pro-gression, by minute steps, in various directions, but always checked and balanced by the necessary conditions, subject to which alone existence can be preserved, may, it is be-lieved, be followed out so as to agree with all the phenom-ena presented by organized beings, their extinction and suc-cession in past ages, and all the extraordinary modifications of form, instinct, and habits which they exhibit.

The Finished Product: Darwin Presents His Theory to the World

Charles Darwin

When Darwin's *Origin of Species* appeared in print toward the end of 1859, it marked the culmination of almost thirty years of investigations and researches and some twenty years of painstaking thought and collection of data to formulate and support the theory of natural selection. Chapter 3 is reproduced here in its entirety. In it, Darwin explains and gives examples of the "struggle for existence," the natural competition in which plants and minerals fight to survive, thereby setting in motion the process of natural selection, which allows the strongest among them to survive and pass on their superior traits to their offspring. For its conceptual brilliance, logical and precise organization and presentation, and clarity of expression, this tract stands on its own as one of the greatest scientific writings of all time. Note also how Darwin frequently and very graciously and professionally mentions and gives credit to others whose ideas and data he has drawn on. These include, among others, philosopher Herbert Spencer, horticulturalist W. Herbert, geologist Charles Lyell, botanists Augustin-Pyrame de Candolle and Hugh Falconer, and economist Thomas Malthus.

CHAPTER III
STRUGGLE FOR EXISTENCE

Its bearing on natural selection—The term used in a wide sense—Geometrical ratio of increase—Rapid increase of naturalised animals and plants—Nature of the checks in increase—Competition universal—Effects of climate—Protection from the number of individuals—Complex relations of all animals and

Reprinted from chapter three of *The Origin of Species*, by Charles Darwin (New York: Collier, 1909).

plants throughout nature—Struggle for life most severe between individuals and varieties of the same species: often severe between species of the same genus—The relation of organism to organism the most important of all relations.

Before entering on the subject of this chapter, I must make a few preliminary remarks, to show how the struggle for existence bears on Natural Selection. It has been seen in the last chapter that amongst organic beings in a state of nature there is some individual variability: indeed I am not aware that this has ever been disputed. It is immaterial for us whether a multitude of doubtful forms be called species or sub-species or varieties; what rank, for instance, the two or three hundred doubtful forms of British plants are entitled to hold, if the existence of any well-marked varieties be admitted. But the mere existence of individual variability and of some few well-marked varieties, though necessary as the foundation for the work, helps us but little in understanding how species arise in nature. How have all those exquisite adaptations of one part of the organisation to another part, and to the conditions of life, and of one organic being to another being, been perfected? We see these beautiful co-adaptations most plainly in the woodpecker and the mistletoe; and only a little less plainly in the humblest parasite which clings to the hairs of a quadruped or feathers of a bird; in the structure of the beetle which dives through the water; in the plumed seed which is wafted by the gentlest breeze; in short, we see beautiful adaptations everywhere and in every part of the organic world.

Again, it may be asked, how is it that varieties, which I have called incipient species, become ultimately converted into good and distinct species which in most cases obviously differ from each other far more than do the varieties of the same species? How do those groups of species, which constitute what are called distinct genera, and which differ from each other more than do the species of the same genus, arise? All these results, as we shall more fully see in the next chapter, follow from the struggle for life. Owing to this struggle, variations, however slight and from whatever cause proceeding, if they be in any degree profitable to the individuals of a species, in their infinitely complex relations to other organic beings and to their physical conditions of life, will tend to the preservation of such individuals, and will generally be inherited by the offspring. The offspring, also, will thus have a better chance of surviving, for, of the many individuals of any species which are periodically born, but a small number can survive. I have called this principle, by which each slight variation, if useful, is preserved, by the term Natural Selection, in order to mark its relation to man's power of selection. But the expression often used by Mr. Herbert Spencer of the Survival of the Fittest is more accurate, and is sometimes equally convenient. We have seen that man by selection can certainly produce great results, and can adapt organic beings to his own uses, through the accumulation of slight but useful variations, given to him by the hand of Nature. But Natural Selection, as we shall hereafter see, is a power incessantly ready for action, and is as immeasurably superior to man's feeble efforts, as the works of Nature are to those of Art.

We will now discuss in a little more detail the struggle for existence. In my future work this subject will be treated, as it well deserves, at greater length. The elder De Candolle and Lyell have largely and philosophically shown that all organic beings are exposed to severe competition. In regard to plants, no one has treated this subject with more spirit and ability than W. Herbert, Dean of Manchester, evidently the result of his great horticultural knowledge. Nothing is easier than to admit in words the truth of the universal struggle for life, or more difficult—at least I have found it so—than constantly to bear this conclusion in mind. Yet unless it be thoroughly engrained in the mind, the whole economy of nature, with every fact on distribution, rarity, abundance, extinction, and variation, will be dimly seen or quite misunderstood. We behold the face of nature bright with gladness, we often see superabundance of food; we do not see or we forget, that the birds which are idly singing round us mostly live on insects or seeds, and are thus constantly destroying life; or we forget how largely these songsters, or their eggs, or their nestlings, are destroyed by birds and beasts of prey; we do not always bear in mind, that, though food may be now superabundant, it is not so at all seasons of each recurring year.

THE TERM, STRUGGLE FOR EXISTENCE, USED IN A LARGE SENSE

I should premise that I use this term in a large and metaphorical sense including dependence of one being on another, and including (which is more important) not only the life of the individual, but success in leaving progeny. Two canine animals, in a time of dearth, may be truly said to struggle with each other which shall get food and live. But a plant on the edge of a desert is said to struggle for life against the drought, though more properly it should be said to be dependent on the moisture. A plant which annually produces a thousand seeds, of which only one of an average comes to maturity, may be more truly said to struggle with the plants of the same and other kinds which already clothe the ground. The mistletoe is dependent on the apple and a few other trees, but can only in a far-fetched sense be said to struggle with these trees, for, if too many of these parasites grow on the same tree, it languishes and dies. But several seedling mistletoes, growing close together on the same branch, may more truly be said to struggle with each other. As the mistletoe is disseminated by birds, its existence depends on them; and it may methodically be said to struggle with other fruit-bearing plants, in tempting the birds to devour and thus disseminate its seeds. In these several senses, which pass into each other, I use for convenience' sake the general term of Struggle for Existence.

GEOMETRICAL RATIO OF INCREASE

A struggle for existence inevitably follows from the high rate at which all organic beings tend to increase. Every being, which during its natural lifetime produces several eggs or seeds, must suffer destruction during some period of its life, and during some season or occasional year, otherwise, on the principle of geometrical increase, its numbers would quickly become so inordinately great that no country could support the product. Hence, as more individuals are produced than can possibly survive, there must in every case be a struggle for existence, either one individual with another of the same species, or with the individuals of distinct species, or with the physical conditions of life. It is the doctrine of Malthus applied with manifold force to the whole animal and vegetable kingdoms; for in this case there can be no artificial increase of food, and no prudential restraint from marriage. Although some species may be now increasing, more or less rapidly, in numbers, all cannot do so, for the world would not hold them.

There is no exception to the rule that every organic being naturally increases at so high a rate, that, if not destroyed, the earth would soon be covered by the progeny of a single pair. Even slow-breeding man has doubled in twenty-five years, and at this rate, in less than a thousand years, there would literally not be standing-room for his progeny. Linnaeus has calculated that if an annual plant produced only two seeds— and there is no plant so unproductive as this—and their seedlings next year produced two, and so on, then in twenty years there should be a million plants. The elephant is reckoned the slowest breeder of all known animals, and I have taken some pains to estimate its probable minimum rate of natural increase; it will be safest to assume that it begins breeding when thirty years old, and goes on breeding till ninety years old, bringing forth six young in the interval, and surviving till one hundred years old; if this be so, after a period of from 740 to 750 years there would be nearly nineteen million elephants alive, descended from the first pair.

But we have better evidence on this subject than mere theoretical calculations, namely, the numerous recorded cases of the astonishingly rapid increase of various animals in a state of nature, when circumstances have been favourable to them during two or three following seasons. Still more striking is the evidence from our domestic animals of many kinds which have run wild in several parts of the world; if the statements of the rate of increase of slow-breeding cattle and horses in South America, and latterly in Australia, had not been well authenticated, they would have been incredible. So it is with plants; cases could be given of introduced plants which have become common throughout whole islands in a period of less than ten years. Several of the plants, such as the cardoon and a tall thistle, which are now the commonest over the whole plains of La Plata, clothing square leagues of surface almost to the exclusion of every other plant, have been introduced from Europe; and there are plants which now range in India, as I hear from Dr. Falconer, from Cape Comorin to the Himalaya, which have been imported from America since its discovery. In such cases, and endless others could be given, no one supposes, that the fertility of the animals or plants has been suddenly and temporarily increased in any sensible degree. The obvious explanation is that the conditions of life have been highly favourable, and that there has consequently been less destruction of the old and young, and that nearly all the young have been enabled to breed. Their geometrical ratio of increase, the result of which never fails to be surprising, simply explains their extraordinarily rapid increase and wide diffusion in their new homes.

In a state of nature almost every full-grown plant annually produces seed, and amongst animals there are very few which do not annually pair. Hence we may confidently assert, that all plants and animals are tending to increase at a geometrical ratio,—that all would rapidly stock every station in which they could anyhow exist,—and that this geometrical tendency to increase must be checked by destruction at some period of life. Our familiarity with the larger domestic animals tends, I think, to mislead us: we see no great destruction falling on them, but we do not keep in mind that thousands are annually slaughtered for food, and that in a state of nature an equal number would have somehow to be disposed of.

The only difference between organisms which annually produce eggs or seeds by the thousand, and those which produce extremely few, is, that the slow-breeders would require a few more years to people, under favourable conditions, a whole district, let it be ever so large. The condor lays a couple of eggs and the ostrich a score, and yet in the same country the condor may be the more numerous of the two; the Fulmar petrel lays but one egg, yet it is believed to be the most numerous bird in the world. One fly deposits hundreds of eggs, and another, like the hippobosca, a single one; but this difference does not determine how many individuals of the two species can be supported in a district. A large number of eggs is of some importance to those species which depend on a fluctuating amount of food, for it allows them rapidly to increase in number. But the real importance of a large number of eggs or seeds is to make up for much destruction at some period of life; and this period in the great majority of cases is an early one. If an animal can in any way protect its own eggs or young, a small number may be produced, and yet the average stock be fully kept up; but if many eggs or young are destroyed, many must be produced, or the species will become extinct. It would suffice to keep up the full number of a tree, which lived on an average for a thousand years, if a single seed were produced once in a thousand years, supposing that this seed were never destroyed, and could be ensured to germinate in a fitting place. So that, in all cases, the average number of any animal or plant depends only indirectly on the number of its eggs or seeds.

In looking at Nature, it is most necessary to keep the foregoing considerations always in mind—never to forget that every single organic being may be said to be striving to the utmost to increase in numbers; that each lives by a struggle at some period of its life; that heavy destruction inevitably falls either on the young or old, during each generation or at recurrent intervals. Lighten any check, mitigate the destruction ever so little, and the number of the species will almost instantaneously increase to any amount.

NATURE OF THE CHECKS TO INCREASE

The causes which check the natural tendency of each species to increase are most obscure. Look at the most vigorous species; by as much as it swarms in numbers, by so much will it tend to increase still further. We know not exactly what the checks are even in a single instance. Nor will this surprise any one who reflects how ignorant we are on this head, even in regard to mankind, although so incomparably better known than any other animal. This subject of the checks to increase has been ably treated by several authors, and I hope in a future work to discuss it at considerable length, more especially in regard to the feral animals of South America. Here I will make only a few remarks, just to recall to the reader's mind some of the chief points. Eggs or very young animals seem generally to suffer most, but this is not invariably the case. With plants there is a vast destruction of seeds, but, from some observations which I have made it appears that the seedlings suffer most from germinating in ground already thickly stocked with other plants. Seedlings, also, are destroyed in vast numbers by various enemies; for instance, on a piece of ground three feet long and two wide, dug and cleared, and where there could be no choking from other plants, I marked all the seedlings of our native weeds as they came up, and out of 357 no less than 295 were destroyed, chiefly by slugs and insects. If turf which has long been mown, and the case would be the same with turf closely browsed by quadrupeds, be let to grow, the more vigorous plants gradually kill the less vigorous, though fully grown plants; thus out of twenty species growing on a little plot of mown turf (three feet by four) nine species perished, from the other species being allowed to grow up freely.

The amount of food for each species of course gives the extreme limit to which each can increase; but very frequently it is not the obtaining food, but the serving as prey to other animals, which determines the average numbers of a species. Thus, there seems to be little doubt that the stock of partridges, grouse, and hares on any large estate depends chiefly on the destruction of vermin. If not one head of game were shot during the next twenty years in England, and, at the same time, if no vermin were destroyed, there would, in all probability, be less game than at present, although hundreds of thousands of game animals are now annually shot. On the other hand, in some cases, as with the elephant, none are destroyed by beasts of prey; for even the tiger in India most rarely dares to attack a young elephant protected by its dam.

Climate plays an important part in determining the average number of a species, and periodical seasons of extreme cold or drought seem to be the most effective of all checks. I estimated (chiefly from the greatly reduced numbers of nests in the spring) that the winter of 1854–5 destroyed four-fifths of the birds in my own grounds; and this is a tremendous destruction, when we remember that ten per cent. is an extraordinarily severe mortality from epidemics with man. The action of climate seems at first sight to be quite independent of the struggle for existence; but in so far as climate chiefly acts in reducing food, it brings on the most severe struggle between the individuals, whether of the same or of distinct species, which subsist on the same kind of food. Even when climate, for instance, extreme cold, acts directly, it will be the least vigorous individuals, or those which have got least food through the advancing winter, which will suffer most. When we travel from south to north, or from a damp region to a dry, we invariably see some species gradually getting rarer and rarer, and finally disappearing; and the change of climate being conspicuous, we are tempted to attribute the whole effect to its direct action. But this is a false view; we forget that each species, even where it most abounds, is constantly suffering enormous destruction at some period of its life, from enemies or from competitors for the same place and food; and if these enemies or competitors be in the least degree favoured by any slight change of climate, they will increase in numbers; and as each area is already fully stocked with inhabitants, the other species must decrease. When we travel southward and see a species decreasing in numbers, we may feel sure that the cause lies quite as much in other species being favoured, as in this one being hurt. So it is when we travel northward, but in a somewhat lesser degree, for the number of species of all kinds, and therefore of competitors, decreases northwards; hence in going northwards, or in ascending a mountain, we far oftener meet with stunted forms, due to the *directly* injurious action of climate, than we do in proceeding southwards or in descending a mountain. When we reach the Arctic regions, or snow-capped summits, or absolute deserts, the struggle for life is almost exclusively with the elements.

That climate acts in main part indirectly by favouring other species, we clearly see in the prodigious number of plants which in our gardens can perfectly well endure our climate, but which never become naturalised, for they cannot compete with our native plants nor resist destruction by our native animals.

When a species, owing to highly favourable circumstances, increases inordinately in numbers in a small tract, epidemics—at least, this seems generally to occur with our game animals—often ensue; and here we have a limiting check independent of the struggle for life. But even some of these so-called epidemics appear to be due to parasitic worms, which have from some cause, possibly in part through facility of diffusion amongst the crowded animals, been disproportionally favoured: and here comes in a sort of struggle between the parasite and its prey.

On the other hand, in many cases, a large stock of individuals of the same species, relatively to the numbers of its enemies, is absolutely necessary for its preservation. Thus we can easily raise plenty of corn and rape-seed, &c., in our fields, because the seeds are in great excess compared with the number of birds which feed on them; nor can the birds, though having a super-abundance of food at this one season, increase in number proportionally to the supply of seed, as their numbers are checked during the winter; but any one who has tried, knows how troublesome it is to get seed from a few wheat or other such plants in a garden: I have in this case lost every single seed. This view of the necessity of a large stock of the same species for its preservation, explains, I believe, some singular facts in nature such as that of very rare plants being sometimes extremely abundant, in the few spots where they do exist; and that of some social plants being social, that is abounding in individuals, even on the extreme verge of their range. For in such cases, we may be-lieve, that a plant could exist only where the conditions of its life were so favourable that many could exist together, and thus save the species from utter destruction. I should add that the good effects of intercrossing, and the ill effects of close interbreeding, no doubt come into play in many of these cases; but I will not here enlarge on this subject.

COMPLEX RELATIONS OF ALL ANIMALS AND PLANTS TO EACH OTHER IN THE STRUGGLE FOR EXISTENCE

Many cases are on record showing how complex and unex-pected are the checks and relations between organic beings, which have to struggle together in the same country. I will give only a single instance, which, though a simple one, in-terested me. In Staffordshire, on the estate of a relation, where I had ample means of investigation, there was a large and extremely barren heath, which had never been touched by the hand of man; but several hundred acres of exactly the same nature had been enclosed twenty-five years previously and planted with Scotch fir. The change in the native vege-tation of the planted part of the heath was most remarkable, more than is generally seen in passing from one quite dif-ferent soil to another: not only the proportional numbers of the heath-plants were wholly changed, but twelve species of plants (not counting grasses and carices) flourished in the plantations, which could not be found on the heath. The ef-fect on the insects must have been still greater, for six insec-tivorous birds were very common in the plantations, which were not to be seen on the heath; and the heath was fre-quented by two or three distinct insectivorous birds. Here we see how potent has been the effect of the introduction of a single tree, nothing whatever else having been done, with the exception of the land having been enclosed, so that cat-tle could not enter. But how important an element enclosure is, I plainly saw near Farnham, in Surrey. Here there are ex-tensive heaths, with a few clumps of old Scotch firs on the distant hilltops: within the last ten years large spaces have been enclosed, and self-sown firs are now springing up in multitudes, so close together that all cannot live. When I as-certained that these young trees had not been sown or planted, I was so much surprised at their numbers that I went to several points of view, whence I could examine hun-dreds of acres of the unenclosed heath, and literally I could not see a single Scotch fir, except the old planted clumps. But on looking closely between the stems of the heath, I found a multitude of seedlings and little trees which had been perpetually browsed down by the cattle. In one square yard, at a point some hundred yards distant from one of the old clumps, I counted thirty-two little trees; and one of them, with twenty-six rings of growth, had during many years tried to raise its head above the stems of the heath, and had failed. No wonder that, as soon as the land was enclosed, it became thickly clothed with vigorously growing young firs. Yet the heath was so extremely barren and so extensive that no one would ever have imagined that cattle would have so closely and effectually searched it for food.

Here we see that cattle absolutely determine the existence of the Scotch fir; but in several parts of the world insects determine the existence of cattle. Perhaps Paraguay offers the most curious instance of this; for here neither cattle nor horses nor dogs have ever run wild, though they swarm southward and northward in a feral state; and Azara and Rengger have shown that this is caused by the greater number in Paraguay of a certain fly, which lays its eggs in the navels of these animals when first born. The increase of these flies, numerous as they are, must be habitually checked by some means, probably by other parasitic insects. Hence, if certain insectivorous birds were to decrease in Paraguay, the parasitic insects would probably increase; and this would lessen the number of the navel-frequenting flies—then cattle and horses would become feral, and this would certainly greatly alter (as indeed I have observed in parts of South America) the vegetation: this again would largely affect the insects; and this, as we have just seen in Staffordshire, the insectivorous birds, and so onwards in ever-increasing circles of complexity. Not that under nature the relations will ever be as simple as this. Battle within battle must be continually recurring with varying success; and yet in the long-run the forces are so nicely balanced, that the face of nature remains for long periods of time uniform, though assuredly the merest trifle would give the victory to one organic being over another. Nevertheless, so profound is our ignorance, and so high our presumption, that we marvel when we hear of the extinction of an organic being; and as we do not see the cause, we invoke cataclysms to desolate the world, or invent laws on the duration of the forms of life!

I am tempted to give one more instance showing how plants and animals remote in the scale of nature, are bound together by a web of complex relations. I shall hereafter have occasion to show that the exotic Lobelia fulgens is never visited in my garden by insects, and consequently, from its peculiar structure, never sets a seed. Nearly all our orchidaceous plants absolutely require the visits of insects to remove their pollen-masses and thus to fertilise them. I find from experiments that humble-bees are almost indispensable to the fertilisation of the heartsease (Viola tricolor), for other bees do not visit this flower. I have also found that the visits of bees are necessary for the fertilisation of some kinds of clover; for instance, 20 heads of Dutch clover (Trifolium repens) yielded 2,290 seeds, but 20 other heads protected from bees produced not one. Again, 100 heads of red clover (T. pratense) produced 2,700 seeds, but the same number of protected heads produced not a single seed. Humble-bees alone visit red clover, as other bees cannot reach the nectar. It has been suggested that moths may fertilise the clovers; but I doubt whether they could do so in the case of the red clover, from their weight not being sufficient to depress the wing petals. Hence we may infer as highly probable that, if the whole genus of humble-bees became extinct or very rare in England, the heartsease and red clover would become vary rare, or wholly disappear. The number of humble-bees in any district depends in a great measure upon the number of field-mice, which destroy their combs and nests; and Col. Newman, who has long attended to the habits of humble-bees, believes that "more than two-thirds of them are thus destroyed all over England." Now the number of mice is largely dependent, as every one knows, on the number of cats; and Col. Newman says, "Near villages and small towns I have found the nests of humble-bees more numerous than elsewhere, which I attribute to the number of cats that destroy the mice." Hence it is quite credible that the presence of a feline animal in large numbers in a district might determine, through the intervention first of mice and then of bees, the frequency of certain flowers in that district!

In the case of every species, many different checks, acting at different periods of life, and during different seasons or years, probably come into play; some one check or some few being generally the most potent; but all will concur in determining the average number or even the existence of the species. In some cases it can be shown that widely-different checks act on the same species in different districts. When we look at the plants and bushes clothing an entangled bank, we are tempted to attribute their proportional numbers and kinds to what we call chance. But how false a view is this! Every one has heard that when an American forest is cut down a very different vegetation springs up; but it has been observed that ancient Indian ruins in the Southern United States, which must formerly have been cleared of trees, now display the same beautiful diversity and proportion of kinds as in the surrounding virgin forest. What a struggle must have gone on during long centuries between the several kinds of trees each annually scattering its seeds by the thousand; what war between insect and insect—between insects, snails, and other animals with birds and beasts of prey—all striving to increase, all feeding on each other, or on the trees, their seeds and seedlings, or on the other plants which first clothed the ground and thus checked the growth of the trees! Throw up a handful of feathers, and all fall to the ground according to definite laws; but how simple is the problem where each shall fall compared to that of the action and reaction of the innumerable plants and animals which have determined, in the course of centuries, the proportional numbers and kinds of trees now growing on the old Indian ruins!

The dependency of one organic being on another, as of a parasite on its prey, lies generally between beings remote in the scale of nature. This is likewise sometimes the case with those which may be strictly said to struggle with each other for existence, as in the case of locusts and grass-feeding quadrupeds. But the struggle will almost invariably be most severe between the individuals of the same species, for they frequent the same districts, require the same food, and are exposed to the same dangers. In the case of varieties of the same species, the struggle will generally be almost equally severe, and we sometimes see the contest soon decided: for instance, if several varieties of wheat be sown together, and the mixed seed be resown, some of the varieties which best suit the soil or climate, or are naturally the most fertile, will beat the others and so yield more seed, and will consequently in a few years supplant the other varieties. To keep up a mixed stock of even such extremely close varieties as the variously-coloured sweet peas, they must be each year harvested separately, and the seed then mixed in due proportion, otherwise the weaker kinds will steadily decrease in number and disappear. So again with the varieties of sheep; it has been asserted that certain mountain-varieties will starve out other mountain-varieties, so that they cannot be kept together. The same result has followed from keeping together different varieties of the medicinal leech. It may even be doubted whether the varieties of any of our domestic plants or animals have so exactly the same strength, habits, and constitution, that the original proportions of a mixed stock (crossing being prevented) could be kept up for half-a-dozen generations, if they were allowed to struggle together, in the same manner as beings in a state of nature, and if the seed or young were not annually preserved in due proportion.

STRUGGLE FOR LIFE MOST SEVERE BETWEEN INDIVIDUALS AND VARIETIES OF THE SAME SPECIES

As the species of the same genus usually have, though by no means invariably, much similarity in habits and constitution, and always in structure, the struggle will generally be more severe between them, if they come into competition with each other, than between the species of distinct genera. We see this in the recent extension over parts of the United States of one species of swallow having caused the decrease of another species. The recent increase of the missel-thrush in parts of Scotland has caused the decrease of the song-thrush. How frequently we hear of one species of rat taking the place of another species under the most different climates! In Russia the small Asiatic cockroach has everywhere driven before it its great congener. In Australia the imported hive-bee is rapidly exterminating the small, stingless native bee. One species of charlock has been known to supplant another species; and so in other cases. We can dimly see why the competition should be most severe between allied forms, which fill nearly the same place in the economy of nature; but probably in no one case could we precisely say why one species has been victorious over another in the great battle of life.

A corollary of the highest importance may be deduced from the foregoing remarks, namely, that the structure of every organic being is related, in the most essential yet often hidden manner, to that of all the other organic beings, with which it comes into competition for food or residence, or from which it has to escape, or on which it preys. This is obvious in the structure of the teeth and talons of the tiger; and in that of the legs and claws of the parasite which clings to the hair on the tiger's body. But in the beautifully plumed seed of the dandelion, and in the flattened and fringed legs of the water-beetle, the relation seems at first confined to the elements of air and water. Yet the advantage of plumed seeds no doubt stands in the closest relation to the land being already thickly clothed with other plants; so that the seeds may be widely distributed and fall on unoccupied ground. In the water-beetle, the structure of its legs, so well adapted for diving, allows it to compete with other aquatic insects, to hunt for its own prey, and to escape serving as prey to other animals.

The store of nutriment laid up within the seeds of many plants seems at first to have no sort of relation to other plants. But from the strong growth of young plants produced from such seeds, as peas and beans, when sown in the midst of long grass, it may be suspected that the chief use of the nutriment in the seed is to favour the growth of the seedlings, whilst struggling with other plants growing vigorously all around.

Look at a plant in the midst of its range, why does it not double or quadruple its numbers? We know that it can perfectly well withstand a little more heat or cold, dampness or dryness, for elsewhere it ranges into slightly hotter or colder, damper or drier districts. In this case we can clearly see that if we wish in imagination to give the plant the power of increasing in number, we should have to give it some advantage over its competitors, or over the animals which prey on it. On the confines of its geographical range, a change of constitution with respect to climate would clearly be an advantage to our plant; but we have reason to believe that only a few plants or animals range so far, that they are destroyed exclusively by the rigour of the climate. Not until we reach the extreme confines of life, in the Arctic regions or on the borders of an utter desert, will competition cease. The land may be extremely cold or dry, yet there will be competition between some few species, or between the individuals of the same species, for the warmest or dampest spots.

Hence we can see that when a plant or animal is placed in a new country amongst new competitors, the conditions of its life will generally be changed in an essential manner, although the climate may be exactly the same as in its former home. If its average numbers are to increase in its new home, we should have to modify it in a different way to what we should have had to do in its native country; for we should have to give it some advantage over a different set of competitors or enemies.

It is good thus to try in imagination to give to any one species an advantage over another. Probably in no single instance should we know what to do. This ought to convince us of our ignorance on the mutual relations of all organic beings; a conviction as necessary, as it is difficult to acquire. All that we can do, is to keep steadily in mind that each organic being is striving to increase in a geometrical ratio; that each at some period of its life, during some season of the year, during each generation or at intervals, has to struggle for life and to suffer great destruction. When we reflect on this struggle, we may console ourselves with the full belief, that the war of nature is not incessant, that no fear is felt, that death is generally prompt, and that the vigorous, the healthy, and the happy survive and multiply.

CHAPTER 3

The Immediate Impact of Darwin's *Origin of Species*

The Conversion of Leading Scientists to Darwinism

Gertrude Himmelfarb

Darwin knew that converting some of the major scientific figures of the day to his theory of natural selection was essential to its receiving a fair hearing, let alone its general acceptance. As City University of New York scholar Gertrude Himmelfarb, a noted authority on Victorian society, explains in this informative essay, Darwin's first formidable hurdle in this endeavor was to win the endorsement of his friends Charles Lyell, J.D. Hooker, and Thomas H. Huxley. Himmelfarb here effectively captures the thinking of scientists of that era, including the intellectual dilemmas of some in accepting so controversial a doctrine and the difficult manner in which such new ideas are so accepted in any age.

Before the publication of *The Origin of Species*, Darwin had confided to Hooker his personal criteria of success:

> I remember thinking, above a year ago, that if ever I lived to see Lyell, yourself, and Huxley come round, partly by my book, and partly by their own reflections, I should feel that the subject is safe, and all the world might rail, but that ultimately the theory of Natural Selection ... would prevail. Nothing will ever convince me that three such men, with so much diversified knowledge, and so well accustomed to search for truth, could err greatly.

It may be that Darwin was subjecting himself to too easy a test when be took as his judges the three men with whom he was most in agreement; he could surely have found others with as much diversified knowledge and as zealous in the pursuit of truth who would have made more impartial examiners. But if his choice was deliberate in weighting the re-

sults in his favor, it was also deliberate in its order of priority, and within this order it was weighted against him. Lyell,
Hooker, and Huxley—this proved to be, in fact, the inverse
sequence of their conversions.

LYELL'S "GRAVE DOUBTS"

Lyell was the decisive test. Of the three, he offered most resistance to Darwin's theory, and, perhaps because of this, his
opinion was most influential among scientists. To Darwin
he was the "Lord High Chancellor" whose verdict would
probably be more influential than the book itself in determining the success of his views. As it happened, the fate of
his book was decided before Lyell could bring himself to
pronounce an unequivocal verdict.

Only a few years earlier, in revulsion against Darwin's
"ugly facts," Lyell had taken refuge in "the orthodox faith." By
1858 his personal distaste for these facts, and his sense of the
impropriety of their public revelation, had so far abated that
he could sponsor them before the Linnean Society and urge
their publication. But it was one thing to think that they ought
to have a hearing and another to subscribe to them. Even on
the subject of their publication, he seems to have vacillated,
agreeing at one point that Darwin would be better advised to
publish a book on pigeons in place of the *Origin*. And when
be read the proof sheets of the book, he characteristically remarked that while he was astonished at the cogency of the
argument, he reserved judgment on its validity. In his address in September 1859 before the Geological Section of the
British Association, he went as far as he could in praise of
Darwin and his forthcoming book: "He appears to me to have
succeeded by his investigations and reasonings in throwing a
flood of light on many classes of phenomena . . . for which no
other hypothesis has been able, or has even attempted to account." He also gave Darwin permission to speak, in the *Origin*, of his former adherence to the theory of immutability
[i.e., the idea that species do not change] and his present
"grave doubts" on that score. At the same time, it appeared
that his grave doubts about immutability were matched by
equally grave ones about mutability. Thus a long and detailed
critique of the proofs of the *Origin* culminated in his opinion
that the "continued intervention of creative power" was necessary for the origin of species.

Lyell would clearly have liked to rest in some halfway

house between immutability and mutability. But neither Darwin nor reason allowed him any repose. Again and again, Darwin welcomed him as a half-convert, only to follow with the warning that there was no compromise, no stopping point short of total conversion: "Do not, I beg, be in a hurry in committing yourself (like so many naturalists) to go a certain length and no further; for I am deeply convinced that it is absolutely necessary to go the whole vast length, or stick to the creation of each separate species." If at any point the necessity for the intervention of a creator was conceded, then the theory of natural selection was utterly nullified. Indeed, it was in testimony to this that Lyell refrained from committing himself, for he himself had always maintained that what was true of animals was necessarily true of man and that if special creation was discarded for the one, it must also be for the other.

DARWIN NO DIFFERENT THAN LAMARCK?

Back and forth went the dialogue between Lyell and Darwin, which was also a dialogue between Lyell and his alter ego. Alternately, Lyell might be found criticizing Darwin for not making his case strong enough, or advising him on how to make it seem stronger than, in fact, it was. "You are a pretty Lord Chancellor," Darwin thanked him, "to tell the barrister on one side bow best to win the cause!" Periodically, he would abdicate the Lord Chancellorship and assure Darwin that he intended publicly to announce himself the attorney for the defense. Darwin would then proclaim him "an entire convert" and praise him for his courage in giving up a position he had held for thirty years: "Considering his age, his former views and position in society, I think his conduct has been heroic on this subject." But no sooner had these congratulations been exchanged than Lyell would revert to type with such double-edged compliments as his praise of Hooker for raising "the variety-making hypothesis to the rank of a theory" and for showing "what grand speculations and results 'the creation by variation' is capable of suggesting, and one day of establishing"—thus, with one stroke, demoting both Darwin and his theory to a rank inferior to Hooker and his systematic work. It was the same strategy of depreciation that prompted Lyell to subsume Darwin's theory under [Jean Baptiste] Lamarck's as if it was only a subcategory, a minor variation of the original classical doctrine. This was what vexed Darwin most: that Lyell should have made the vulgar mistake of confusing his "principle of improvement" with Lamarck's "power of adaptation." If the two were basically the same, he asked Lyell, why had he been so adamant against Lamarck's theory in the *Principles of Geology,* and why had his conversion to mutability come only with the *Origin?* The answer, of course, which Darwin was too polite to suggest, was that Lyell cared no more for Lamarck now than then and that he invoked his name only because it was easier to make his obeisance to [bow down before] a senior and long-deceased master than to a junior and all-too-active competitor.

Originally, Lyell had proposed making his submission in a new edition of his *Geology.* By the beginning of 1860, inspired perhaps by the success of the *Origin,* he had decided to put it in the form of a book on the "geological history of man," to appear later that year. For three years Darwin waited for the pronouncement that would put Lyell unequivocally on his side, venturing the jest that as Lyell used to caution him about man, so he now had to return the caution a hundredfold. When the long-awaited *Antiquity of Man* was finally published in 1863, it became apparent that neither cautions nor hopes had been warranted. For although Lyell conscientiously summarized the evidence for mutability as it applied to species in general and to man in particular, he did not commit himself to it. From such expressions as "should it ever become highly probable that the past changes of the organic world have been brought about by the subordinate agency of such causes as 'Variation' and 'Natural Selection' . . . ," or "Mr. Darwin labours to show . . . ," he intimated that Darwinism remained what it had always been: an interesting and respectable theory, but one that was far from proved. Again he featured Darwinism as a variation of Lamarckism and Hooker as a peer of Darwin. Again he suggested that man was the result of a leap of nature separating him at one bound from the species below him. And he concluded with the observation that transmutation in no way invalidated the idea of design or of a designer, the whole course of nature being "the material embodiment of a preconcerted arrangement."

LYELL JUSTIFIES HIS POSITION

Darwin's disappointment amounted almost to a sense of betrayal. He could not see how this book could be reconciled with Lyell's private assurances on the subject, or how it fulfilled his promise to "go the whole orang." "The best of the joke," he wryly commented to Hooker, "is that he thinks he has acted with the courage of a martyr of old." On the theory that to be neutral at this stage of the controversy was, in effect, to be hostile, Darwin wished that Lyell had kept silent rather than declare himself so equivocally. Lyell, for his part, refused to take affront at Darwin's outspoken criticisms, justifying himself by arguing, first, that his book honestly represented his opinions as best he could make them out, and, second, that strategically it was better calculated to win supporters to evolution than any frontal attack. As usual, his rationale was a nice blend of reason, sentiment, and calculation:

I find myself after reasoning through a whole chapter in favor of man's coming from the animals, relapsing to my old views whenever I read again a few pages of the "Principles" or yearn for fossil types of intermediate grade. . . . Hundreds who have bought my book in the hope that I should demolish heresy, will be awfully confounded and disappointed. As it is, they will at best say with Crawford, who still stands out, "You have put the case with such moderation that one cannot complain." But when he read Huxley, he was up in arms again.

My feelings, however, more than any thought about policy or expediency, prevent me from dogmatising as to the descent of man from the brutes, which, though I am prepared to accept it, takes away much of the charm from my speculations on the past relating to such matters. . . .

I cannot go Huxley's length in thinking that natural selection and variation account for so much, and not so far as you, if I take some passages of your book separately.

I think the old "creation" is almost as much required as ever, but of course it takes a new form if Lamarck's view improved by yours are adopted.

What I am anxious to effect is to avoid positive inconsistencies in different parts of my book, owing probably to the old trains of thought, the old ruts, interfering with the new course.

But you ought to be satisfied, as I shall bring hundreds towards you, who if I treated the matter more dogmatically would have rebelled.

I have spoken out to the utmost extent of my tether, so far as my reason goes, and farther than my imagination and sentiment can follow, which I suppose has caused occasional incongruities.

As Hooker simplified it: Lyell was "half-hearted and whole-headed."

LYELL IS FINALLY CONVERTED

This tenuous balance was beyond Darwin's understanding. It was even difficult for Lyell to sustain, and in the second edition of the *Antiquity*, published only a few months after the first, he inserted a parenthetical phrase that went further to commit him than almost anything else in the book, although it was as deliberately awkward and evasive as only Lyell could have put it: "Yet we ought by no means to undervalue the importance of the step which will have been made, should it hereafter become the generally received opinion of men of science (as I fully expect it will), that the past changes of the organic world have been brought about by the subordinate agency of such causes as 'Variation' and 'Natural Selection.'" Darwin was somewhat mollified by this and other small emendations, such as the alteration of "Mr. Darwin labours to show" to "Mr. Darwin argues, and with no small success"; and even more when Lyell finally and unequivocally, in the tenth edition of the *Principles* published in 1867, announced his conversion to mutability (although still with the tantalizing allusions to Lamarck).

Lyell may have given himself away in an ambiguous remark concluding one of his apologias at the time of the *Antiquity:* "I see too many difficulties to be in the danger of many new converts who outrun their teacher in faith." It is not clear whether the "teacher" was intended to refer to Darwin or to himself, whether he was cautioning against Darwin's impetuous converts or against his own—that is, Darwin. There are intimations that he resented the subversion of their natural relationship, the elevation of Darwin to the status of master and his own debasement to that of convert. Even while he was opposing the *Origin,* he took a perverse pleasure in criticisms directed against "Lyell and his friend." And later, when Darwin's critics as well as his converts neglected to mention him, he felt slighted and resentful. The German biologist, Ernst Haeckel, in his *History of Creation,* was one of the few to pay homage to him as one of the founders of the theory of evolution, whereupon Lyell wrote to thank him:

> Most of the zoologists forget that anything was written between the time of Lamarck and the publication of our friend's

Origin of Species. . . . I had certainly prepared the way in this country, in six editions of my work before the *Vestiges of Creation* appeared in 1842, for the reception of Darwin's gradual and insensible evolution of species, and I am very glad that you noticed this.

HOOKER: AN UNWILLING CONVERT AND EFFECTIVE WITNESS

Hooker was the second in Darwin's triumvirate [group of three] of judges, outranked by Lyell in seniority and power but not in ability; in ability, Darwin pronounced him—although only after Hooker had announced his conversion— "by far the most capable judge in Europe." It was with great satisfaction, therefore, that Darwin heard from him: "I expect to think that I would rather be author of your book than of any other on Natural History Science."

Hooker was not only one of the first and most distinguished of Darwin's converts; he was also the first to apply the theory to a particular scientific problem. His introductory essay to the *Flora Tasmaniae,* completed and published only a few weeks before the *Origin* appeared, was a conscious attempt to apply the hypothesis of natural selection to the case of the Australian flora. While admitting that he had not proved the truth of the hypothesis, he insisted that it explained more of the peculiarities of that flora than any alternative theory and that it promoted inquiry where others hindered it. It was as a minor exercise in humdrum science, a ragged handkerchief flying beside the royal standard, that he compared his own essay with Darwin's, so that he was all the more astonished and distressed to find Lyell praising it so fulsomely, and to Darwin's obvious derogation. Had he known, he protested, that the *Origin* would appear so soon after his essay, he would have delayed its publication rather than seem to be antedating or competing with Darwin.

Unlike Lyell, Hooker was not in the least abashed by his position as convert. He had, to be sure, some minor disagreements with Darwin; he thought, for example, that Darwin had attached too much, perhaps too exclusive an importance to natural selection. But these, he felt, were matters to be arbitrated by scientists working on the lines laid down in the *Origin.* Of the importance of the theory in general, he had no doubts. And he was the more firmly convinced of this, knowing how long he himself had resisted it. When he publicly announced his adherence, at the meeting of the British Association in 1860, he described himself as one who had been apprised of the theory fifteen years earlier, had vigorously argued against it, even while engaging in the scientific researches which had carried him around the world, and had only been persuaded of its truth when facts otherwise inexplicable became intelligible as a result of it. Thus, as he described it, conviction was "forced upon an unwilling convert."

It is the unwilling convert who makes the most effective witness in a cause and is likely to be its most enthusiastic communicant. The eyes of the world and of posterity were upon science, Hooker warned one lagging colleague, and for the "credit of the age we live in," it was important that naturalists should have something better to show than was current a quarter of a century earlier. "Above all things," he counseled, "remember that this reception of Darwin's book is the exact parallel of the reception that every great progressive move in science has met with in all ages." The difficulties of the theory might be, as he confessed, appalling, but as long as the alternative was worse and as long as history gave promise of its ultimate vindication, progressive scientists had the duty of supporting it.

HUXLEY: THE GREAT AVENGER

If Darwin's opponents are sometimes charged with a partiality for the past, his friends may as justly be charged with a partiality for the future. It cannot be said that this partiality actually determined their conversion; for some time, indeed, it was in doubt which party the future would favor. But, having been converted, they were not long in arrogating the future to themselves. As Hooker was warning his friends not to offend posterity, so Huxley was predicting the inauguration of a new Augustan age in English science.

Huxley, rather than either Hooker or Darwin, was preeminently the modem intellectual. Regarding heresy rather than orthodoxy as the hallmark of truth, he deliberately flaunted the novelty of his views instead of smuggling them in, as was the older fashion, in the guise of tradition. Every great physical truth, he declared, had come into the world under the onus of blasphemy, and Darwinism was no exception. "In this nineteenth century, as at the dawn of modern physical science, the cosmogony of the semi-barbarous Hebrew is the incubus of the philosopher and the opprobrium of the orthodox." But the patient seekers after truth had learned to avenge themselves. "Extinguished theologians lie about the cradle of every science as the strangled snakes beside that of Hercules; and history records that whenever science and orthodoxy have been fairly opposed, the latter has been forced to retire from the lists, bleeding and crushed if not annihilated; scotched, if not slain."

Huxley was the great avenger. Raging against the inferior status of scientists compared with clergymen, he looked forward to the time when he could get his heel "into their mouths and scr-r-unch it round." The *Origin* gave him the opportunity. As self-designated bulldog, he announced that he was sharpening his claws to do battle with the pack of yelping curs at Darwin's heels. His first engagement was in the December issue of *Macmillan's Magazine* in an article called "Time and Life," based on a lecture given earlier that year before the Royal Institution and expanded to include an analysis of the *Origin.* By a stroke of luck and quick thinking, he was also able to capture the coveted review in the *Times.* As a matter of routine, the book had been handed for review to a regular staff writer, who, bemoaning his ignorance of science, was by chance referred to Huxley. Huxley promptly relieved him of the chore by writing the review himself, which appeared in the *Times* of December 26, prefaced only by a few paragraphs by the staff writer. He carried the battle into the next year with a lecture before the Royal Institution in February and a long article in the *Westminster Review* in April.

THE VERDICT OF POSTERITY

Years later, reviewing his pleadings on behalf of Darwin, Huxley insisted that his zeal never reduced him to the role of a mere advocate or blind partisan. It had been, he claimed, a matter of indifference to him whether Darwin's theory was ultimately proved true, so long as it was fully and fairly examined. And he did, in fact, often take the precaution of introducing it as a working hypothesis rather than an established fact. "Either it would prove its capacity to elucidate the facts of organic life, or it would break down under the stress," he reasonably proposed, thus disarming the opposition and insuring against the future. But he made it clear that the hypothesis agreed with all the available facts—the "many apparent anomalies in the distribution of living beings" and the "main phenomena of life and organization"—

and that it was utterly different from such speculative hypotheses as that of the *Vestiges*. Darwin, he insisted, "abhors mere speculation as nature abhors a vacuum"; "he is as greedy of cases and precedents as any constitutional lawyer, and all the principles he lays down are capable of being brought to the test of observation and experiment." Admitting that Darwin had not proved that natural selection *did* actually operate to produce new species, he went on to say that such proof was unobtainable, that Darwin had proved all that was provable, which was that natural selection *must* so operate. And he concluded by saying that even if natural selection should turn out to be an inadequate explanation for the origin of species, Darwin would still have superseded all previous thinkers, much as Copernicus superseded Ptolemy [in astronomy]; a Kepler or Newton might be required to correct his details, but they would not vitiate his great achievement.

Thus Huxley managed to recover at the end what he had pretended to forfeit in the beginning. The working hypothesis turned out to be indistinguishable from an established theory, the "test of observation and experiment" was discounted in advance, and the verdict of posterity was assured from the start.

Even these small concessions to neutrality irked Darwin, who was piqued to have his theory passed off as a mere hypothesis. And other of Huxley's criticisms were serious enough to disturb him, such as the remark that the theory was faulty in not providing a *vera causa* [true cause] of variation, or that species ought to be defined primarily in terms of sterility. What Darwin did not comment on was Huxley's strongest and most imaginative point of criticism. While Hooker was rejoicing because the *Origin* had revealed to him once again the truth of the dictum, "*Natura non facit saltum* [nature does not make leaps]," Huxley was deploring the fact that Darwin had unnecessarily burdened himself with so specious a principle. The strength of natural selection, he believed, was precisely the fact that it allowed for such jumps in nature, that, in his favorite formula, it accounted for transmutation without transition.

Huxley's occasional reservations, however, were more than made up for by his enthusiasms in other directions. He gave Darwin fair warning that after a slow start he was gravitating toward his theories at such an accelerated pace that he would soon pass him. While Lyell was slowly and painfully feeling his way to the *Antiquity of Man,* Huxley was boldly lecturing to working men on "The Relation of Man to the rest of the Animal Kingdom" and publishing monographs demonstrating the humanlike structure of the brain of the higher ape. His professional colleagues remained unconverted, but his working men were so loyal that, as he reported to his wife, "by next Friday evening they will all be convinced that they are monkeys."

In 1863 he published the substance of these lectures as *Man's Place in Nature,* and, by contrast to Lyell's book appearing at the same time, Huxley's seemed to Darwin all the more admirable. . . .

ACCEPTANCE IN AMERICA

Huxley and Hooker were Darwin's advance guard, with Lyell bringing up the rear. But it was not long before others joined the ranks. By March 1863 enough had committed themselves, to one degree or another, for Darwin to draw up a table of organization of the names and professions of fifteen of his more prominent adherents. One of these, reviewing the *Origin* in the *National Review,* observed hopefully that as species emerged from a war of nature, so truth would emerge from the intellectual collision precipitated by this work. Yet even Darwin's partisans could not agree as to the exact nature of the new truth.

The American botanist Asa Gray had so special an interpretation of it that Darwin represented him on his table as only a partial adherent. Yet Gray was Darwin's chief agent in America as Huxley was in England. He was one of those who had first read an abstract of the *Origin* and then the proof sheets of the individual chapters as they came from the printer, but who was not converted until he had experienced the dramatic effect of the printed, bound book. Once converted, however, he worked tirelessly in Darwin's interest, arranging for an American edition and extracting a token payment from the publishers of the pirated edition, reviewing the book and defending it against its detractors. He opened his campaign in March 1860 with an article in the *American Journal of Science and Arts* (more commonly known as "Silliman's Journal"), continued it with a discussion in the *Proceedings of the American Academy* in April, and brought it to a climax with a series of three articles in the *Atlantic Monthly* which were reprinted as a pamphlet and eventually incorporated in his book *Darwiniana.*

Gray's first reaction to the theory was typically American, although surprising in so ardent an abolitionist: "The prospect of the future is encouraging. It is only the backward glance that reveals anything alarming. . . . The very first step backward makes the Negro and the Hottentot blood relations. . . . Not that reason or Scripture objects to that, though pride may." Reason and Scripture triumphed, and Darwin's prediction that Gray would come around was fulfilled: "For it is futile to give up very many species, and stop at an arbitrary line at others. It is what my grandfather called Unitarianism, 'a feather bed to catch a falling Christian.'"

Unitarianism, indeed, proved to be not only capacious enough to accommodate fallen Christians but also fallen scientists, including Darwinists of several varieties. It is not surprising that the first sustained and sympathetic religious reading of the *Origin* should have come from America, where scientists were as jealous of their religious and moral reputations as theologians, where the leading naturalist, Louis Agassiz, might be described as "a sort of demagogue . . . [who] always talks to the rabble" and the geologist James Dwight Dana as too "idealistic" to appreciate Darwin's naturalism. Gray himself, whose descriptions these were, was none the less idealistic, or theistic, for all of his Darwinist naturalism. It was his thesis, that natural selection was "not inconsistent with natural theology," which later attracted so many converts and distressed so many others, leaving Darwin himself in a "hopeless muddle" about the whole affair. His friends, Darwin was to discover, could be almost as quarrelsome as his enemies.

How Huxley Came to Accept the Doctrine of Evolution

Leonard Huxley

Darwin's chief advocate and supporter in the years following the publication of *The Origin of Species* was the eminent British biologist Thomas H. Huxley (his other two primary defenders being British botanist Joseph D. Hooker and British geologist Charles Lyell). Huxley had long been familiar with but had rejected theories of transmutation, the supposed change of one species into another. He had, for instance, read *Vestiges of the Natural History of Creation,* an evolutionary tract published anonymously by Scottish writer Robert Chambers in 1844, but had brushed it aside. As Huxley's son, Leonard, chronicles here (partly through his father's own writings), it was Darwin's landmark book that finally won over the man who would become known as "Darwin's bulldog."

In November 1859 the *Origin of Species* was published, and a new direction was given to Huxley's activities. Ever since Darwin and [Alfred Russel] Wallace had made their joint communication to the Linnean Society in the proceeding July, expectation had been rife as to the forthcoming book. Huxley was one of the few privileged to learn Darwin's argument before it was given to the world; but the greatness of the book, mere installment as it was of the long accumulated mass of notes, almost took him by surprise. Before this time, he had taken up a thoroughly agnostic attitude with regard to the species question, for he could not accept the creational theory, yet sought in vain among the transmutationists for any cause adequate to produce transmutation. He had had many talks with Darwin, and though ready enough to accept the main point, maintained such a critical attitude on many

Excerpted from Leonard Huxley, *Life and Letters of Thomas Henry Huxley,* vol. 1 (New York: Appleton, 1900).

others, that Darwin was not by any means certain of the effect the published book would produce upon him. . . . Darwin was the more anxious, as, when he first put pen to paper, he had fixed in his mind three judges, by whose decision he determined mentally to abide. These three were Lyell, Hooker, and Huxley. If these three came round, partly through the book, partly through their own reflections, he could feel that the subject was safe. "No one," writes Darwin on November 13, "has read it, except Lyell, with whom I have had much correspondence. Hooker thinks him a complete convert, but he does not seem so in his letters to me; but is evidently deeply interested in the subject." And again: "I think I told you before that Hooker is a complete convert. If I can convert Huxley I shall be content."

On all three, the effect of the book itself, with its detailed arguments and overwhelming array of evidence, was far greater than that of previous discussions. With one or two reservations as to the logical completeness of the theory, Huxley accepted it as a well-founded working hypothesis, calculated to explain problems otherwise inexplicable.

A DESIRE FOR EVIDENCE

Two extracts from the chapter he contributed to the *Life of Darwin* show very clearly his attitude of mind when the *Origin of Species* was first published:

> I think I must have read the *Vestiges* before I left England in 1846; but, if I did, the book made very little impression upon me, and I was not brought into serious contact with the "Species" question until after 1850. At that time, I had long done with the Pentateuchal cosmogony [biblical explanation of creation], which had been impressed upon my childish understanding as Divine truth, with all the authority of parents and instructors, and from which it had cost me many a struggle to get free. But my mind was unbiassed in respect of any doctrine which presented itself, if it professed to be based on purely philosophical and scientific reasoning. It seemed to me then (as it does now) that "creation," in the ordinary sense of the word, is perfectly conceivable. I find no difficulty in conceiving that, at some former period, this universe was not in existence; and that it made its appearance in six days (or instantaneously, if that is preferred), in consequence of the volition of some pre-existing Being. Then, as now, the so-called *a priori* arguments [those accepted without evidence one way or another] against Theism, and given a Deity, against the possibility of creative acts, appeared to me to be devoid of reasonable foundation. I had not then, and I have

not now, the smallest *a priori* objection to raise to the account of the creation of animals and plants given in *Paradise Lost*, in which [John] Milton so vividly embodies the natural sense of Genesis. Far be it from me to say that it is untrue because it is impossible. I confine myself to what must be regarded as a modest and reasonable request for some particle of evidence that the existing species of animals and plants did originate in that way, as a condition of my belief in a statement which appears to me to be highly improbable.

And, by way of being perfectly fair, I had exactly the same answer to give to the evolutionists of 1851–58. Within the ranks of the biologists, at that time, I met with nobody, except Dr. Grant of University College, who had a word to say for Evolution—and his advocacy was not calculated to advance the cause. Outside these ranks, the only person known to me whose knowledge and capacity compelled respect, and who was, at the same time, a thorough-going evolutionist, was Mr. Herbert Spencer, whose acquaintance I made, I think, in 1852, and then entered into the bonds of a friendship which, I am happy to think, has known no interruption. Many and prolonged were the battles we fought on this topic. But even my friend's rare dialectic skill and copiousness [large amount] of apt illustration could not drive me from my agnostic position. I took my stand upon two grounds:—Firstly, that up to that time, the evidence in favour of transmutation was wholly insufficient; and secondly, that no suggestion respecting the causes of transmutation assumed, which had been made, was in any way adequate to explain the phenomena. Looking back at the state of knowledge at that time, I really do not see that any other conclusion was justifiable.

EARLY EXPOSURE TO EVOLUTIONIST IDEAS

In those days I had . . . studied [Jean Baptiste] Lamarck attentively, and I had read the *Vestiges* with due care; but neither of them afforded me any good ground for changing my negative and critical attitude. As for the *Vestiges*, I confess that the book simply irritated me by the prodigious ignorance and thoroughly unscientific habit of mind manifested by the writer. If it had any influence on me at all, it set me against Evolution; and the only review I ever have qualms of conscience about, on the ground of needless savagery, is one I wrote on the *Vestiges* while under that influence. . . .

But, by a curious irony of fate, the same influence which led me to put as little faith in modern speculations on this subject as in the venerable traditions recorded in the first two chapters of Genesis, was perhaps more potent than any other in keeping alive a sort of pious conviction that Evolution, after all, would turn out true. I have recently read afresh the first edition of the *Principles of Geology* [Lyell's book]; and when I consider that this remarkable book had been nearly thirty years in everybody's hands, and that it brings home to any reader of ordinary intelligence a great principle and a great fact,—the principle that the past must be explained by the present, unless good cause be shown to the contrary; and the fact that so far as our knowledge of the past history of life on our globe goes, no such cause can be shown,—I cannot but believe that Lyell, for others, as for myself, was the chief agent in smoothing the road for Darwin. For consistent uniformitarianism postulates Evolution as much in the organic as in the inorganic world. The origin of a new species by other than ordinary agencies would be a vastly greater "catastrophe" than any of those which Lyell successfully eliminated from sober geological speculation.

Thus, looking back into the past, it seems to me that my own position of critical expectancy was just and reasonable, and must have been taken up, on the same grounds, by many other persons. If [American scientist Louis] Agassiz told me that the forms of life which have successively tenanted the globe were the incarnations of successive thoughts of the Deity, and that He had wiped out one set of these embodiments by an appalling geological catastrophe as soon as His ideas took a more advanced shape, I found myself not only unable to admit the accuracy of the deductions from the facts of paleontology, upon which this astounding hypothesis was founded, but I had to confess my want of any means of testing the correctness of his explanation of them. And besides that, I could by no means see what the explanation explained. Neither did it help me to be told by an eminent anatomist that species had succeeded one another in time, in virtue of "a continuously operative creational law." That seemed to me to be no more than saying that species had succeeded one another in the form of a vote-catching resolution, with "law" to catch the man of science, and "creational" to draw the orthodox. . . .

A Light in the Darkness

I remember, in the course of my first interview with Mr. Darwin, expressing my belief in the sharpness of the lines of demarcation between natural groups and in the absence of transitional forms, with all the confidence of youth and imperfect knowledge. I was not aware, at that time, that he had then been many years brooding over the species-question; and the humorous smile which accompanied his gentle answer, that such was not altogether his view, long haunted and puzzled me. . . .

As I have already said, I imagine that most of those of my contemporaries who thought seriously about the matter, were very much in my own state of mind—inclined to say to both Mosaists [creationists] and Evolutionists, "a plague on both your houses!" [a line spoken by the character Mercutio in Shakespeare's *Romeo and Juliet*] and disposed to turn aside from an interminable and apparently fruitless discussion, to labour in the fertile fields of ascertainable fact. And I may therefore suppose that the publication of the Darwin and Wallace paper in 1858, and still more that of the "Origin" in 1859, had the effect upon them of the flash of light which, to a man who has lost himself on a dark night, suddenly reveals a road which, whether it takes him straight home or not, certainly goes his way. That which we were looking for, and could not find, was a hypothesis respecting the origin of known organic forms which assumed the operation of no causes but such as could be proved to be actually at work. We wanted, not to pin our faith to that or any other speculation, but to get hold of clear and definite conceptions which could be brought face to face with facts and have their validity tested. The "Origin" provided us with the working hypothesis we sought. Moreover, it did the immense service of freeing us for ever from the dilemma—Refuse to accept the creation hypothesis, and what have you to propose that can be accepted by any cautious reasoner? In 1857 I had no answer ready, and I do not think that anyone else had. A year later we reproached ourselves with dulness for being perplexed with such an inquiry. My reflection, when I first made myself master of the central idea of the "Origin" was, "How extremely stupid not to have thought of that!" I suppose that Columbus' companions said much the same when he made the egg stand on end. The facts of variability, of the struggle for existence, of adaptation to conditions, were notorious enough; but none of us had suspected that the road to the heart of the species problem lay through them, until Darwin and Wallace dispelled the darkness, and the beacon-fire of the "Origin" guided the benighted.

COMMON SENSE CARRIED THE DAY

Whether the particular shape which the doctrine of Evolution, as applied to the organic world, took in Darwin's hands, would prove to be final or not, was to me a matter of indifference. In my earliest criticisms of the "Origin" I ventured to point out that its logical foundation was insecure so long as experiments in selective breeding had not produced varieties which were more or less infertile; and that insecurity remains up to the present time. But, with any and every critical doubt which my sceptical ingenuity could suggest, the Darwinian hypothesis remained incomparably more probable than the creation hypothesis. And if we had none of us been able to discern the paramount significance of some of the most patent and notorious of natural facts, until they were, so to speak, thrust under our noses, what force remained in the dilemma—creation or nothing? It was obvious that hereafter the probability would be immensely greater, that the links of natural causation were hidden from our purblind eyes, than that natural causation should be incompetent to produce all the phenomena of nature. The only rational course for those who had no other object than the attainment of truth was to accept "Darwinism" as a working hypothesis and see what could be made of it. Either it would prove its capacity to elucidate the facts of organic life, or it would break down under the strain. This was surely the dictate of common sense, and, for once, common sense carried the day.

Even before the "Origin" actually came out, Huxley had begun to act as what Darwin afterwards called his "general agent." He began to prepare the way for the acceptance of the theory of evolution by discussing, for instance, one of the most obvious difficulties, namely, How is it that if evolution is ever progressive, progress is not universal? It was a point with respect to which Darwin himself wrote soon after the publication of the "Origin":—"Judging from letters . . . and from remarks, the most serious omission in my book was not explaining how it is, as I believe, that all forms do not necessarily advance, how there can now be *simple* organisms existing."(May 22, 1860.)

Huxley's idea, then, was to call attention to the persistence of many types without appreciable progression during geological time; to show that this fact was not explicable on any other hypothesis than that put forward by Darwin; and by paleontological arguments, to pave the way for consideration of the imperfection of the geological record.

A Critical Review of *The Origin of Species*

Adam Sedgwick

This unfavorable review of Darwin's landmark 1859 book was written by his old teacher, a man whom he once had held in high regard—Adam Sedgwick—and published in the widely read *Spectator* on April 7, 1860. Sedgwick begins with an overview of the main points of the theories expounded in the book and then proceeds to reject them outright. In the first place, he claims, the "purpose" and "design" of a creator are clearly visible everywhere. Second, he condemns the idea of natural selection because it does not seem to account for the extinction of species, including the dinosaurs (an erroneous criticism it turns out, since we now know that the dinosaurs were destroyed by a cosmic catastrophe). Sedgwick's biggest complaint about Darwin's theory, however, is that it is all too materialistic; that is, it reduces the nobility of human intelligence and morals to mechanical and bestial principles, which in itself seems to go against God's intentions.

Before writing about the transmutation [evolution] theory, I must give you a skeleton of what the theory is:

1st. *Species* are *not permanent; varieties* are the beginning of new species.

2nd. Nature began from the simplest forms—probably from one form—the primaeval *monad,* the parent of all organic life.

3d. There has been a continual ascent on the organic scale, till organic nature became what it is, by one continued and unbroken stream of onward movement.

4th. The organic ascent is secured by a Malthusian principle through nature,—by a battle of life, in which the best in

Reprinted from Adam Sedgwick, "Objections to Mr. Darwin's Theory of the Origin of Species," *The Spectator*, April 7, 1860.

organization (the best varieties of plants and animals) encroach upon and drive off the less perfect. This is called the theory of *natural selection.*

It is admirably worked up, and contains a great body of important truth; and it is eminently amusing. But it gives no element of strength to the fundamental theory of transmutation; and without specific transmutations natural selection can do nothing for the general theory. The flora and fauna of North America are very different from what they were when the Pilgrim Fathers were driven out from old England; but changed as they are, they do not one jot change the collective fauna and flora of the actual world.

5th. We do not mark any great organic changes *now,* because they are so slow that even a few thousand years may produce no changes that have fixed the notice of naturalists.

6th. But *time is the agent,* and we can mark the effects of time by the organic changes on the great geological scale. And on every part of that scale, where the organic changes are great in two contiguous deposits of the scale, there must have been a corresponding lapse of time between the periods of their deposition—perhaps millions of years.

I think the foregoing heads give the substance of Darwin's theory; and I think that the great broad facts of geology are directly opposed to it.

ALL AROUND US A DESIGN, A PURPOSE

Some of these facts I shall presently refer to. But I must in the first place observe that Darwin's theory is not *inductive,*—not based on a series of acknowledged facts pointing to a *general conclusion,*—not a proposition evolved out of the facts, logically, and of course including them. To use an old figure, I look on the theory as a vast pyramid resting on its apex, and that apex a mathematical point. The only facts he pretends to adduce, as true elements of proof, are the *varieties* produced by domestication, or the *human artifice* of cross-breeding. We all admit the varieties, and the very wide limits of variation, among domestic animals. How very unlike are poodles and greyhounds! Yet they are of one species. And how nearly alike are many animals,—allowed to be of distinct species, on any acknowledged views of species. Hence there may have been very many blunders among naturalists in the discrimination and enumeration of species. But this does not undermine the grand truth of nature, and the continuity of true species. Again, the varieties, built upon by Mr. Darwin, are varieties of domestication and human *design.* Such varieties could have no existence in the old world. Something may be done by cross-breeding; but mules are generally sterile, or the progeny (in some rare instances) passes into one of the original crossed forms. The Author of Nature will not permit His work to be spoiled by the wanton curiosity of Man. And in a state of nature (such as that of the old world before Man came upon it) wild animals of different species do not desire to cross and unite.

Species have been constant for thousands of years; and time (so far as I see my way) though multiplied by millions and billions would never change them, so long as the conditions remained constant. Change the conditions, and old species would disappear; and new species *might* have room to come in and flourish. But how, and by what causation? I say by *creation.* But, what do I mean by creation? I reply, the operation of a power quite beyond the powers of a pigeon-fancier, a cross-breeder, or hybridizer; a power I cannot imitate or comprehend; but in which I can believe, by a legitimate conclusion of sound reason drawn from the laws and harmonies of Nature. For I can see in all around me a design and purpose, and a mutual adaptation of parts which I *can* comprehend,—and which prove that there is exterior to, and above, the mere phenomena of Nature a great prescient and designing cause. Believing this, I have no difficulty in the repetition of new species during successive epochs in the history of the earth.

But Darwin would say I am introducing a *miracle* by the supposition. In one sense, I am; in another, I am not. The hypothesis does not suspend or interrupt in established law of Nature. It does suppose the introduction of a new phenomenon unaccounted for by the operation of any *known* law of Nature; and it appeals to a power above established laws, and yet acting in harmony and conformity with them.

The pretended physical philosophy of modern days strips Man of all his moral attributes, or holds them of no account in the estimate of his origin and place in the created world. A cold atheistical materialism is the tendency of the so-called material philosophy of the present day. Not that I believe that Darwin is an atheist; though I cannot but regard his materialism as atheistical; because it ignores all rational conception of a final cause. I think it untrue because opposed to the obvious course of Nature, and the very opposite of inductive truth. I therefore think it intensely mischievous.

Let no one say that it is held together by a cumulative argument. Each series of facts is laced together by a series of assumptions, which are mere repetitions of the one false principle. You cannot make a good rope out of a string of air-bubbles.

WHAT HAPPENED TO THE DINOSAURS?

I proceed now to notice the manner in which Darwin tries to fit his principles to the facts of geology.

I will take for granted that the known series of fossil-bearing rocks or deposits may be divided into the Palaeozoic; the Mesozoic; the Tertiary or Neozoic; and the Modern—the Fens, Deltas, &c., &c., with the spoils of the actual flora and fauna of the world, and with wrecks of the works of Man.

To begin then, with the Palaeozoic rocks. Surely we ought on the transmutation theory, to find near their base great depositis with *none but the lowest forms of organic life.* I know of no such deposits. . . . Neither do we find beds exclusively of hard corals and other humble organisms, which ought, on the theory, to mark a period of vast duration while the primaeval monads were working up into the higher types of life. Our evidence is, no doubt, very scanty; but let not our opponents dare to say that it makes *for them.* So far as it is positive, it seems to me pointblank *against them.* If *we* build upon imperfect evidence, they commence without any evidence whatsoever, and against the evidence of actual nature. As we ascend in the great stages of the Palaeozoic series (through Cambrian, Silurian, Devonian, and Carboniferous rocks) we have in each a *characteristic* fauna; we have no wavering of species,—we have the noblest cephalopods and brachiopods that ever existed; and they preserve their typical forms till they disappear. And a few of the types have endured, with specific modifications, through all succeeding ages of the earth. It is during these old periods that we have some of the noblest icthyc forms that ever were created. The same may be said, I think, of the carboniferous flora. As a whole, indeed, it is lower than the living flora of our own period; but many of the old types were grander and of higher organization than the corresponding families of the living flora; and there is no wavering, no wanting of organic definition, in the old types. We have some land reptiles (batrachians), in the higher Palaeozoic periods, but not of a very low type; and the reptiles of the permian groups (at the very top of the Palaeozoic rocks), are of a high type. If all this be true, (and I think it is), it gives but a sturdy grist for the transmutation-mill, and may soon break its cogs.

We know the complicated organic phenomena of the Mesozoic (or Oolitic) period. It defies the transmutationist at every step. Oh! but the document, says Darwin, is a fragment. I will interpolate long periods to account for all the changes. I say, in reply, if you deny my conclusion grounded on positive evidence, I toss back your conclusions, derived from negative evidence—the inflated cushion on which you try to bolster up the defects of your hypothesis. The reptile fauna of the Mesozoic period is the grandest and highest that ever lived. How came these reptiles to die off, or to degenerate? And how came the Dinosaurs to disappear from the face of Nature, and leave no descendants like themselves, or of a corresponding nobility? By what process of *natural selection* did they disappear? Did they tire of the land, and become Whales, casting off their hind-legs? And, after they had lasted millions of years as whales, did they tire of the water, and leap out again as Pachyderms? I have heard of both hypotheses; and I cannot put them into words without seeming to use the terms of mockery. This I do affirm, that if the transmutation theory were proved true in the actual world, and we could hatch rats out of eggs of geese, it would still be difficult to account for the successive forms of organic life in the old world. They appear to me to give the lie to the theory of transmutation at every turn of the pages of Dame Nature's old book.

A COUNTLESS LAPSE OF AGES

The limits of this letter compel me to omit any long discussion of the Tertiary Mammals, of course including man at their head. On physical grounds, the transmutation theory is untrue, if we reason (as we ought to do) from the known to the unknown. To this rule, the Tertiary Mammals offer us no exception. Nor is there any proof, either ethnographical or physical, of the bestial origin of man.

And now for a few words upon Darwin's long inter*polated periods of* geological ages. He has an eternity of past time to draw upon; and I am willing to give him ample measure; only let him use it logically, and in some probable accordance with facts and phenomena.

1st. I place the theory against facts viewed collectively. I see no proofs of enormous *gaps* of geological time, (I say nothing of years or centuries,) in those cases where there is a sudden change in the ancient fauna and flora. . . .

2d. Towards the end of the carboniferous period, there was a vast extinction of animal and vegetable life. We can, I think, account for this extinction mechanically. The old crust was broken up. The sea bottom underwent a great change. The old flora and fauna went out; and a new flora and fauna appeared, in the ground, now called permian, at the base of the new red sandstone, which overlies the carboniferous rocks. I take the fact as it *is*, and I have no diffi-

---

SEDGWICK EXPOSES TO DARWIN THE GRANDEUR OF CREATION

In this brief excerpt from Adrian Desmond's and James Moore's biography of Darwin, young Darwin is duly impressed by Sedgwick's lectures, not realizing that he and Sedgwick would one day become intellectual enemies.

For his part, Darwin was fired up by Sedgwick's lectures that spring. They were incomparably better than Jameson's at Edinburgh, which he had hated. Sedgwick's reminded him of [naturalist Alexander von] Humboldt, [astronomer John] Herschel, and [theologian William] Paley, wrapped into one. They opened up new vistas of God's world, exposed the grandeur of creation. 'What a capital hand is Sedgewick [sic] for drawing large cheques upon the Bank of Time!' Darwin marvelled. And as for space, the professor revealed how much more of the globe remained to be conquered. 'It strikes *me*,' Darwin reflected, 'that all our knowledge about the structure of our Earth is very much like what an old hen w^d [would] know of the hundred-acre field in a corner of which she is scratching.'

Undaunted by his ignorance, Darwin was—as usual—anxious to please and took the initiative. When Sedgwick mentioned a local spring, flowing from a chalk hill, which deposited lime in a delicate tracery on twigs, Darwin rode out, found it, and threw a whole bush in. Later he retrieved it, an extraordinary white-coated spray, so exquisite that Sedgwick exhibited it in class; whereupon others followed suit, and encrusted branches were soon adorning rooms all over the university.

Adrian Desmond and James Moore, *Darwin*. New York: Warner Books, 1992, pp. 94–95.

culty. The time in which all this was brought about *may* have been very long, even upon a geological scale of time. But where do the *intervening* and connecting types exist, which are to mark the *work of natural selection*? We do not find them. Therefore, the step onwards gives no true resting-place to a baseless theory; and is, in fact, a stumbling-block in its way.

3d. Before we rise through the new red sandstone, we find the muschel-kalk (wanting in England, though its place on the scale is well-known) with an *entirely new* fauna: where have we a proof of any enormous lapse of geological time to account for the change? We have no proof in the desposits themselves: the presumption they offer to our senses is of a contrary kind.

4th. If we rise from the muschel-kalk to the Lias, we find again a new fauna. All the anterior species are gone. Yet the passage through the upper members of the new red sandstone to the Lias is by insensible gradations, and it is no easy matter to fix the physical line of their demarcation. I think it would be a very rash assertion to affirm that a great geological interval took place between the formation of the upper part of the new red sandstone and the Lias. Physical evidence is against it. To support a baseless theory, Darwin would require a countless lapse of ages of which we have no commensurate physical monuments; and he is unable to supply any of the connecting organic links that ought to bind together the older fauna with that of the Lias.

DARWIN IS TOO MATERIALISTIC

I cannot go on any further with these objections. But I will not conclude without expressing my deep aversion to the theory; because of its unflinching materialism;—because it has deserted the inductive track,—the only track that leads to physical truth;—because it utterly repudiates final causes, and thereby indicates a demoralized understanding on the part of its advocates. By the word, demoralized, I mean a want of capacity for comprehending the force of moral evidence, which is dependent on the highest faculties of our nature. What is it that gives us the sense of right and wrong, of law, of duty, of cause and effect? What is it that enables us to construct true theories on good inductive evidence? Theories which enable us, whether in the material or the moral world, to link together the past and the present. What is it that enables us to anticipate the future, to act wisely with reference to future good, to believe in a future state, to acknowledge the being of a God? These faculties, and many others of like kind, are a part of ourselves quite as much so as our organs of sense. All nature is subordinate to law. Every organ of every sentient being has its purpose bound up in the very law of its existence. Are the highest conceptions of man, to which he is led by the necessities of his moral nature, to have no counterpart or fruition? I say *no*, to all such questions; and fearlessly affirm that we cannot speculate on man's position in the actual world of nature, on his destinies, or on *his origin*, while we keep his highest faculties out of our sight. Strip him of these faculties, and he becomes entirely bestial; and he may well be (under such a false and narrow view) nothing better than the natural progeny of a beast, which has to live, to beget its likeness, and then die for ever.

By gazing only on material nature, a man may easily have his very senses bewildered (like one under the cheatery of an electro-biologist); he may become so frozen up, by a too long continued and exclusively material study, as to lose his relish for moral truth, and his vivacity in apprehending it. I think I can see traces of this effect, both in the origin and in the details of certain portions of Darwin's theory; and, in confirmation of what I now write, I would appeal to all that he states about those marvellous structures,—the comb of a common honey-bee, and the eye of a mammal. His explanations make demands on our credulity, that are utterly beyond endurance, and do not give us one true natural step towards and explanation of the phenomena—viz., the perfection of the structures, and their adaptation to their office. There *is* a light by which a man may see and comprehend facts and truths such as these. But Darwin wilfully shuts it out from our senses; either because he does not apprehend its power, or because he disbelieves in its existence. This is the grand blemish of his work. Separated from his sterile and contracted theory, it contains very admirable details and beautiful views of nature,—especially in those chapters which relate to the battle of life, the variations of species, and their diffusion through wide regions of the earth.

In some rare instances, Darwin shows a wonderful credulity. He . . . seems to believe that a white bear, by being confined to the slops floating in the Polar basin, might be turned into a whale; that a Lemur might easily be turned into a bat; that a three-toed Tapir might be a great grandfather of a horse! Or the progeny of a horse (in America) have gone back to the tapir.

But any startling and (supposed) novel paradox, maintained very boldly and with something of imposing plausibility, produces, in some minds, a kind of pleasing excitement, which predisposes them in its favour; and if they are unused to careful reflection, and averse to the labour of accurate investigation, they will be likely to conclude that what is (apparently) *original* must be a production of original *genius*, and that anything very much opposed to prevailing notions must be a grand *discovery*,—in short, that whatever comes from "the bottom of a well" must be the "truth" supposed to be hidden there.

A Favorable Review of *The Origin of Species*

Joseph D. Hooker

Darwin's longtime friend, the brilliant British botanist Joseph Dalton Hooker (1817–1911), wrote the following review of Darwin's *Origin of Species* for the December 31, 1859, issue of the *Gardener's Chronicle*. In support of Darwin's thesis, Hooker points out that plant and animal breeders have long demonstrated the ability to breed what appear to be new species, and/or genera, a phenomenon that cannot be explained by—and indeed seems to contradict—the doctrine of special creation. In addition, he notes that variations in species can actually be observed and quantified, whereas special creation must be accepted on faith.

To how many of our gardening readers has it ever occurred to investigate the origin of any of the "favoured races" of plants with which they are familiar in the garden, the orchard, or the forest? Many know or take for granted that the most dissimilar kinds of Strawberries, Apples, and Potatoes have all sprung from one stock, and that most of them have originated within a very recent period; as also that the history of many is attainable, did they think it worth the trouble of searching for. Even this limited knowledge is seldom acquired; and it is rarer still to find a gardener who has ever reflected upon the possible origin of the wild plants that surround him; though he not only knows that these are composed of the very same elements as are contained in the soil and air, but that they are themselves the immediate ancestors of the cultivated plants whose nurture provides him with remunerative labour, and whose increase at the same time supplies him abundantly with food. Little, however, as our gardening friends may have thought of these matters,

Reprinted from Joseph Dalton Hooker, review of *The Origin of Species, Gardeners' Chronicle*, December 31, 1859 (published anonymously).

still the terms "favoured race" and "origin of species," are more or less intelligible to most: but it is very different with "struggle for life." In its application to man civilized and savage, at peace and at war, and in a certain degree to the lower animals, the significance of the phrase is obvious enough; but how it can apply to the vegetable kingdom is not so evident at first sight, and still less evident is its connection with the "origin of species" and with "favoured races."

A BOLD, FRANK, AND COURTEOUS BOOK

Perplexed with these thoughts on reading for the first time the title of Mr. DARWIN'S new volume ON THE ORIGIN OF SPECIES [i.e., the book's full title, *On the Origin of Species by Means of Natural Selection; or the Preservation of Favoured Races in the Struggle for Life*], and knowing that the author is of first-rate standing in science, of great popularity, and a frequent contributor to our columns, we awaited the publication of his book with great curiosity and interest. It is true that we had been referred to a notice in the *Gardeners' Chronicle* (1858, p. 735) of a paper communicated by Mr. DARWIN to the Linnean Society, which gives a clue to the general nature of his work, but rather whetted the curiosity than allayed it; being little more than an indication of one method of research now fully developed, and giving little idea of the extent, variety, and suggestive value of that research, and still less of the comprehensiveness and talent of the present work.

From the above expressions it will be inferred that we have risen from the perusal of Mr. DARWIN'S book much impressed with its importance, and have moreover found it to be so dependent on the phenomena of horticultural operations, for its facts and results, and so full of experiments that may be repeated and discussed by intelligent gardeners, and of ideas that may sooner fructify in their minds than in those of any other class of naturalists, that we shall be doing them (and we hope also science) a service by dwelling in some detail upon its contents. Thus much we may premise, that it is a book teeming with deep thoughts on numberless simple and complex phenomena of life; that its premises in almost all cases appear to be correct; that its reasoning is apparently close and sound, its style clear, and we need hardly add its subject and manner equally attractive and agreeable; it is also a perfectly ingenuous book, bold in expressions as

in thought where the author adduces what he considers
clear evidence in his favour, frank in the statement of objections to the hypotheses or conclusions founded on its facts
and reasonings; and uniformly courteous to antagonistic
doctrines. In fine, whatever may be thought of Mr. DAR-
WIN'S ultimate conclusions it cannot be denied that it would
be difficult in the whole range of the literature of science to
find a book so exclusively devoted to the development of theoretical inquiries, which at the same time is throughout so
full of conscientious care, so fair in argument, and so con-
siderate in tone.

NATURE HAS MOCKED US?

Before entering upon an analysis of those parts of Mr. DAR-
WIN'S work which more immediately concern our readers,
we may explain that it is devoted to the inquiry of how it is
that the world has come to be peopled by so many and such
various kinds of plants and animals as now inhabit it; and
why it is that these do not all present a continuous, instead
of an interrupted series, capable of being divided into varieties, species, genera, orders, &c. To all careless and many
careful naturalists the assertion is sufficient, that they were
so created, and have been endowed with power to remain
unchanged; but there are considerable difficulties in the
way of the adoption of this theory, which all reflecting naturalists allow; whilst more to our present purpose is the fact,
that in Mr. DARWIN'S opinion the objections to it are more
numerous and some of them more conclusive than the arguments in its favour. In the first there is the fact, that gardeners and cattle and bird breeders have made races which
are not only more dissimilar than many species in a state of
nature are, but if found in a state of nature would unques-
tionably be ranked as species and even genera; while the
possibility of their reversion to their parent forms is doubted
by many and denied by some. Then, there is the fact, that in
a great many genera many so-called species present a graduated series of varieties which have puzzled the best naturalists; and that in such genera at any rate it is easier to suppose that the species are not separate creations than that
they are so. Again, the whole system of animal and plant
classification into individuals, species, genera, &c., presents
a series strictly analogous to that of the members of the human or any other family; and we further express our notions

of the mutual relations of animals and plants in the very terms that would represent their affinities as being due to a blood relationship; so that either Nature has mocked us by imitating hereditary descent in her creations, or we have misinterrupted her in assuming that she has followed one method for families and another for species.

ORIGINAL CREATIONS OR CREATION BY VARIATION?

There is then the geological evidence of species not having all been introduced at one period on the globe, but at various successive periods, and in like manner there is abundant evidence that they are being extinguished one by one; and as geologists are now pretty unanimous in believing that the past changes of the globe were the same in kind and degree as those now going on, we can no longer cling to the old vague belief that species were created at a time when all other conditions were different from those now existing; and thus hide one mystery under another. Again, if we hold to original creations we must also admit that it is more likely that a new kind of Strawberry, as different from all the wild as the British Queen is from the Alpine, should naturally originate in England or elsewhere out of air and earth and water, than that it should have originated in accordance with the laws that favoured the gardener's skill in producing the above-mentioned form. Finally, we know that on the one hand all changes of the surface of the globe (of climate, geographical limits, elevation and depression) are extremely slow; and that on the other relations of co-adaptation subsist between the climate, &c., of every country and the animals and plants which it contains; but such co-adaptations could not harmoniously exist if the physical changes were slow, and the creations of species sudden, for in such cases the species must be created either before or after they were wanted, a state of things which no orthodox naturalist would admit; but if, on the contrary, the organisms are supposed to change with the changed conditions of the country they inhabit, perfect adaptation and continuous fitness would be the necessary result.

Such ideas as these, either in whole or in part, have occurred to many naturalists, when in endeavouring to classify their animals and plants, or to account for their distribution, they have found themselves forced to face the difficulty of accounting for their origin. Hitherto most have, as we have already observed, contented themselves with the hypothesis that they were independently created, and the minority have clung to the only other explanation hitherto conceived, that they have all been created by variation from a single first-created living organism, or a few such. Now it must be borne in mind that both these views are mere hypotheses in a scientific point of view; neither has any inherent or prescriptive right to a preference in the mind of the impartial inquirer; but the most superficial observation will show that the hypothesis of original creations is incapable of absolute proof, except the operation be witnessed by credible naturalists, and can only be supported by facts that are either not conclusive against the opposite doctrine, or may be regarded as equally favourable to it; and this hypothesis is hence placed at a disadvantage in comparison with that of the creation of species by variation, which takes its stand on the fa-

HOOKER CONGRATULATES DARWIN ON HIS BOOK

In this note to Darwin, dated Monday, November 21, 1859, Hooker comments that the finished book is even more impressive than the original manuscript, which Hooker had seen.

MY DEAR DARWIN,—I am a sinner not to have written you ere this, if only to thank you for your glorious book—what a mass of close reasoning on curious facts and fresh phenomena—it is capitally written, and will be very successful. I say this on the strength of two or three plunges into as many chapters, for I have not yet attempted to read it. [Charles] Lyell, with whom we are staying, is perfectly enchanted, and is absolutely gloating over it. I must accept your compliment to me, and acknowledgment of supposed assistance from me, as the warm tribute of affection from an honest (though deluded) man, and furthermore accept it as very pleasing to my vanity; but, my dear fellow, neither my name nor my judgment nor my assistance deserved any such compliments, and if I am dishonest enough to be pleased with what I don't deserve, it must just pass. How different the *book* reads from the MS. I see I shall have much to talk over with you. Those lazy printers have not finished my luckless Essay: which, beside your book, will look like a ragged handkerchief beside a Royal Standard.

Quoted in Francis Darwin, ed., *The Autobiography of Charles Darwin and Selected Letters.* New York: Dover Publications, 1958, pp. 223–24.

miliar fact that species do depart from the likeness of their progenitors, both in a wild and domestic state.

A PLAUSIBLE METHOD OF VARIATION

On the other hand the hypothesis of creation by variation labours under the disadvantage of being founded upon a series of phenomena, the action of each of which individually, as explained by Mr. DARWIN, would appear to prevent the possibility of species retaining their characters for any length of time, and it therefore appears at first sight opposed to the undisputed fact, that many hundreds of animals and plants have transmitted their characters unchanged (or nearly so) through countless generations, and covered, even within the historic period, many square miles of country each with millions of its exact counterpart. To explain this anomaly and to raise this hypothesis of creations by variation to the rank of a scientific theory, is the object of Mr. DARWIN'S book, and to do this he has endeavoured to invent and prove such an intelligible rationale of the operation of variation, as will account for many species having been developed from a few in strict adaptation to existing conditions, and to show good cause how these apparently fleeting changelings may by the operation of natural laws be so far fixed as to reconcile both the naturalist and the common observer to the idea, that what in all his experience are immutable forms of life may have once worn another guise. The hypothesis itself is a very old one; it was, as all the world knows, strongly advocated by [Jean Baptiste] LAMARCK, and later still by the author of the "Vestiges of the Natural History of the Creation" [Robert Chambers], but neither of these authors were able to suggest even a plausible method according to which Nature might have proceeded in producing suitable varieties, getting rid of intermediate forms, and giving a temporary stability to such as are recognised as species by all observers. Mr. DARWIN has been more successful, though whether completely so or not the future alone can show. We shall proceed to examine his method in another article.

The Famous Oxford Debate of Darwin's Theory

Francis Darwin (and various eyewitnesses)

Following is a combination of commentary and eye-witness accounts first published by Charles Darwin's son, Francis, in 1892. The event described is the now famous public meeting of the British Association for the Advancement of Science, held at Oxford University on June 28, 1860. It was here that the major anti-Darwinian figures, including the noted scientist Richard Owen, planned to gather and blacken the reputation of Darwin and his recently published book, *The Origin of Species*. As these eyewitness recollections attest, their champion, the popular Bishop Samuel Wilberforce, spoke eloquently but ultimately revealed that, despite his having been coached by Owen beforehand, he had no real idea what he was talking about. Contrary to what many had expected, Darwin's own champions, J.D. Hooker and Thomas Huxley, eventually won the day, convincing the vast majority of those gathered that Darwin's theory at least deserved a fair hearing.

The meeting of the British Association at Oxford in 1860 is famous for two pitched battles over the *Origin of Species*. Both of them originated in unimportant papers. On Thursday, June 28th, Dr. Daubeny of Oxford made a communication to Section D: "On the final causes of the sexuality of plants, with particular reference to Mr. Darwin's work on the *Origin of Species*." Mr. [Thomas] Huxley was called on by the President, but tried (according to the *Athenæum* report) to avoid a discussion, on the ground "that a general audience, in which sentiment would unduly interfere with intellect, was not the public before which such a discussion should be carried on."

Excerpted from *Charles Darwin: His Life Told in an Autobiographical Chapter and in a Selected Series of his Published Letters*, edited by Francis Darwin (New York: Appleton, 1892).

However, the subject was not allowed to drop. Sir R. Owen (I quote from the *Athenæum*, July 7th, 1860), who "wished to approach this subject in the spirit of the philosopher," expressed his "conviction that there were facts by which the public could come to some conclusion with regard to the probabilities of the truth of Mr. Darwin's theory." He went on to say that the brain of the gorilla "presented more differences, as compared with the brain of man, than it did when compared with the brains of the very lowest and most problematical of the Quadrumana." Mr. Huxley replied, and gave these assertions a "direct and unqualified contradiction," pledging himself to "justify that unusual procedure elsewhere," a pledge which he amply fulfilled. On Friday there was peace, but on Saturday 30th, the battle arose with redoubled fury, at a conjoint meeting of three Sections, over a paper by Dr. Draper of New York, on the "Intellectual development of Europe considered with reference to the views of Mr. Darwin."

THE BISHOP'S DULCET TONES

The following account is from an eye-witness of the scene.

"The excitement was tremendous. The Lecture-room, in which it had been arranged that the discussion should be held, proved far too small for the audience, and the meeting adjourned to the Library of the Museum, which was crammed to suffocation long before the champions entered the lists. The numbers were estimated at from 700 to 1000. Had it been term-time, or had the general public been admitted, it would have been impossible to have accommodated the rush to hear the oratory of the bold Bishop [Samuel Wilberforce]. Prof. Henslow, the President of Section D, occupied the chair, and wisely announced . . . that none who had not valid arguments to bring forward on one side or the other, would be allowed to address the meeting: a caution that proved necessary, for no fewer than four combatants had their utterances burked by him, because of their indulgence in vague declamation.

"The Bishop was up to time, and spoke for full half-an-hour with inimitable spirit, emptiness and unfairness. It was evident from his handling of the subject that he had been 'crammed' up to the throat, and that he knew nothing at first hand; in fact, he used no argument not to be found in his *Quarterly Review* article. He ridiculed Darwin badly, and Huxley savagely, but all in such dulcet tones, so persuasive a manner, and in such well-turned periods, that I who had been inclined to blame the President for allowing a discussion that could serve no scientific purpose, now forgave him from the bottom of my heart."

HUXLEY'S APE ANCESTRY?

What follows is from notes most kindly supplied by the Hon. and Rev. W.H. Fremantle, who was an eye-witness of the scene.

"The Bishop of Oxford attacked Darwin, at first playfully but at last in grim earnest. It was known that the Bishop had written an article against Darwin in the last *Quarterly Review*: it was also rumoured that Prof. [Richard] Owen had been staying at Cuddesden and had primed the Bishop, who was to act as mouthpiece to the great Palæontologist, who did not himself dare to enter the lists [contest]. The Bishop, however, did not show himself master of the facts, and made one serious blunder. A fact which had been much dwelt on as confirmatory of Darwin's idea of variation, was that a sheep had been born shortly before in a flock in the North of England, having an addition of one to the vertebræ of the spine. The Bishop was declaring with rhetorical exaggeration that there was hardly any actual evidence on Darwin's side. 'What have they to bring forward?' he exclaimed. 'Some rumoured statement about a long-legged sheep.' But he passed on to banter: 'I should like to ask Professor Huxley, who is sitting by me, and is about to tear me to pieces when I have sat down, as to his belief in being descended from an ape. Is it on his grandfather's or his grandmother's side that the ape ancestry comes in?' And then taking a graver tone, he asserted in a solemn peroration that Darwin's views were contrary to the revelations of God in the Scriptures. Professor Huxley was unwilling to respond: but he was called for and spoke with his usual incisiveness and with some scorn. 'I am here only in the interest of science,' he said, 'and I have not heard anything which can prejudice the case of my august client.' Then after showing how little competent the Bishop was to enter upon the discussion, he touched on the question of Creation. 'You say that development [change, evolution] drives out the Creator. But you assert that God made you; and yet you know that you yourself were originally a little piece of matter no bigger than the end of this gold pencil-case.' Lastly as to the descent from a monkey, he said: 'I should feel it no shame to have risen from such an origin. But I should feel it a shame to have sprung from one who prostituted the gifts of culture and of eloquence to the service of prejudice and of falsehood.'

THOSE MOST CAPABLE ACCEPT DARWIN'S CONCLUSIONS

"Many others spoke. Mr. Gresley, an old Oxford don, pointed out that in human nature at least orderly development was not the necessary rule; Homer was the greatest of poets, but he lived 3000 years ago, and has not produced his like.

"Admiral [Robert] Fitz-Roy [skipper of the *Beagle*, the ship that had carried Darwin on his voyage of discovery years before] was present, and said that he had often expostulated with his old comrade of the *Beagle* for entertaining views which were contradictory to the First Chapter of Genesis.

"Sir John Lubbock declared that many of the arguments by which the permanence of species was supported came to nothing, and instanced some wheat which was said to have come off an Egyptian mummy and was sent to him to prove that wheat had not changed since the time of the Pharaohs; but which proved to be made of French chocolate. Sir Joseph (then Dr.) Hooker spoke shortly, saying that he had found the hypothesis of Natural Selection so helpful in explaining the phenomena of his own subject of Botany, that he had been constrained to accept it. After a few words from Darwin's old friend Professor Henslow who occupied the chair, the meeting broke up, leaving the impression that those most capable of estimating the arguments of Darwin in detail saw their way to accept his conclusions."

Many versions of Mr. Huxley's speech were current: the following report of his conclusion is from a letter addressed by the late John Richard Green, then an undergraduate, to a fellow-student, now Professor Boyd Dawkins:—"I asserted, and I repeat, that a man has no reason to be ashamed of having an ape for his grandfather. If there were an ancestor whom I should feel shame in recalling, it would be a *man*, a man of restless and versatile intellect, who, not content with an equivocal success in his own sphere of activity, plunges into scientific questions with which he has no real acquaintance, only to obscure them by an aimless rhetoric, and distract the attention of his hearers from the real point at issue by eloquent digressions, and skilled appeals to religious prejudice."

Darwin's Follow-Up to *Origin—The Descent of Man*

William Irvine

In this essay, William Irvine, the noted modern biographer of both Darwin and Thomas Huxley, describes the appearance of Darwin's *Descent of Man* in 1871. Contrary to the assumption still made by many who are unfamiliar with the actual content of Darwin's works, *The Origin of Species* does not deal directly with human evolution. Darwin therefore felt compelled to produce a follow-up volume that did so, and the result was *Descent*. After summarizing the book's principal ideas and viewpoints, Irvine follows up with a brief discussion of its critical reception, which, he points out, was surprisingly less outraged and mean-spirited that the one that had greeted *Origin*.

In 1870 Darwin worked almost without interruption on *The Descent of Man*. It grew longer and longer, so that he saved it from the interminability of *Variation* [*The Variation of Animals and Plants Under Domestication*] only by amputating *The Expression of the Emotions*. As the manuscript neared completion, he turned it over to [his daughter] Henrietta [for proofreading]. . . . Looking over the corrections, Charles was as usual astonished, and when after its appearance the book was admired for its "lucid, vigorous style," he attributed this unwonted virtue wholly to his daughter's efforts and presented her with thirty pounds from his royalties. "By Jove, how hard you must have worked," he exclaimed, "and how thoroughly you have mastered my MS." By 1871, having labored three years and driven himself to the extremity of boredom and disgust with his subject, be sent the last corrections to John Murray [his publisher]. . . .

It was published in February, 1871.

The Descent of Man is usually considered Darwin's second best book. As a matter of fact, despite much amputation and other drastic surgery, it is really two books in one pair of covers. Having dealt with man for 206 pages, the author digresses to sexual selection and persists indefatigably in that digression to the last and 688th page. Considered apart from its giant appendage, the *Descent* is undoubtedly Darwin at a disadvantage—Darwin at grips with an uncongenial animal in uncongenial environments, Darwin without the miracles of inspiration and discovery, in large part without even the exhaustive, first-hand research and the tireless, sympathetically understanding observation which were among his most dependable gifts. . . .

The *Descent* is just good enough to fill up the space between a great thinker and a great opportunity. It sums up and evaluates, sometimes with authority and always with balance and common sense, a decade of brilliant anthropological thinking.

ANIMAL ANECDOTES

Studying man somewhat less exhaustively than the barnacle, Darwin maintains that his preeminence is due not to any one characteristic, like the acquisition of language, but to many— to his upright position, the freedom and delicacy of his hands, the use of tools and language, and above all, the mental capacity which made tools and language possible. Nevertheless, Darwin believes that increasing powers of expression must have interacted with increasing mental powers to bring intelligence to a genuinely human level. Like [British philosopher Herbert] Spencer, he regards mind as an adaptation to environment and a weapon in the struggle for survival, but, unlike Spencer, he soberly refrains from pursuing the metaphysical implications of this view. He insists on the great gap between man and the higher mammals, and disagrees with [his colleague, naturalist Alfred Russel] Wallace that the savage could have discovered fire or developed language with a brain little better than that of the ape; yet he insists also that, as a product of natural selection, man differs from animals physically, mentally and morally not in kind but in degree. Monkeys use sticks and stones as tools; dogs exhibit loyalty and other moral virtues; and many of the higher species are capable of very elementary reasoning.

Darwin is always at his best with animal anecdotes:

> One female baboon had so capacious a heart that she not only adopted young monkeys of other species, but stole young dogs and cats, which she continually carried about. . . . An adopted kitten scratched this affectionate baboon, who certainly had a fine intellect, for she was much astonished at being scratched, and immediately examined the kitten's feet, and without more ado bit off the claws.

Like a good Darwinian, he is cautious about theories which . . . involve inherited memory and the recording of thought patterns on the nervous system of succeeding generations. Deeply ingrained habits may transmit tendencies, but scarcely, perhaps, the habits themselves. Otherwise, absurd customs, like the Hindoo's aversion to certain foods, ought to be inherited.

HUMAN SOCIAL PROGRESS

Making no pretensions as an ethical thinker, Darwin does not attempt any elaborate account of moral experience, nor is he entirely free from confusion and inconsistency. Nevertheless, his general position is pretty clear. Broadly consid-

WHY ARE WOMEN LESS HAIRY THAN MEN?

In this brief excerpt from Chapter 20 of The Descent of Man, *Darwin suggests that the tendency for women to be less hairy than men is a result of sexual selection.*

The absence of hair on the body is to a certain extent a secondary sexual character; for in all parts of the world women are less hairy than men. Therefore we may reasonably suspect that this character has been gained through sexual selection. We know that the faces of several species of monkeys, and large surfaces at the posterior end of the body of other species, have been denuded of hair; and this we may safely attribute to sexual selection, for these surfaces are not only vividly coloured, but sometimes, as with the male mandrill and female rhesus, much more vividly in the one sex than in the other, especially during the breeding-season. I am informed . . . that, as these animals gradually reach maturity, the naked surfaces grow larger compared with the size of their bodies. The hair, however, appears to have been removed, not for the sake of nudity, but that the colour of the skin may be more fully displayed. So again with many birds, it appears as if the head and

ered, conscience arises from the evolutionary process; more particularly—first, from sympathy and the social instincts, which are supported by opinion, and second, from rational reflection on the consequences of actions and from the emergence of the idea of *ought*, which may, in idealistic individuals, rise above mere public opinion. Darwin had prepared himself for the moral problem by extensive reading in [the works of great social philosophers, such as] Bain, Mill, Adam Smith, Hume, Bacon, and even Marcus Aurelius. . . . He follows Smith in stressing the importance of sympathy, and Hume in emphasizing the nonrational basis of conduct. Yet he avoids the speculative subtleties of the Utilitarians, and particularly their tendency to turn moral consciousness into an epicurean balance sheet of pains and pleasures— keeping as close as possible to the broad generalities of common sense on the one hand and the solid facts of animal behavior on the other. In general, he sees clearly that the moral life consists in a struggle between duty and desire, and that virtue and happiness depend first on humility and self-knowledge and second on effort and rational discipline.

His discussion of man in society is equally sound but less

---

neck had been divested of feathers through sexual selection, to exhibit the brightly-coloured skin.

As the body in woman is less hairy than in man, and as this character is common to all races, we may conclude that it was our female semi-human ancestors who were first divested of hair, and that this occurred at an extremely remote period before the several races had diverged from a common stock. Whilst our female ancestors were gradually acquiring this new character of nudity, they must have transmitted it almost equally to their offspring of both sexes whilst young; so that its transmission, as with the ornaments of many mammals and birds, has not been limited either by sex or age. There is nothing surprising in a partial loss of hair having been esteemed as an ornament by our ape-like progenitors, for we have seen that innumerable strange characters have been thus esteemed by animals of all kinds, and have consequently been gained through sexual selection. Nor is it surprising that a slightly injurious character should have been thus acquired; for we know that this is the case with the plumes of certain birds, and with the horns of certain stags.

The Descent of Man. New York: Random House, n.d., pp. 903–904.

definite and clear-cut. Within the community, physical, mental, and moral excellence tends to be preserved both by natural selection and by deliberate cultivation. Social achievement is spread within the community by imitation and beyond it by . . . natural selection of communities. Darwin sees only a partial truth in the arguments . . . that civilization preserves weaklings and failures. Successful men in all walks of life tend to leave more offspring; and the diseased, the pathological, and the criminal tend to be eliminated. The total result is apparently that all peoples progress biologically at a very slow rate, and a few peoples progress socially at a very rapid rate.

MAKING ANIMALS TOO HUMAN?

Undoubtedly, the *Descent* encouraged the trend toward naturalism, but it also pointed the way toward that more complex, cautious, and critical naturalism which recognizes salient differences, as well as a basic unity, in the immense region of organic phenomena. It emphasizes that as man grows more civilized, the natural process is in all its higher and determining phases superseded by an ethical. Darwin was no crude leveler down to origins. He may more readily be accused of making animals too human, than of making men too animal. With regard to method, he is of course extremely modern in emphasizing behavior rather than introspection,

The first part of the *Descent* concludes with a chapter on race, for which Darwin promises to account by sexual selection. He is thus led to his Olympian tour de force on sex, in which he explains everything in order to explain something. In short, he analyzes another kind of biological warfare, in which, for the possession of a mate, the males of a species not only fight each other physically, but compete in erotic dances, in artistic displays of plumage and other ornamentation, or in musical concerts with instruments, voice, or penetrating odors, sometimes accumulating aesthetic extravagance upon extravagance until the principle of utility seems actually to give way to that of beauty. Moreover, behind the outward display of instinctive art is the inward intensity of erotic passion. Certainly, the *Descent* adds new and violent colors to Darwin's picture of nature.

Returning at last to man in the final chapters, Darwin explains race differentiation by divergent masculine conceptions of female beauty. Negroes are black and flat-nosed because the remote male ancestors of Negroes preferred women with dark skins and flattened noses. The strongest and most virile males mated with such women, and by rearing more children than their weaker rivals, brought their tribe, and ultimately their race, to a closer approximation of their ideal. Darwin also maintains that sexual selection made women more tender, affectionate, and unselfish, and men more courageous, energetic, and intelligent—thereby proving once more that biology was a soundly Victorian science. The three primary masculine qualities are, in Darwin's opinion, closely bound together. In their highest manifestations, they constitute genius, which is essentially "patience," or "unflinching, undaunted perseverance."

CRITICAL REVIEWS OF THE BOOK

Darwin awaited publication in his usual state of superficial collapse and exhaustion resting on a broad basis of latent eagerness and curiosity. He protested he hardly knew whether the book had been worth writing. Nevertheless, he wanted Murray to send him all out-of-the-way reviews and notices. The public response was a very pleasant surprise. One indignant Welshman, it is true, did in a personal letter abuse him "as an old Ape with a hairy face and a thick skull." But, on the whole, having steeled himself for fresh waves of virtuous horror and pious vituperation, he was astonished to find that everybody was interested without being in the least shocked.

> A happy change [pronounced Thomas Huxley in his most authoritative tone as Darwin's vicar in the world outside Down] has come over Mr. Darwin's critics. The mixture of ignorance and insolence which, at first, characterised a large proportion of the attacks with which he was assailed, is no longer the sad distinction of anti-Darwinian Criticism.

The new politeness, though certainly a tribute to the *Origin*, was perhaps scarcely so to the *Descent* itself. Its fame might last longer, if at its first appearance clerical tempers had been shorter. [Religious commentator] Sir Alexander Grant, writing thoughtfully on the side of the angels in *The Contemporary Review*, grumbled a little that Darwin thought so well of monkeys and so ill of Tories and churchmen, but exhibited no symptoms of shock or intellectual dazzlement. Darwin had given us simply "the theory of Epicurus with the atheism removed." Grant's final pronouncement, uttered with just the suspicion of a yawn, was, "There is very little that is absolutely new."

Darwin feared the worst from scientists, especially from those who had one foot in religion. "I shall probably receive a few stabs from your polished stiletto of a pen," be wrote [American botanist] Asa Gray. He was partly right. Most scientists admired his science, but a few objected to his theology. Wallace was as usual full of praise but reiterated his view that something more than natural selection was necessary to produce man. The Roman Catholic St. George Mivart, whose *Genesis of Species* had appeared shortly after the *Descent*, agreed with Wallace, adding that new types in particular must be explained by teleological forces acting within the organism. Mivart also objected that Darwin made morality too little self-conscious and rational. On the other hand, he not only accepted evolution but, citing the medieval Jesuit Suárez, declared it in accord with the doctrines of the Catholic Church.

CHAPTER 4

Modern Reevaluations of and Objections to Darwin's Ideas

The Course of Evolutionary Theory Since Darwin

Robert Wesson

In the years since Darwin presented his case for evolution driven by inherited variations and natural selection, hundreds of scientists have refined his ideas and/or offered variations on his theory. In this essay, Robert Wesson, a research fellow at the Hoover Institute in Stanford, California, summarizes over a century of post-Darwinian research and hypotheses about evolution. He makes the point that, despite differing opinions about its exact workings, all evolutionary biologists accept Darwin's theory of natural selection as the underlying basis of their work.

A generation before Darwin, Jean-Baptiste Lamarck, who coined the word *biology*, related fossils to living organisms and proposed a consistent theory of evolution to explain their differences. Charles's grandfather Erasmus and others had put forward the idea that species grew out of one another. Several writers in the first part of the nineteenth century also proposed something like natural selection of those more capable of self-propagation. But Darwin crystallized these ideas in the intellectual atmosphere and mustered a mass of evidence in their support. No one else treated the matter with comparable learning and persuasiveness and Darwin's passion for detail appealed to experimental scientists.

Darwin's claim to greatness rests not on his advocacy of the idea of common origins of species but on his simple and logical explanation by inheritable variation and natural selection. This idea was by no means as clear, however, as the thesis of evolution ("We are descended from apes"), and it raised many questions. It was not thoroughly accepted until much later when it was fortified with Mendelian genetics [the theories of Austrian botanist Gregor Mendel] and, in [the twentieth] century, formed the neo-Darwinist synthesis regnant today.

Without Darwin, the doctrine of evolution would probably have been named Wallaceism, after Alfred Russell Wallace. Wallace came to conclusions very close to Darwin's about the same time but received much less credit, partly because he did not support his ideas with such a mass of observations. . . .

Darwin—who was better situated, presented more evidence, and was more consistent in his scientific attitude—became the symbol of evolution personified. Acceptance or denial of the theory of evolution came to be and has remained nearly equivalent to loyalty or opposition to Darwin. Nonetheless, his theory of change by natural selection was based more on plausibility and analogy than solid evidence. It was fairly clear that variations like those observed in domestic animals brought about some changes in nature; Darwin extrapolated to assert that all differences between living creatures were thus caused, ultimately back to the separation of humans, fish, protozoa, and plants. In order to exclude anything savoring of divine intervention, Darwin also assumed that change had to be gradual and random.

DARWINISM AND GENETICS

A serious weakness of the theory was ignorance regarding how variations are transmitted. Darwin theorized that particles from all parts of the body gather in the reproductive organs to determine the inheritance of the offspring (pangenesis), but he had no evidence. The theory also had the defect that it led back to Lamarck's earlier idea, which Darwin wanted to supersede, that evolution progresses by the inheritance of acquired traits. In the conventional example, the giraffe came about because a gazellelike animal stretched to reach higher foliage, its offspring were born with longer necks, and, after many generations, voilà: a giraffe.

Without knowledge of genetics, it was difficult to understand how random variations could change a species. Any rare improvement would be diluted by half through mating with an animal without the improvement, and it would be lost in the general population, critics argued, in a few generations. . . .

There seemed to be no answer until the work of Gregor

Mendel. Darwin, however, ignored this work when he published his findings in 1866. . . . But in 1900 three investigators rediscovered Mendel's theory that traits are inherited in simple unitary fashion; hence they are not diluted by mating and reproduction but can reappear in subsequent generations. This meant that the features making up the plant or animal are mechanically transmitted and are more or less independent of the rest of the organism. It became difficult to conceive of acquired characteristics being somehow rather mysteriously incorporated into the genetic makeup, or genotype, of the individual and species. . . .

Mendelian genetics initially seemed to contradict Darwin's gradualist variation. But in the first decades of [the twentieth] century, biologists melded Mendelism with Darwinism to make what came to be regarded as a definitive synthesis of evolutionary theory. In a research binge, geneticists working with cages of fruit flies discovered [enough complex evidence] to construct what seemed to be a solid theory of evolution. The synthesis completed in the 1940s became an imposing theoretical edifice.

This success, however, was more imposing than solid. Genetics proved to be unexpectedly and confusingly complicated. Mendel's experiments had worked out well partly because he had extraordinarily good luck: the several genes that lie traced through generations of peas happened to occur on different chromosomes and manifested themselves in simpler fashion than usually occurs. Genes were found to combine variously, to have multiple effects, and to change, or mutate, in ways difficult to explain. Moreover, the mountain of data produced little understanding of evolution. Fruit flies had mutations of eye color or even sprouted a leg from the head, but nothing was learned about how new organs originated and little about how different species . . . may have arisen.

Accident and Chance

Consequently, many biologists looked for forces or directions in evolution beyond those postulated by the basic Darwinist theory. Some resorted to vitalism—the theory that living beings are alive by virtue of a special life force—or to some variant of Lamarckism, or to a teleology—the belief in a built-in purposiveness of evolution.

The variation-selection theory was refortified, however, by

another big advance of genetics. The discovery in the 1950s that nucleic acid (DNA and RNA) is the carrier of heredity, demonstrating the physical materiality of the genes, restored confidence in the materialistic explanation of evolution. Because nucleic acid both replicated itself and transmitted information to proteins, molecular biologists concluded that information flows only from the nucleic acid to the body, never in the reverse direction. This implied that changes in the genetic apparatus, or genome, could come about only by errors of replication. Variation had to be accidental; there could be feedback only through the relative success or failure of variants in propagating themselves. This beautifully mechanical-materialistic idea was hardly to be questioned. As a biochemist put it, "Advances in understanding of the details of genetics [through discovery of DNA] confirmed Darwin's theory and documented the processes to the same extent that Newton laws of physics had been validated."

The successes of the new molecular biology in analyzing and manipulating enzymes and nucleic acids made it easy to believe that unraveling the material substance of heredity would reveal the secrets of evolution. Again, however, answers remained elusive. Relations between genes and organism turned out be excessively complicated, and the voluminous information coming out of the laboratories was of little help in interpreting the fossil record or understanding structures and behaviors. But the treatment of heredity in concrete molecular terms set the tone of the discussion for most practicing biologists. . . .

An unconditional thesis of neo-Darwinism is that "Chance the only source of true novelty." This means that innovations spring from errors in the reproductive process. A large majority of the mistakes are insignificant or harmful, dislocations in a well-organized and tested apparatus, but these are weeded out by the stern culling of the environment. A few errors are improvements, enabling the organism to cope better and reproduce itself more abundantly, especially when environmental changes raise new demands. As variations accumulate, the interbreeding population changes indefinitely, eventually altering the species or making a new species. Darwin assumed that variation could tend in any direction without definite limits, and the modern theory tends to favor this assumption, which leaves the organism subject to the roulette wheel of variation and the pressures of its world. . . .

The important point is that there can be nothing purposive or teleological in evolution; any notion of inherent purpose would make nature less amenable to objective analysis. For a biologist to call another a teleologist is an insult. Even the idea of direction in evolution caused by internal factors, or orthogenesis, is disliked. The sole force for change must be adaptation.

Many biologists go on to refuse to recognize any overall direction in evolution. They even dislike the notion that some creatures are in any important way "higher" than others. In spite of the fact that natural selection implies improvement and that a mammal is much further from its presumed one-celled ancestor than is an amoeba, they sense a contradiction between the idea of "higher" forms and mechanistic means of change. . . .

OF GENES AND MOTHS

Conventional theorists also prefer to think as much as possible in terms of the material particles of heredity, the genes. For Darwin, the unit of selection was the individual, which might be enabled by its qualities (plus good luck) to give rise to more than its share of the new generation. The discoveries of genetics led to a shift of emphasis, however, from the organism to its reproductive material. In the view of population genetics, as developed by Sewall Wright, Ronald Fisher, and others, a species is characterized simply by the frequency of various genes and their alternatives at any given site. . . . Evolutionary change thus was reduced to a matter of gene statistics. . . . The product is a set of impressive and sometimes useful equations governing the probable alteration of a population (that is, evolutionary change), equations that are sometimes taken as the biological equivalent of Newton's laws.

Population genetics is less firm, however, than classical mechanics. Its chief variable, gene frequency, is seldom measurable in practice; its principal independent variable, fitness, can only be guessed because it is impossible to determine to what degree survival is a matter of special genes or accident or special circumstances. More broadly, an organism cannot be treated simply as the product of a number of proteins, each produced by the corresponding gene. Genes have multiple effects, and most traits depend on multiple genes. The selection of individual genes is most important in very simple organisms. That is, population genetics is best applicable to bacteria and it does not tell much about the evolution of organs and higher animals. . . .

The stark affirmation of the "selfish gene" appeals for it counterintuitive boldness. But to say that the genes are in some indefinable way primary is more of an ideological than a scientific statement. Genes are not independent entities but dependent parts of an entirety that gives them effect. All parts of the cell interact, and the combinations of genes are at least as important as their individual effects in the making of the organism. Selection operates not on genes but on organisms or perhaps groups (and possibly species). . . .

The selection-variation theory is a useful approximation. It doubtless accounts for, or helps to account for, very much. Natural selection serves to eliminate those less qualified in the competition; that is, it stabilizes forms. Darwin, however, thought of selection not so much as elimination of the unfit as the opportunity of the fitter, that is, adaptive change.

The best studied and most frequently cited example is the alteration of the British peppered moth (*Biston betularia*). In this species, as in many other species of moths and other insects, a dark-colored variety has taken over in areas where industrial smoke has blackened much of the landscape, replacing a mottled gray form, that was camouflaged on lichen-covered surfaces. This adaptation is selected for by natural agents; birds have difficulty spotting dark-colored moths on a dark background. A clean air act was followed by a return of lighter-colored. But things are not simple. The dark (carbonaria) gene was not fully dominant at first but became so. Melanic moths have invaded rural areas with lichen-covered tree trunks; it seems that they may have become more viable for reasons other than camouflage. The victory of the darker variety is interesting, but it does not prove that such a selective process can account for the ability of chameleons to camouflage themselves by reflex in a few minutes.

GENETIC DRIFT AND STASIS-PUNCTUATION

To meet problems abundantly arising many biologists, while adhering in principle to Darwinism, have suggested modifications to the basic theory, and evolutionary doctrine has become less coherent. In principle it is held correct, but when one tries to apply it—as in the question of human origins—controversy arises.

A mild challenge to the theory is the idea that populations change not only through adaptation but through mutations that are neutral or at least not seriously negative. Strict adaptationists claim that there "must be an evolutionary advantage to a trait if we only look hard enough." But for each positive change, there must be thousands or tens of thousands that are not clearly useful, and unuseful traits (except for those harmful enough to be eliminated by selection) can lead to changes of the population as variants are increased or eliminated by the workings of pure chance. Suppose one has a barrel filled with a mixture of black beans and white beans. After stirring it, one removes half and throws them away, and then doubles the other half and returns it to the barrel, like a new generation being born, and repeats the operation. The proportions of black and white will change in each "generation." After enough times, one will have all black or all white beans. How many "generations" it will take depends on luck and the number of beans.

Such change, called "genetic drift" by Sewall Wright, takes part of the honor of driving evolution away from the principle of adaptation. That drift is a reality is indicated by the universality of molecular change in proteins and its greater frequency where selection is less important. . . .

A sharper challenge to mainstream theory is the rejection of gradualism in favor of "stasis-punctuation," the idea that change does not simply flow along but is sharply punctuated. Darwin insisted (despite an occasional contrary remark) on gradualism, although his theory did not really require it. The continuity of nature was a major discovery of his age; the corollary of present-day continuity was that the past was to be understood in terms of forces at work in the present. Attributing change of species to an accumulation of small variations made everything seem most natural and understandable. This idea also filled Darwin's philosophical outlook: gradualism was the opposite of the special creationism that he combated.

The conviction that change must have been gradual harmonizes with the rejection of any idea of purpose in evolution. If organisms grope their way, so to speak, into new adaptations, they do it by little steps. Hence, biologists for the most part prefer the gradualism that Darwin preferred. But the fossil record fails to show continuous series linking different groups, and some biologists early in [the twentieth] century, led by Richard Goldschmidt, attempted to show that evolution must have proceeded by radical leaps—in Goldschmidt's phrase, "hopeful monsters." This idea was pretty much abandoned. It was argued that no such leaps have been observed, and when gross mutational changes do appear in the laboratory, such as a doubled thorax in a fruit fly or a leg coming out of the head, they consist of errors in the formation or placement of old parts, never the appearance of a new organ. . . .

Recently, however, some theorists, led by Stephen J. Gould and Niles Eldredge, have forcefully argued on a more sophisticated level that evolution is by no means a mere accumulation of tiny, continually occurring changes. They contend that there is a dichotomy [division] between stability of species and rapid change, or "stasis and punctuation." More conventional theorists dislike this non-Darwinian thesis because it seems to contradict the strictly mechanistic approach, at least in spirit. . . .

INDIVIDUAL VERSUS GROUP ADVANTAGE

Evolutionists also differ in their emphasis on single genes or combinations, on genes that make proteins or on genes that turn other genes on or off. If most traits are the effect of multiple genes, regulatory genes, or gene-enzyme systems, large changes become more conceivable as results of recombinations, and mutations to make new proteins are correspondingly less important. The process of inheritance is evidently much more complicated than appeared from Mendel's tracing simple, unitary traits in peas—smooth or wrinkled, yellow or green, dwarf or tall. This implies shifting emphasis from relatively well-understood structural genes (which produce no structures but proteins that may or may not go into structures) to the poorly understood regulatory genes, which turn batteries of genes on and off. No simple theory can cope with the enormous complexity revealed by modern genetics.

A different problem is the existence of many traits that are evidently advantageous for the group but not for the individual. One prairie dog stands guard while others feed, forgoing a meal and exposing itself to predators. A honeybee not only rushes out to defend the hive but sacrifices its life by leaving its barbed stinger in the flesh of the intruder, along with the poison sac and part of the bee's guts. To resolve this contradiction, evolutionists have postulated that selection operates not only on the basis of individual but of group advantage: a group possessing traits useful for its collective success would prosper and reproduce, eventually perhaps replacing groups lacking the socially useful trait.

On the other hand, individuals lacking the altruistic gene would presumably have greater individual reproductive success, and the social trait would be wiped out. To overcome this contradiction, William Hamilton in the 1960s and 1970s elaborated the idea of indirect fitness, a significant addition to the Darwinist canon. An animal has "direct fitness" in its ability to propagate is lineage; it also has "indirect fitness" insofar as it helps other individuals with which it is related by sharing genes. This idea has proved handy in evolutionary theory despite its logical weaknesses.

Evolutionary theory may be modified to meet such difficulties, and evolutionists differ widely in their views regarding the pace, focus, and mechanics of change. They firmly maintain, however, the central ideas: there is nothing purposive, and organisms adapt genetically only by success or failure in leaving descendants. In the words of Ernst Mayr, "The one thing about which modern authors are unanimous is that adaptation is not teleological."

TRUE UNLESS PROVED FALSE

Darwin answered the intellectual need of the day, and the age recognized itself in him. He has been elevated as perhaps the greatest of scientists, and his name stands for a theory that has grown far beyond his work. What is commonly called the neo-Darwinian synthesis, or simply the modern synthesis, has taken on somewhat ideological overtones, especially in the United States. It becomes a little like a revelation by a prophet, whose every word in his major works is recorded in concordances. . . .

In a common view, the accepted evolutionary doctrine, rough hewn as it may be, has to be regarded as true unless it is proved false, even though the evidence for it is admittedly incomplete. Mark Ridley, for example, again and again makes the case for natural selection simply on the grounds that we have no other plausible explanation. This perspective is understandable, perhaps persuasive. Theories in which many scientists have invested their careers are not set aside until they can be replaced by more satisfactory theories, usually brought forward by younger thinkers. Neo-Darwinism is an accepted "mode of cognition" as conceived by historians of science.

Science advances by testing, modifying, and so far as necessary replacing hypotheses, but standard evolutionary theory is not usually treated as a hypothesis to be investigated. A single counterexample refutes a mathematical theorem, but evolutionary theory is in practice not falsifiable. Many very simple facts, such as that all the million of species of insects and no species of noninsects have six legs might well be considered to disprove natural selection as generalization. But such broad problems are usually ignored and it is assumed that any puzzle must be solvable in its term if adequately studied. . . .

Despite the infrequency of any useful mutation, it can always be postulated that the appropriate mutations came along by accident and were selected, bringing about the adaptation in question. For example, it is hypothesized that natural selection has led the female sedge warbler to prefer full-throated male because they should make good foragers for the family. On the other hand, the female lyrebird supposedly has been selected to prefer the male who neglects his offspring and so avoids bringing the nest to the attention of predators. The female spotted hyena, in the opinion of some, has a set of external genitals like those of the male in order the better to greet her friends. Some weaverbirds are monogamous because food is scarce, others because food is abundant. Marmot families stay together longer at high altitudes because there is less vegetation; if the young ones dispersed sooner at high altitudes, it would probably be because where food is scarce they have to seek new pastures. . . .

In practice, however, biologists are usually rather realistic. They think of more evolved plants and animals as "advanced" or "higher," and they use those words. However scrupulously they avoid teleological language, they recognize certain directions in evolution. They are likely to speak of animals having purposes and acting to secure ends, if only because it is awkward to say that the animal has genes causing its limbic system to direct certain actions conducive to its reproductive success. Having devotedly spent thousands of hours observing lions or jays or damselflies doing nothing in particular, they faithfully report facts that do not accord with the standard theory.

It is comforting, however, to see nature as basically mechanical, and hence totally understandable. "To maximize fitness" is an offhand explanation for almost anything, usually persuasive until critically examined. . . .

The principle of variation-selection represents a mental economy and suggests a way to seek answers, a key to unraveling the infinite variety and complexity of living nature. It gives a clear-cut orientation whether or not its explanations are adequate.

No other science has such a comfortable foundation. The physicists had something like it in the Newtonian synthesis, but they lost it because they learned too much. Sociologists and other social scientists (except for devotees of certain schools) have never been able to cherish even an illusion of total intellectual mastery. But the neo-Darwinian synthesis gives biologists a satisfying basis on which to work, most suitable for those who simply want to get on with their interesting investigations. The variation-selection theory even offers an uncomplicated view of the human condition and promises a means of coming to grips with the bafflements of human nature. The doctrine being axiomatically true, there must be a basis in natural selection for all human as well as other animal behavior; we have only to search for it. Sociobiologists find satisfaction in the bold assertion of a firmly scientific attitude in a controversial area where no one else can offer satisfactory answers. . . .

There are strong reasons for reluctance to admit any modification of evolutionary theory that might lead away from its mechanistic essence. Humans have adhered much more blindly to many less rational beliefs.

Evidence for Evolution in the Fossil Record

Theodore H. Eaton Jr.

Scientists have found plentiful physical evidence for the process of evolution by examining fossils, the surviving remains or imprints of ancient animals and plants. For the most part, the fossil record is jerky; that is, it has gaps in the lines of descent of most particular kinds of animals and plants. However, a few modern species can be traced backwards in time, with only a few such gaps, providing scientists with an almost unbroken record of one species giving rise to a family tree of descendant species. One of the most clear-cut and stunning examples is that of the horse, summarized here by Theodore H. Eaton Jr., a former professor at the Museum of Natural History at the University of Kansas in an excerpt from his textbook on evolution.

Although much of the current interest in evolution among biologists is concerned with the processes by which the genetic characters of populations change, more and better work than ever before is being published on the long-range results of evolution, that is, on the phylogenetic relationships of ancestors and descendants in various groups of organisms. The nature of this work and its conclusions are often somewhat taken for granted by those who do it and tend to be disregarded by others who are not directly concerned. Therefore it seems advisable to discuss in this chapter some examples of the kind of information that is available and the way in which it can be used to obtain a broad picture of evolutionary relationships. . . .

SCARCELY ANY GAP IN THE RECORD

The horses of today and their relatives, the zebras and wild asses, belong to the genus *Equus,* which stands at the end of a long line of evolutionary history extending back about 50 million years to the beginning of the family Equidae in the early Eocene. This history is probably unique in its completeness, for it is possible to trace back the ancestry of modern horses to preceding genera and species, and these to their ancestors, and so on with scarcely any gap in the record. The evolution of the horse family is not in a single line, but, as with other histories, it shows many branches that diverge from one another. All have led to extinction except that represented by the modern genus *Equus.* . . .

The completeness of the record introduces an unusual factor in its interpretation, for in going from the recent horses to those of a slightly but not much earlier time, there is no need to search among mammals of various types for one that could be considered ancestral to a horse. Instead, the earlier horses themselves are clearly, unmistakably recognizable among all other mammals contemporary with them, simply because they do not differ greatly from horses of today. Likewise, in comparing fossils of a particular age to those of either a later or an earlier time not far removed, the same problem is solved in the same way by recognition of animals that are very little different from those already being considered. The same principle holds for the comparison of any particular parts of these animals, for example, the pattern of the molar teeth, the shape of the skull, or the arrangement of bones in the feet. Through a succession of ages in which horses are known, the result is a sequence of changing characteristics in which the stages differ only slightly from one another. In fact, through much of this history the changes are of scarcely more than a statistical nature, such as would be seen in overlapping populations.

Long before the fossil record had become known as completely as this, it seemed that the changes in characteristics of the horse family beginning in the Eocene represented a very regular progression in several features, especially the size of the animal; the proportions of the limbs, body, and head; the number of digits on the feet; the form and pattern of molar teeth; and the size and proportions of the brain. The closely coordinated regularity of these changes suggested that the horses were an excellent example of evolution in a straight line. There are two aspects to this concept of *orthogenesis.* One is that the changes seemed to proceed without deviation and might lead in the course of time to an extreme that was no longer able to survive because it had passed the limits of adaptation. The other is that this straight line of evolution could be explained by an innate controlling force in the genetic makeup of the animals that produces gradual change regardless of circumstances or adaptive advantage, even though it lead to extinction. But fuller understanding of evolutionary processes and the more complete elucidation of the fossil record of horses have shown that neither of these aspects of orthogenesis is true or is necessary from the evidence, and the whole orthogenetic principle is a fallacy based on insufficient knowledge.

THE MOST ANCIENT HORSES KNOWN

The oldest genus of horses, once widely known as *Eohippus*, but by priority of name correctly *Hyracotherium*, appeared in the early Eocene of both Europe and North America at a time when the two continents were connected by land across what is now Bering Strait. Several species of these small animals are known, varying in height from less than 1 foot to about 20 inches. The front feet had four toes, each tipped with a small pad-like hoof, the thumb being absent and the longest toe the second (which would be third if the thumb were present). The hind foot had three toes with hoofs, the first and fifth being reduced to tiny vestiges. The body, instead of straight, was somewhat arched and the actual tail (in contrast to the hairs that it may have carried) was relatively longer and heavier than in any later horses. On the head, in contrast to modern horses, the muzzle in front of the eyes was no longer than the cranium behind the eyes. The brain was small and without convolutions but quite similar in general appearance to that of the modern opossum. The teeth of *Hyracotherium* numbered 44, as in the early insectivores and primitive members of several other orders of mammals. The four premolars were recognizably different from and simpler in pattern than the three molars behind them. The animal evidently fed on soft leafy vegetation and it differed very little from some members of the extinct order Condylarthra from which several orders of herbivorous mammals evolved.

There is a small but definite gap in our knowledge between the earliest horses and the earlier Condylarthra of the Paleocene, immediately preceding the Eocene. During the middle and late Eocene the connection between Asia and

North America was again submerged, with the result that horses of the Old World and New World went their own ways in evolution. Those of Europe died out finally at the end of the Eocene, but in North America the line was more successful. The genera *Orohippus* and *Epihippus* succeeded *Hyracotherium* in the middle and late Eocene, respectively,

---

GAPS IN THE FOSSIL RECORD

Noted scientist Richard Dawkins here describes the unevenness of the evidence in the fossil record for many species (the horse being a fortunate exception) and points out how the theory of stasis punctuation might partially explain the gaps.

From Darwin onwards evolutionists have realized that, if we arrange all our available fossils in chronological order, they do *not* form a smooth sequence of scarcely perceptible change. We can, to be sure, discern long-term trends of change—legs get progressively longer, skulls get progressively more bulbous, and so on—but the trends as seen in the fossil record are usually jerky, not smooth. Darwin, and most others following him, have assumed that this is mainly because the fossil record is imperfect. Darwin's view was that a complete fossil record, if only we had one, *would* show gentle rather than jerky change. But since fossilization is such a chancy business, and finding such fossils as there are is scarcely less chancy, it is as though we had a cine film with most of the frames missing. We can, to be sure, see movement of a kind when we project our film of fossils, but it is more jerky than Charlie Chaplin, for even the oldest and scratchiest Charlie Chaplin film hasn't completely lost ninetenths of its frames.

The American palaeontologists Niles Eldredge and Stephen Jay Gould, when they first proposed their theory of punctuated equilibria in 1972, made what has since been represented as a very different suggestion. They suggested that, actually, the fossil record may not be as imperfect as we thought. Maybe the 'gaps' are a true reflection of what really happened, rather than being the annoying but inevitable consequences of an imperfect fossil record. Maybe, they suggested, evolution really did in some sense go in sudden bursts, punctuating long periods of 'stasis', when no evolutionary change took place in a given lineage.

Richard Dawkins, *The Blind Watchmaker: Why the Evidence of Evolution Reveals a Universe Without Design.* New York: W.W. Norton, 1987, p. 229.

with some changes in the characteristics of premolar and molar teeth but little progress in size or other features.

DISTINCTLY LARGER BRAINS

Following *Epihippus* in the early and middle Oligocene there came a somewhat larger horse, *Mesohippus,* having longer legs, three toes on each foot, the bones of the toes and the hoofs being larger and stronger than in the Eocene horses, the body straighter, and the tail relatively shorter. The height was about 2 to 3 feet. The brain was distinctly larger and the cerebral hemispheres somewhat convoluted. The part of the skull anterior to the eyes was slightly longer than the cranium behind the eyes. All the cheek teeth except the first premolar now had essentially the same pattern of cusps and ridges but were still adapted to browsing on soft vegetation rather than harsh grass, which was not yet available.

With relatively little structural change but some increase in size, the characters of *Mesohippus* blended into those of the late Oligocene and early Miocene genus *Miohippus,* although this involved merely a small detail in the structure of the molar teeth and a slightly more rigid contact among the bones of the hind foot. There was then a divergence of evolutionary lines in different directions from *Miohippus.* At least two of these lines retained relatively simple, short-crowned, browsing-type teeth. One branch, *Archaeohippus,* was reduced in size to something like that of the earlier Oligocene horses and then became extinct. Another short-crowned group continued to increase in size through the Pliocene. It is probable that these animals continued to be forest dwellers, whereas the third line, starting with *Parahippus,* may have initiated the habit of grazing in open grassy fields, which apparently were beginning to appear in some parts of the world during the Miocene. *Parahippus,* although still three-toed, developed what are known as hypsodont molar and premolar teeth, capable of continuing growth at a rate compensating for the wearing down of their grinding surfaces and also resisting such wear by development of complicated ridges of enamel to do the grinding. The special significance of this is that grass is unusually abrasive, as it contains silica and, for that matter, dust and grit near the ground, and only animals that were adapted to chewing great quantities of grass could take full advantage of the opportunity provided by this successful family of plants.

MODERN HORSES EMERGE

Parahippus was followed in the middle and late Miocene by the highly successful grazing genus *Merychippus*. This animal resembled fairly closely the modern horses in its proportions but had not yet attained their size. In the forelegs, the radius and ulna became fused into a single bone instead of remaining separate as in more primitive horses. The middle toe of each foot was much larger than the two lateral toes and carried most or all of the weight. At least five branches of the three-toed horses appeared in the late Miocene and Pliocene but had disappeared by the middle Pleistocene.

Meanwhile, in the Pliocene the genus *Pliohippus* became one-toed by the complete loss of the two reduced side toes. From among the widely distributed species of *Pliohippus* there arose in the late Pliocene the genus *Equus* and a peculiar South American group of three genera, whose ancestral stock was able to reach that continent when the isthmus of Panama arose from the sea. Thus, for a while, single-toed horses lived on all the continents except Australia. The Pliocene invaders of South America were replaced there, perhaps competitively, by species of *Equus* during the Pleistocene. It was not until the very late Pleistocene that horses became entirely extinct in the western hemisphere, and they did not appear again until they were brought from Europe by the Spanish explorers. The wild species of *Equus* of historic times are in Africa, eastern Europe, and central Asia. Domestic horses of Europe and Asia probably originated from two or three sources somewhere in western Asia.

Darwinian Evolution Unsupported by the Fossil Record

Phillip E. Johnson

It must be emphasized that, although the vast majority of modern scientists and researchers consider Darwin's overall thesis to be a fact rather than a working hypothesis, there are still a few prominent dissenters. Most often, these dissenters suggest that too few fossils have been discovered to prove Darwin's ideas in any conclusive way, as does Phillip E. Johnson, a law professor at the University of California at Berkeley, in this excerpt from his book *Darwin on Trial*. There are simply too many major gaps and inconsistencies in the fossil record, Johnson asserts. In other words, too few transitional forms, especially between apes and humans, have been positively identified. According to Johnson, the major error made by modern biologists who accept Darwin's thesis is that they first assume that thesis is correct and then go looking for evidence to support it, instead of subjecting the thesis to rigorous testing.

Darwinists claim that amphibians and modern fish descended from all ancestral fish; that reptiles descended from an amphibian ancestor; and that birds and mammals descended separately from reptile ancestors. Finally, they say that humans and modern apes had a common simian ancestor, from which modern humans descended through transitional intermediates that have been positively identified. According to Gould, fossils in the reptile-to-mammal and ape-to-human transitions provide decisive confirmation of the "fact of evolution."

Before going to the evidence I have to impose an important condition which is sure to make Darwinists very uncomfortable. It is that the evidence must be evaluated independently of any assumption about the truth of the theory being tested.

Paleontology . . . has taken Darwinian descent as a deductive certainty and has sought to flesh it out in detail rather than to test it. Success for fossil experts who study evolution has meant success in identifying ancestors, which provides an incentive for establishing criteria that will permit ancestors to be identified. Gareth Nelson of the American Museum of Natural History has expressed in plain language what this has meant in practice:

> "We've got to have some ancestors. We'll pick those." Why? "Because we know they have to be there, and these are the best candidates." That's by and large the way it has worked. I am not exaggerating.

Obviously, "ancestors" cannot confirm the theory if they were labelled as such only because the theory told the researchers that ancestors had to be there.

Now let's look at the vertebrate sequence.

FISH TO AMPHIBIANS

The story to be tested is that a fish species developed the ability to climb out of the water and move on land, while evolving the peculiar reproductive system of amphibians and other amphibian features more or less concurrently. No specific fossil fish species has been identified as an amphibian ancestor, but there is an extinct order of fish known as the rhipidistians which Darwinists frequently describe as an "ancestral group." The rhipidistians have skeletal features resembling those of early amphibians, including bones that look like they could have evolved into legs. But according to Barbara J. Stahl's comprehensive textbook, *Vertebrate History*, "none of the known fishes is thought to be directly ancestral to the earliest land vertebrates. Most of them lived after the first amphibians appeared, and those that came before show no evidence of developing the stout limbs and ribs that characterized the primitive tetrapods."

In 1938, a coelacanth (pronounced see-la-kanth), an ancient fish thought to have been extinct for about seventy million years, was caught by fishermen in the Indian Ocean. Many paleontologists considered the coelacanth to be closely related to the rhipidistians, and thus a living specimen was expected to shed light on the soft body parts of the immediate ancestors of amphibians. When the modern coelacanth was dissected, however, its internal organs showed no signs of being preadapted for a land environment and gave no indication of how it might be possible for a fish to become an amphibian. The experience suggests that a rhipidistian fish might be equally disappointing to Darwinists if its soft body parts could be examined.

AMPHIBIANS TO REPTILES

No satisfactory candidates exist to document this transition. There are fossil amphibians called *Seymouria* that have some reptile-like skeletal characteristics, but they appear too late in the fossil record and recent evidence indicates that they were true amphibians. The transition is in any case one which would be hard to confirm with fossils, because the most important difference between amphibians and reptiles involves the unfossilized soft parts of their reproductive systems. Amphibians lay their eggs in water and the larvae undergo a complex metamorphosis before reaching the adult stage. Reptiles lay a hard shell-cased egg and the young are perfect replicas of adults on first emerging. No explanation exists for how an amphibian could have developed its reptilian mode of reproduction by Darwinian descent.

REPTILES TO MAMMALS

We come at last to the crown jewel of the fossil evidence for Darwinism, the famous mammal-like reptiles cited by Gould and many others as conclusive proof. The large order *Therapsida* contains many fossil species with skeletal features that appear to be intermediate between those of reptiles and mammals. At the boundary, fossil reptiles and mammals are difficult to tell apart. The usual criterion is that a fossil is considered reptile if its jaw contains several bones, of which one, the articular bone, connects to the quadrate bone of the skull. If the lower jaw consists of a single dentary bone, connecting to the squamosal bone of the skull, the fossil is classified as a mammal. . . .

Douglas Futuyma makes a confident statement about the therapsids that actually reveals how ambiguous the therapsid fossils really are. He writes that "The gradual transition from therapsid reptiles to mammals is so abundantly documented by scores of species in every stage of transition that it is impossible to tell which therapsid species were the actual ancestors of modern mammals." But large numbers of eligible candidates are a plus only to the extent that they can be placed in a single line of descent that could conceivably lead from a particular reptile species to a particular early mammal descendant. The presence of similarities in many different species that are outside of any possible ancestral line only draws attention to the fact that skeletal similarities do not necessarily imply ancestry. The notion that mammals-in-general evolved from reptiles-in-general through a broad clump of diverse therapsid lines is not Darwinism. Darwinian transformation requires a single line of ancestral descent.

It seems that the mammal-like qualities of the therapsids were distributed widely throughout the order, in many different subgroups which are mutually exclusive as candidates for mammal ancestors. An artificial line of descent can be constructed, but only by arbitrarily mixing specimens from different subgroups, and by arranging them out of their actual chronological sequence. If our hypothesis is that mammals evolved from therapsids only once . . . then most of the therapsids with mammal-like characteristics were not part of a macroevolutionary transition. If most were not then perhaps all were not. . . .

If one does not stop with the reptile-mammal transition but continues the attempt to provide a coherent account of macroevolution into the mammal class itself, it becomes immediately apparent that there is a great deal more to explain than the differences in jaw and ear bone structure between reptiles and mammals. The mammal class includes such diverse groups as whales, porpoises, seals, polar bears, bats, cattle, monkeys, cats, pigs, and opossums. If mammals are a monophyletic group, then the Darwinian model requires that every one of the groups have descended from a single unidentified small land mammal. Huge numbers of intermediate species in the direct line of transition would have had to exist, but the fossil record fails to record them.

REPTILES TO BIRDS

Archaeopteryx ("old wing"), a fossil bird which appears in rocks estimated to be 145 million years old, was discovered soon after the publication of *The Origin of Species*, and it thus helped enormously to establish the credibility of Darwinism and to discredit skeptics like Agassiz. *Archaeopteryx* has a number of skeletal features which suggest a close kinship to a small dinosaur called *Compsognathus*. It is on the whole bird-like, with wings, feathers, and wishbone, but it has claws on its wings and teeth in its mouth. No modern bird has teeth, although some ancient ones did, and there is a modern bird, the hoatzin, which has claws.

Archaeopteryx is an impressive mosaic. The question is whether it is proof of a reptile (dinosaur) to bird transition, or whether it is just one of those odd variants, like the contemporary duck-billed platypus, that have features resembling those of another class but are not transitional intermediates in the Darwinian sense. Until very recently, the trend among paleontologists was to regard *Archaeopteryx* as an evolutionary dead end rather than as the direct ancestor of modern birds. The next oldest bird fossils were specialized aquatic divers that did not look like they could be its direct descendants.

The picture has changed somewhat following discoveries of fossil birds, one in Spain and the other in China, in rocks dated at 125 million and 135 million years. The new specimens have reptilian skeletal features which qualify them as possible intermediates between *Archaeopteryx* and certain modern birds. The evidence, however, is too fragmentary to justify any definite conclusions. According to a 1990 review article by Peter Wellnhofer, a recognized authority, it is impossible to determine whether *Archaeopteryx* actually was the ancestor of modern birds. Wellnhofer concludes that "this correlation is not of major importance," because the *Archaeopteryx* specimens "provide clues as to how birds evolved," and because "They are documents without which the idea of evolution would not be as powerful."

In *Archaeopteryx* we therefore have a possible bird ancestor rather than a certain one. As in the cases of mammals, there is plenty of difficulty in imagining how any single ancestor could have produced descendants as varied as the penguin, the hummingbird, and the ostrich, through viable intermediate stages. The absence of fossil evidence for the transitions is more easily excused, however, because birds pursue a way of life that ensures that their bodies will rarely be fossilized.

Archaeopteryx is on the whole a point for the Darwinists, but how important is it? Persons who come to the fossil evidence as convinced Darwinists will see a stunning confirmation, but skeptics will see only a lonely exception to a consistent pattern of fossil disconfirmation. If we are testing Darwinism rather than merely looking for a confirming example or two, then a single good candidate for ancestor status is not enough to save a theory that posits a worldwide history of continual evolutionary transformation. . . .

FROM APES TO HUMANS

In . . . 1981 . . . Gould cited the "half-dozen human species discovered in ancient rocks" as proof that humans evolved from apes. When he published a revised version of the same argument in 1987, the number of species had been reduced to five, one of which was Homo sapiens itself, but the point was the same:

> Would God—for some inscrutable reason, or merely to test our faith—create five species, one after the other (*Australopithecus afarensis, A. africanus, Homo habilis, H. Erectus, and H. Sapiens*), to mimic a continuous trend of evolutionary change?

That way of putting the question makes it sound as if Darwin proposed his theory because the presence of an abundance of fossil intermediates between apes and humans required some explanatory hypothesis. Of course what actually happened is that the theory was accepted first, and the supporting evidence was discovered and interpreted in the course of a determined effort to find the "missing links" that the theory demanded. The question this sequence of events raises is not whether God has been planting fossil evidence to test our faith in Genesis, but whether the Darwinist imagination might have played an important role in construing the evidence which has been offered to support Darwin's theory.

Physical anthropology—the study of human origins—is a field that throughout its history has been more heavily influenced by subjective factors than almost any other branch of respectable science. From Darwin's time to the present the "descent of man" has been a cultural certainty begging for empirical confirmation, and worldwide fame has been the reward for anyone who could present plausible fossil evidence for missing links. The pressure to find confirmation was so great that it led to one spectacular fraud, Piltdown Man—which British Museum officials zealously protected from unfriendly inspection, allowing it to perform forty years of useful service in molding public opinion.

Museum reconstructions based on the scanty fossil evidence have had a powerful impact on the public imagination, and the fossils themselves have had a similar effect upon the anthropologists. The psychological atmosphere that surrounds the viewing of hominid fossils is uncannily reminiscent of the veneration of relics at a medieval shrine. That is just how Roger Lewin described the scene at the 1984 *Ancestors* exhibition at the American Museum of Nat-

DARWINIAN EVOLUTION A MYTH

In this short tract from his widely distributed book, Evolution: A Theory in Crisis, *Australian medical doctor Michael Denton supports Johnson's view that Darwinian evolution remains an unproven hypothesis.*

There can be no question that Darwin had nothing like sufficient evidence to establish his theory of evolution. Neither speciation nor even the most trivial type of evolution had ever actually been observed directly in nature. He provided no direct evidence that natural selection had ever caused any biological change in nature and the concept was in itself flawed because it was impossible to reconcile with the theory of heredity in vogue at that time. The idea of evolution on a grand scale was entirely speculative and Darwin was quite unable to demonstrate the "infinitude of connecting links", the existence of which he repeatedly admitted was crucial to his theory. . . .

The overriding supremacy of the myth has created a widespread illusion that the theory of evolution was all but proved one hundred years ago and that all subsequent biological research—paleontological, zoological and in the newer branches of genetics and molecular biology—has provided ever-increasing evidence for Darwinian ideas. Nothing could be further from the truth. The fact is that the evidence was so patchy one hundred years ago that even Darwin himself had increasing doubts as to the validity of his views, and the only aspect of his theory which has received any support over the past century is where it applies to microevolutionary phenomena. His general theory, that all life on earth had originated and evolved by a gradual successive accumulation of fortuitous mutations, is still, as it was in Darwin's time, a highly speculative hypothesis entirely without direct factual support and very far from that self-evident axiom some of its more aggressive advocates would have us believe.

Michael Denton, *Evolution: A Theory in Crisis.* Bethesda, MD: Adler and Adler, 1985, pp. 69, 77.

ural History, an unprecedented showing of original fossils relating to human evolution from all over the world. . . .

Lewin considers it understandable that anthropologists observing tile bones of their ancestors should be more emotionally involved with their subject than other kinds of scientists. "There *is* a difference. There *is* something inexpressibly moving about cradling in one's hands a cranium drawn from one's own ancestry." Lewin is absolutely correct, and I can't think of anything more likely to detract from the objectivity of one's judgment. Descriptions of fossils from people who yearn to cradle their ancestors in their hands ought to be scrutinized as carefully as a letter of recommendation from a job applicant's mother. In his book *Human Evolution,* Lewin reports numerous examples of the subjectivity that is characteristic of human origins research, leading him to conclude that the field is invisibly but constantly influenced by humanity's shifting self-image. In plain English, that means that we see what we expect to see unless we are extremely rigorous in checking our prejudice.

Anthropologists *do* criticize each other's work, of course— —their ferocious personal rivalries are partly responsible for the subjectivity of their judgments—but the question they debate is *whose* set of fossil candidates tells the story of human evolution most accurately, not *whether* fossil proof of the ape-human transition exists. For those who have chosen to devote their lives to exploring exactly how humans evolved from apes, persons who doubt the basic premise are by definition creationists, and hence not to be taken seriously. That there might be no reliable fossil evidence of human evolution is out of the question.

A prestigious outsider, however, has proposed the unthinkable. Solly Zuckerman, one of Britain's most influential scientists and a leading primate expert, is a good scientific materialist who regards the evolution of man from apes as self-evident, but who also regards much of the fossil evidence as poppycock. Zuckerman subjected the *Australopithecines* to years of intricate "biometric" testing, and concluded that "the anatomical basis for the claim that [they] walked and ran upright like man is so much more flimsy than the evidence which points to the conclusion that their gait was some variant of what one sees in subhuman Primates, that it remains unacceptable.". . .

Zuckerman's methodological premise was that the first

priority of human origins researchers should be to avoid embarrassments like the Piltdown Man fiasco, not to find fossils that they can plausibly proclaim as ancestors. His factual premise was that the variation among ape fossils is sufficiently great that a scientist whose imagination was fired by the desire to find ancestors could easily pick out some features in an ape fossil and decide that they were "prehuman." Granted these two premises, it followed that all candidates for "ancestor" status should be subjected to a rigorous objective analysis, and rejected if the analysis was either negative or inconclusive.

Zuckerman understood that it was probable that none of the ape-like hominid fossils would be able to pass this kind of test, and that as a consequence fossil evidence of human evolution might be limited to specimens like Neanderthal Man that are human or nearly human. The absence of direct evidence for an ape-man transition did not trouble him, because he assumed that the Darwinian model was established for humans as well as other species on logical grounds. Besides, evidence of ancestral relationships is in general absent from the fossil record. That being the case, it should be cause for suspicion rather than congratulation if there were a surfeit of ancestors in the one area in which human observers are most likely to give way to wishful thinking. . . .

For all these reasons I do not accept the alleged hominid species as independently observed data which can confirm the Darwinian model. I should add, however, that this degree of skepticism is not necessary to make the point that the hominid series cited by Gould is open to question. Some experts in good standing doubt, for example, that *A. Afarensis* and *A. Africanus* were really distinct species, and many deny that there ever was such a species as *Homo habilis.* The most exciting hypothesis in the field right now is the "mitochondrial Eve" theory . . . , which asserts that modern humans emerged from Africa less than 200,000 years ago. If that hypothesis is accepted, then all the *Homo erectus* fragments found outside of Africa are necessarily outside the ancestral chain, because they are older than 200,000 years.

Still, I am happy to assume . . . that small apes (the *Australopithecines)* once existed which walked upright, or more nearly upright than apes of today, and that there may also have been an intermediate species *(Homo erectus)* that walked upright and had a brain size intermediate between that of modern men and apes. On that assumption there are possible transitional steps between apes and humans, but nothing like the smooth line of development that was proclaimed by . . . neo-Darwinists. . . .

The hominids, like the mammal-like reptiles, provide at most some plausible candidates for identification as ancestors, if we assume in advance that ancestors must have existed. That 130 years of very determined efforts to confirm Darwinism have done no better than to find a few ambiguous supporting examples is significant negative evidence. It is also significant that so much of the claimed support comes from the human evolution story, where subjectivity in evaluation is most to be expected.

The fossils provide much more discouragement than support for Darwinism when they are examined objectively, but objective examination has rarely been the object of Darwinist paleontology. The Darwinist approach has consistently been to find some supporting fossil evidence, claim it as proof for "evolution," and then ignore all the difficulties. The practice is illustrated by the use that has been made of a newly-discovered fossil of a whale-like creature called *Basilosaurus.*

Basilosaurus was a massive serpent-like sea monster that lived during the early age of whales. It was originally thought to be a reptile (the name means "king lizard"), but was soon reclassified as a mammal and a cousin of modern whales. Paleontologists now report that a *Basilosaurus* skeleton recently discovered in Egypt has appendages which appear to be vestigial hind legs and feet. The function these could have served is obscure. They are too small even to have been much assistance in swimming, and could not conceivably have supported the huge body on land. The fossil's discoverers speculate that the appendages may have been used as an aid to copulation.

Accounts of the fossil in the scientific journals and in the newspapers present the find as proof that whales once walked on legs and therefore descended from land mammals. None of these accounts mentions the existence of any unresolved problems in the whale evolution scenario, but the problems are immense. . . . Even the vestigial legs present problems. By what Darwinian process did useful hind limbs whither away to vestigial proportions, and at what stage in the transformation from rodent to sea monster did this occur? Did rodent forelimbs transform themselves by gradual adaptive stages into whale flippers? We hear nothing of the difficulties because to Darwinists unsolvable problems are not important.

Darwin conceded that the fossil evidence was heavily against his theory, and this remains the case today.

The Creationist Explanation for Life's Origins

Institute for Creation Research

That some people still refuse to accept Darwin's theory of evolution and all the biological, geological, and historical implications that go with it, is well illustrated in the beliefs of modern creationists. In their view, the earth is only a few thousand years old, so that there has not been enough time for Darwinian evolution to take place; and at any rate, the miraculous acts of creation attributed to God in the Bible constitute a fully logical and satisfying explanation for how the universe and life came into existence. Among the many groups and religious sects that advocate creationist doctrines, the Institute for Creation Research (ICR), in Santee, California, is one of the most prominent and well organized. Following is ICR's official statement of the tenets of creationism. It is divided into two broad sections—"Scientific Creationism" and "Biblical Creationism"; however, ICR maintains "that the two are compatible and that all genuine facts of science support the Bible."

Tenets of Scientific Creationism

• The physical universe of space, time, matter, and energy has not always existed, but was supernaturally created by a transcendent personal Creator who alone has existed from eternity.

• The phenomenon of biological life did not develop by natural processes from inanimate systems but was specially and supernaturally created by the Creator.

• Each of the major kinds of plants and animals was cre-

From "ICR Tenets of Creationism" published by the Institute for Creation Research, Santee, California, at www.icr.org/abouticr/tenets.htm. Reprinted by permission.

ated functionally complete from the beginning and did not evolve from some other kind of organism. Changes in basic kinds since their first creation are limited to "horizontal" changes (variation) within the kinds, or "downward" changes (e.g., harmful mutations, extinctions).

• The first human beings did not evolve from an animal ancestry, but were specially created in fully human form from the start. Furthermore, the "spiritual" nature of man (self-image, moral consciousness, abstract reasoning, language, will, religious nature, etc.) is itself a supernaturally created entity distinct from mere biological life.

• The record of earth history, as preserved in the earth's crust, especially in the rocks and fossil deposits, is primarily a record of catastrophic intensities of natural processes, operating largely within uniform natural laws, rather than one of gradualism and relatively uniform process rates. There are many scientific evidences for a relatively recent creation of the earth and the universe, in addition to strong scientific evidence that most of the earth's fossiliferous [fossil-bearing] sedimentary rocks were formed in an even more recent global hydraulic cataclysm [catastrophe].

• Processes today operate primarily within fixed natural laws and relatively uniform process rates but, since these were themselves originally created and are daily maintained by their Creator, there is always the possibility of miraculous intervention in these laws or processes by their Creator. Evidences for such intervention should be scrutinized critically, however, because there must be clear and adequate reason for any such action on the part of the Creator.

• The universe and life have somehow been impaired since the completion of creation, so that imperfections in structure, disease, aging, extinctions, and other such phenomena are the result of "negative" changes in properties and processes occurring in an originally-perfect created order.

• Since the universe and its primary components were created perfect for their purposes in the beginning by a competent and volitional Creator, and since the Creator does remain active in this now-decaying creation, there do exist ultimate purposes and meanings in the universe. Teleological considerations [i.e., considerations of design and purpose in nature], therefore, are appropriate in scientific studies whenever they are consistent with the actual data of observation, and it is reasonable to assume that the creation presently awaits the consummation of the Creator's purpose.

• Although people are finite and scientific data concerning origins are always circumstantial and incomplete, the human mind (if open to the possibility of creation) is able to explore the manifestations of that Creator rationally and scientifically, and to reach an intelligent decision regarding one's place in the Creator's plan.

HOW DIFFERENT RACES CAME TO BE

In this excerpt from his book, Evolution: The Fossils Say No!, *noted creationist Duane T. Gish explains how, according to creationist doctrine, variations can occur within a single species.*

The concept of special creation does not exclude the origin of varieties and species from an original created kind. It is believed that each kind was created with sufficient genetic potential, or gene pool, to give rise to all of the varieties within that kind that have existed in the past and those that are yet in existence today.

Each kind was created with a great variety of genes. These genes can be sorted out during the sexual reproductive process in an enormous number of different ways. For instance, there are approximately 4 billion human beings in the world today, and except for identical twins and other cases of multiple births, no two individuals are exactly alike. None have the same gene combination. This sorting out process has not only given rise to many different individuals but also to distinctively different races. All remain, however, members of one species, *Homo sapiens.*

Another example familiar to all of us is that of the dog. All of the dogs, from the tiny Chihuahua to the Great Dane, and from the bulldog to the greyhound have been derived from a single species, *Canis familiaris.* The process has been exaggerated by man, of course, through artificial selection and inbreeding.

Many other examples could be cited. In each case the great variety of genes responsible for the variations that have taken place was present in the original created kind. There has merely occurred a sorting out in many different ways. No matter what combinations may occur, however, the human kind always remains human, and the dog kind never ceases to be dog kind. The transformations proposed by the theory of evolution never take place.

Duane T. Gish, *Evolution: The Fossils Say No!,* San Diego: Creation-Life Publishers, 1978, pp. 40–41.

TENETS OF BIBLICAL CREATIONISM

• The Creator of the universe is a triune God-Father, Son, and Holy Spirit. There is only one eternal and transcendent God, the source of all being and meaning, and He exists in three Persons, each of whom participated in the work of creation.

• The Bible, consisting of the thirty-nine canonical books of the Old Testament and the twenty-seven canonical books of the New Testament, is the divinely-inspired revelation of the Creator to man. Its unique, plenary, verbal inspiration guarantees that these writings, as originally and miraculously given, are infallible and completely authoritative on all matters with which they deal, free from error of any sort, scientific and historical as well as moral and theological.

• All things in the universe were created and made by God in the six literal days of the creation week described in Genesis 1:1–2:3, and confirmed in Exodus 20:8–11. The creation record is factual, historical, and perspicuous [clearly presented]; thus all theories of origins or development which involve evolution in any form are false. All things which now exist are sustained and ordered by God's providential care. However, a part of the spiritual creation, Satan and his angels, rebelled against God after the creation and are attempting to thwart His divine purposes in creation.

• The first human beings, Adam and Eve, were specially created by God, and all other men and women are their descendants. In Adam, mankind was instructed to exercise "dominion" over all other created organisms, and over the earth itself (an implicit commission for true science, technology, commerce, fine art, and education) but the temptation by Satan and the entrance of sin brought God's curse on that dominion and on mankind, culminating in death and separation from God as the natural and proper consequence.

• The Biblical record of primeval earth history in Genesis I–II is fully historical and perspicuous, including the creation and fall of man, the curse on the creation and its subjection to the bondage of decay, the promised Redeemer, the worldwide cataclysmic deluge in the days of Noah, the postdiluvian renewal of man's commission to subdue the earth (now augmented by the institution of human government) and the origin of nations and languages at the tower of Babel.

• The alienation of man from his Creator because of sin can only be remedied by the Creator Himself, who became man in the person of the Lord Jesus Christ, through miraculous conception and virgin birth. In Christ were indissolubly united perfect sinless humanity and full deity, so that His substitutionary death is the only necessary and sufficient price of man's redemption. That the redemption was completely efficacious is assured by His bodily resurrection from the dead and ascension into heaven; the resurrection of Christ is thus the focal point of history, assuring the consummation of God's purposes in creation.

• The final restoration of creation's perfection is yet future, but individuals can immediately be restored to fellowship with their Creator, on the basis of His redemptive work on their behalf, receiving forgiveness and eternal life solely through personal trust in the Lord Jesus Christ, accepting Him not only as estranged Creator but also as reconciling Redeemer and coming King. Those who reject Him, however, or who neglect to believe on Him, thereby continue in their state of rebellion and must ultimately be consigned to the everlasting fire prepared for the devil and his angels.

Why Darwin's View of Life's Origins Remains the Most Convincing

Chet Raymo

Darwin's theory of evolution is often attacked by creationists, those who advocate that life was created miraculously by God. For decades creationists have advocated teaching "creation science" alongside evolution in high school biology classes. Chet Raymo, professor of physics and astronomy at Stonehill College, argues in this essay that creationists have so far failed to offer a valid scientific hypothesis of their own that plausibly explains the observed biological and geological evidence. Raymo explores the basic intellectual approaches the opposing groups—Darwinians and creationists, which he calls skeptics and true believers respectively—take in examining nature. Citing Darwin's own views, as well as recent research both in the wild and in labs, he maintains that creationism has no credibility in the scientific community and therefore has no place in science classes. However, Raymo's argument is ultimately less a refutation of creationism's claims and agenda and more an explanation of, first, what a scientific theory actually is and, second, why most modern scientists presently see no logical alternative to Darwinism.

There are people who prefer that things remain the same; there are people who like change. We call them respectively reactionaries and progressives. Charles Darwin was a reluctant progressive. In early 1844, eight years after the voyage of the *Beagle,* he wrote to his friend Joseph Hooker, "I am convinced (quite contrary to the opinion I started with) that species are not (it is like confessing a murder) immutable."

Species change! Most species that existed in the past have

become extinct. New species will exist in the future, having descended from species that exist today. All present animals and plants (including ourselves) are but a momentary snapshot in an ever-changing flux of life. Here was one of the most progressive ideas in the history of human thought, and Darwin was reluctant to admit it. To think such a thing was akin to murder. He would delay publication of his great book for sixteen years, then publish only when his priority was threatened by Alfred Wallace.

Darwin was keenly aware of the political, social, and religious implications of his new idea. If species change, then so might established institutions: the church, the landed gentry, the ruling class. Religion, especially, appeared to have much to lose, grounded as it was in scriptural cosmology. If the Bible was wrong in the very first chapter of Genesis, then the veracity of the entire enterprise was called into question. Evolution was not just a scientific idea, it was a bombshell, taken up by progressives as justification for social reform, damned by reactionaries as subversive of the social order, welcomed by atheists, feared by theists. It pitted against each other the two great hankerings of humankind—for fixity and for change—and the corresponding postures of mind—True Believer and Skeptic. . . .

Two Great Worldviews

Darwin was not an ardent Skeptic, but neither was he a True Believer. Evolution was *forced* upon him by his meticulous examination of the evidence. Everything in his life—his social position, his religiously conservative wife, his personal temperament—inclined him toward established doctrine. . . .

Now, more than a century later, we are still locked in a battle between those who believe what makes them feel good and those who trust the evidence of their senses. The battle lines are drawn in about the same place as they were in the immediate aftermath of the publication of Darwin's *Origin of Species*. At issue are two great worldviews: In the one, humans are coeval with the world itself and reside at its center; in the other, the human species is a recent and contingent offshoot of evolution in a typical corner of a universe that is vast beyond our knowing. Americans are divided down the middle on this issue. Evolution of species by natural selection remains the great bugbear of religious fundamentalists, the issue upon which they have chosen to stake all. If the nonfixity of species is admitted, then their whole edifice of True Belief comes tumbling down.

Biologists vigorously debate the details of evolution and the sufficiency of natural selection as the agent of change, but no one within the scientific community doubts that life evolved over billions of years from simple beginnings, that all life is related by common descent, and that humans are part of the web of life. Most scientists would say that these statements are facts, not theories—or at least as close to being facts as our rational instruments of knowing can make them. . . . In fact, the issue is so cut-and-dried I feel a little embarrassed even talking about it. However, not to talk about it is to put science teaching in our public schools at risk. The teaching of evolutionary biology is under nationwide assault by fundamentalist Christians, led by the powerful Traditional Values Coalition, a group that represents thousands of conservative churches.

WARM AND FUZZY SCIENCE

Reverend Louis Sheldon, spokesperson for the coalition, was quoted in the press as saying: "When they teach kids that they came from monkeys, that's a dead dinosaurial kind of thing. It's a negative. It's not a warm, fuzzy kind of thing.". . .

In the late twentieth century, science is the source of our health, wealth, and physical well-being but provides little in the way of emotional comfort. As a culture, we divide our time between science and religion, going to the former when in need of physical sustenance (technology, medicine, creation of wealth), but spending most of our time clinging to the latter. When faced with a large and frightening universe filled with unfamiliar objects, we do not turn to science for reassurance, but to the "warm and fuzzy" truths of fundamentalist faith.

Can I take the metaphor further? Growing up has something to do with putting aside our teddy bears and security blankets. The spokesperson for the Traditional Values Coalition underestimates our children when he insists that schoolkids can't handle cold and clammy truths like descent from reptilian or amoebic ancestors. It would be comforting to think, as did our ancestors, that we live in a nurturing universe, centered upon ourselves, embraced by nearby, consoling stars. The truth, however, is rather different. Our Earth is a typical planet in an "infinite immensity of spaces," and it is a measure of our adulthood that we have the courage to accept this more difficult truth. It is comforting to imagine that our species had its origin in a secure nursery—a garden perhaps—presided over by a watchful parent, but again the truth turns out to be otherwise.

Evolution is not warm and fuzzy. It can even be capricious and sometimes cruel. It does, however, have much that recommends it to the adult mind; it is a *fact* by every criterion of science. Our schoolkids do not need intellectual security blankets. By insisting that science textbooks be warm and fuzzy, fundamentalists encourage the infantization of the next generation of Americans.

FACTS AND THEORIES

I grew up in the Bible Belt, not far from Dayton, Tennessee, the site of the Scopes monkey trial [a 1925 trial in which high school teacher John T. Scopes was tried and convicted for teaching Darwin's theory in his classes]. Early on I moved to New England so that my children could be raised in the thoughtful tradition of the Adamses, Emerson, Thoreau, Agassiz, and Gray. (I was influenced in this decision by two books in my mother's library when I was a child: Van Wyck Brooks's *The Flowering of New England* and *New England: Indian Summer.*) Now the Bible Belt has been loosened to encompass the expanding girth of fundamentalism. Even in New England, strident voices on school committees are agitating to have "creation science" taught in the classroom along with the "theory" of evolution.

There are some fundamental misapprehensions at work here. First, there is the so-called opposition of "fact" and "theory." Scientists speak of any group of related assertions about the world as a "theory." Some theories are firmly held, such as the atomic theory of matter or the cell theory of life, so firmly held that atoms and cells are spoken of as facts. Other theories are highly speculative, such as the theory that quasars are black holes forming at the centers of galaxies in the early universe; astronomers are cautious about calling galactic black holes "facts." There is much about the theory of evolution that scientists would call 99.9 percent fact, such as the idea that life developed on this planet over hundreds of millions of years from simple beginnings. There is much about the theory of evolution that remains speculative, including the pace of change and the sufficiency of natural selection as a driving force. These topics are hotly debated by evolutionary biologists.

The idea that life was created essentially as it is today some time within the last 10,000 years has zero standing as scientific fact. I know of no research anywhere in the peer-reviewed scientific literature that supports such a theory. Of course, creationists claim that science is ruled by dogma, that dissenting views are not given a fair hearing. Nothing could be further from the truth. If there were any solid, reproducible evidence supporting a young Earth, scientists would be falling over each other to publish it. Being on top of a revolutionary and successful idea is the way scientific careers are made. Every scientist I know is as happy to have something proved wrong as proved right. Either outcome advances us toward truth.

WON OVER BY THE EVIDENCE

An instructive example of how science *actually* works is afforded by an article called "Phylogeny Reconstruction and the Tempo of Speciation in Cheilostome Bryozoa," published in 1994, by Jeremy Jackson and Alan Cheetham, both associated with the Smithsonian Institution.

First, a little background. Darwin believed that species arise by the gradual and *continuous* accumulation of tiny changes within isolated populations of animals or plants; for example, mainland invaders of the newly formed Galápagos Islands slowly diverge from their ancestral populations on the mainland until they are different enough so that they can no longer interbreed.

In 1972, evolutionary biologists Niles Eldredge and Stephen Gould introduced a new idea, called "punctuated equilibrium." They proposed that new species appear rapidly in the geological record, presumably at times of environmental change or stress, followed by long periods when species remain relatively unchanged; continuing with the same example, while the Galápagos invaders rapidly evolved to adapt to their new environments, their well-adapted stay-at-home mainland cousins remained relatively unchanged.

Alan Cheetham, coauthor of the 1994 article, had long been opposed to punctuated equilibrium, championing instead the classic Darwinian idea that populations evolve gradually and continuously through millions of years of natural selection, occasionally giving rise to new species. With his colleague Jackson, he set out to provide the most detailed reading yet of the fossil record of Bryozoa (coral-like animals well represented in the fossil record), confident that the Darwinian view would be sustained. He writes: "I came reluctantly to the conclusion that I wasn't finding evidence for gradualism." What he found instead were individual species of Bryozoa persisting virtually unchanged for millions of years, then in brief moments of geologic time giving rise to new species. Cheetham switched his allegiance to punctuated equilibrium. The lesson is clear: *What we want to believe is not necessarily true.* The only way to discern the truth is to observe nature. Like Darwin, Cheetham was won over by the evidence of nature.

AN ASTONISHING VARIETY OF EYES

Let's pursue these issues a bit further. The human eye is dear to creationists. It is so exquisitely suited for its purpose—to provide sharp visual images of the outside world to the brain—that no sequence of random variations acting over time would seem sufficient for its design. Michael Pitman, an influential creationist writer, says, "That such an instrument should undergo a succession of blind but lucky accidents which by necessity led to perfect sight is as credible as if all the letters of the *Origin of Species,* being placed in a box, shaken and poured out, should at last come together in the order in which they occur in that diverting work." This is typical of what creationists want to teach our children in public school science classes. It's an argument I often hear from respondents to my occasional *Globe* columns on evolution. Like other creationists, Pitman wonders how natural selection could have favored anything less than the perfect organ. "The eye must be perfect or near perfect," he writes. "Otherwise, it is useless."

My own eyes are far from perfect; without glasses I could not read Pitman's diverting book. Nevertheless, my imperfect eyes are not useless. Even the ability to vaguely perceive light and dark makes life easier. The one-celled marine organism *Euglena* has an eyespot containing a few specks of pigment by which it orients itself toward the light, which it uses to manufacture nutrients by photosynthesis. *Euglena*'s eyespot is hardly a perfect visual instrument by human standards, yet it is crucial to the organism's survival. The scallop has dozens of eyespots, each with its own lens and light-sensitive cells. These organs are crude, but they serve the scallop well as it scoots across the ocean floor. A scallop without eyespots would be at a considerable disadvantage in the struggle for life. The variety of eyes in nature is aston-ishing. Virtually every image-forming method devised by human technology has been anticipated by nature: lenses, mirrors, pinhole cameras, and fiber-optic bundles. Eyes of one sort or another have independently evolved at least forty times during the history of life.

PERSONAL INCREDULITY

Of course, creationists are most enamored with the eyes of the higher vertebrates, including ourselves. The human eye, with its lid, lashes, adjustable iris, adjustable lens, and 125 million light-sensitive receptors, is considered by creation-ists to be the crowning glory of the creation. A creationist writer, I.L. Cohen, says of the human eye: "The whole sys-tem came into being at precisely the same time. . . . It is not possible, under any stretch of the imagination, that all these parts of the optical mechanisms could haphazardly become functional through random mutations."

Not possible? Under any stretch of the imagination? This is the sort of thinking that biologist Richard Dawkins calls "The Argument from Personal Incredulity": *If it seems im-possible to me, then it must be impossible.* This hugely an-thropocentric fallacy assumes that nature conforms to the limitations of our imaginations. The Argument from Per-sonal Incredulity is a kind of idolatry: making the Creator in our own image. The only way to decide whether something is possible or impossible (I am not talking about logical con-tradictions) is to go to nature and observe. Or, as is increas-ingly the case in science today, to model natural processes on a computer.

A computer study by evolutionists Dan Nilsson and Su-sanne Pelger suggests that the evolution of the eye by natural selection may be less difficult than previously estimated even by biologists. They modeled evolution of the eye com-putationally. They started with something akin to an eyespot, a flat patch of light-sensitive cells sandwiched between a transparent protective layer and a layer of dark pigment, equivalent to the simple eyespot of *Euglena.* They allowed the eyespot to deform itself at random, with the requirement that any change be only 1 percent bigger or smaller than what went before. They also provided for random changes in refractive index of the transparent layer. (Refractive index is a measure of the speed of light in a medium compared to the speed in a vacuum, and affects the amount an oblique ray of light is bent upon entering the medium.) The image quality at each step was calculated using elementary optics. The two researchers made assumptions about heritability and intensity of natural selection based on research with living species in the field, choosing the most conservative numbers in each case. They then set the computer program running and observed the results.

Here is Richard Dawkins's description of what happened: "The results were swift and decisive. A trajectory of steadily improving acuity led unhesitatingly from the flat beginning through a shallow cup to a steady deepening cup. The transparent layer thickened to fill the cup and smoothly curved its outer surface. And then, almost like a conjuring trick, a portion of the transparent filling condensed into a local, spherical subregion of higher refractive index." In other words, an eye socket, a curved retina, and a lens appeared on the screen of the computer. Using the most conservative assumptions about how changes are propagated through offspring, the researchers found that the time taken to evolve a vertebrate eye from a flat patch of light-sensitive skin was 400,000 generations. That's half a million years or so for typical small animals, a mere blink of the eye in geological time.

Charles Darwin himself expressed occasional doubts that natural selection could have produced the vertebrate eye, even with millions of years to work with. However, as Dawkins suggests, personal incredulity is not a reliable guide to truth. What seemed unlikely to Darwin, and seems impossible to creationists, has been shown to be quite reasonable by high-speed computer modeling. Not only reasonable, but given the proven premises of random mutations and natural selection, virtually inevitable. Will successful computer simulations make any difference to creationist True Believers? Not likely. Although creationists claim they want to expose our schoolchildren to alternate "scientific" accounts of creation, there is nothing remotely scientific about the Argument from Personal Incredulity. All we learn from the argument is that the Creator is more resourceful than the creature can possibly imagine.

EVOLUTION HAPPENING ALL AROUND US

Charles Darwin was in the Galápagos Islands only for a matter of days. He did not observe the flora and fauna of the islands evolve. His theory of evolution by natural selection was based on logical deduction, not observation. In the mid-1800s, no one, not even Darwin, had ever seen a new species emerge in nature. Evolution, as Darwin imagined it, takes place on a time scale that is vast compared to human experience. For that reason, it has long been thought impossible to observe natural selection in action. Creationists make much of this fact to emphasize that evolution is "just a theory."

By the same argument, it is "just a theory" that there once lived a person named George Washington who was the first president of the United States. Evolution is a historical science, confirmed by historical evidence, primarily the fossil record. For a long time, even biologists were inclined to admit that evolution might *never* be an experimental science. Now it turns out that evolution is happening all around us, day by day—most dramatically and dangerously in the case of pathogenic bacteria evolving resistance to antibiotics. For example, the bacterial agent of malaria has evolved resistance to many of the drugs that formerly held that disease in check. This is compounded by the evolution of DDT resistance by the mosquito that carries the malaria pathogen during part of its life cycle. After a period during which malaria worldwide was on the decline, the disease is now making a roaring comeback as the world's biggest killer of children. Creationists who deny evolution not only contribute nothing to the resolution of the malaria problem but also undermine the scientific education that will help the next generation solve the problem.

Creationists who doubt the reality of evolution should read Jonathan Weiner's wonderful book *The Beak of the Finch: A Story of Evolution in Our Time.* The central protagonists are Peter and Rosemary Grant, of Princeton University, who for twenty years have observed generation after generation of finches on one of Darwin's Galápagos Islands—measuring, weighing, tracking, and analyzing the birds' struggle for existence. The Grants have come to know every one of thousands of birds individually. They have watched populations evolve—yes, physically evolve—in times of stress and in times of plenty. It is a brilliant story, beautifully told, which stunningly confirms in scope and particulars Charles Darwin's reluctantly progressive leap of faith. Weiner also catalogs ongoing evolution observed by scientists in other places: guppies in the Caribbean, soapberry bugs in the American South, stickleback fish in ponds of the Canadian West, and, of course, bacteria worldwide.

LIFE A FLAME?

Evolution has at last become an experimental science. It cannot be long before we will observe the holy grail of experimental evolutionary studies, the emergence of a new vertebrate species by natural selection under controlled conditions.

The Institute for Creation Research (ICR) in California is this country's most prolific font of religion-inspired anti-evolution propaganda. "These are scientists," one of my *Globe* correspondents insisted, "and they are finding evidence that evolution is wrong." Nonsense. ICR "scientists" are conspicuously deficient in primary research and publish nothing in peer-reviewed scientific journals. They have negligible standing within the scientific community. The real scientists are the ones like Peter and Rosemary Grant or Jeremy Jackson and Alan Cheetham who get out in the field or go into the lab and do the nitty-gritty work that is always involved in asking nature an answerable question. What the ICR crowd is best at is cataloging gaps or supposed inconsistencies in evolutionary science. (The "impossibility" of the eye evolving by natural selection is an example of a supposed inconsistency.) Any evolutionary biologist can list as many gaps in our knowledge as can creationists, and probably more. If there were no gaps, science would be at an end.

Scientists look at the overwhelming success of evolutionary science and assume that the gaps will be filled as our knowledge becomes more complete. Creationists point gleefully to the gaps: "See," they shout, "evolution is a shambles." They assume that because we don't know everything, we know nothing.

Science is a dynamic social activity, made up of millions of men and women of all religious faiths, races, nationalities, and political persuasions. It is preposterous to suggest, as do creationists, that this vast and diverse assemblage of scientists, many of them devoutly religious, is guided by blind commitment to Darwinian dogma. As noted earlier, the evolution of life over hundreds of millions of years has virtually 100 percent support of the organized scientific community, whereas biblical creationism has essentially zero support. To suggest that creationism should get equal billing in our public schools not only is unconstitutional (violating separation of Church and State) but is simply silly. One might as well give equal billing to those who believe the Earth is flat.

By supposing that evolutionary science and religion are in conflict, creationists impoverish religion. Science reveals a creation story worthy of a Creator who is more, much more, than a warm and fuzzy projection of ourselves. If we are to find him, we had best look to the creation rather than into the dusty mirror of Personal Incredulity. If we want knowledge of the creation, our best instructors are the researchers who spend years scrambling across Galápagos rocks tagging finches or in the laboratory patiently measuring and cataloging thousands of fossils, rather than to those nit-picking creationists doing secondhand "science" in California.

Life is a flame that dances on the face of creation, never still, infinitely creative, with a prodigiously creative past and, it seems to me, bright potential for the future. I guess that makes me progressive in temperament. Others of a more reactionary bent will continue to plump for fixity of species, regardless of the progress of empirical research, clinging to their terry-cloth mother of archaic cosmology for all it's worth. Attitudes toward evolution can be as much a matter of temperament as of evidence.

DISCUSSION QUESTIONS AND RESEARCH PROJECTS

CHAPTER 1

1. Explain some of the ways that Pierre Maupertuis's ideas about evolution foreshadowed those of Darwin.

2. What was the central principle of the concept of spontaneous generation?

3. What objections did naturalists and other scientists raise to Robert Chambers's 1844 volume, *Vestiges of the Natural History of Creation*?

CHAPTER 2

1. How did Thomas Malthus's essay about population inspire Darwin to conceive the principle of natural selection?

2. Explain Darwin's view of the struggle for existence, using examples given by Darwin himself in Chapter 3 of his *Origin of Species*.

3. Why was Darwin worried when he learned that Alfred Russel Wallace had also conceived a theory of natural selection?

CHAPTER 3

1. Summarize how biologist T.H. Huxley came to accept the doctrine of evolution.

2. What were the main objections raised by Adam Sedgwick, Darwin's old teacher, to Darwin's book and theory?

3. How, according to botanist Joseph Hooker, do the results of the artificial breeding of plants and animals support Darwin's theory?

CHAPTER 4

1. What is punctuated equilibrium (or stasis punctuation)? And how does it differ from the "gradualist" concept of evolution proposed by Darwin?

2. Compare and contrast the arguments of Theodore Eaton and Phillip Johnson about the evidence for evolution in the fossil record. Which argument do you find more convincing, and why?

3. Summarize the creationist view of life's origins. Why is there no room for Darwinian concepts in this view?

4. List at least three reasons given by scientist Chet Raymo that the tenets of creationism are inadequate to explain the development of life on earth.

APPENDIX

EXCERPTS FROM ORIGINAL DOCUMENTS PERTAINING TO CHARLES DARWIN

DOCUMENT 1: OBSERVATIONS FROM THE VOYAGE OF THE *BEAGLE*

The main source Darwin used in writing his Journal *of the voyage of the* Beagle *was a diary he kept on the trip. He did not seem to have much interest in evolution at this time; however, in the following passages he deals with topics he was to confront later in his evolutionary researches, including extinction and the Malthusian relationship between population and food supply.*

January 4, 1835, Cape Tres Montes, Chile: "The entire absence of all Indians amongst these islands is a complete puzzle. That they formerly lived here is certain, & some even within a hundred years; I do not think they could migrate anywhere, & indeed, what could their temptation be? For we here see the great abundance of the Indians' highest luxury;—seal's flesh. I should suppose the tribe has become extinct; one step to the final extermination of the Indian race in S. America."

January 12, 1836, New South Wales: "At Sunset by good fortune a party of a score of the Aboriginal Blacks passed by, each carrying, in their accustomed manner, a bundle of spears & other weapons. By giving a leading young man a shilling they were easily detained & they threw their spears for my amusement. They were all partly clothed & several could speak a little English; their countenances were good-humoured & pleasant & they appeared far from such utterly degraded beings as usually represented. In their own arts they are admirable; a cap being fixed at thirty yards distance, they transfixed it with the spear delivered by the throwing stick, with the rapidity of an arrow from the bow of a practised Archer; in tracking animals & men they show most wonderful sagacity & I heard many of their remarks, which manifested considerable acuteness. They will not, however, cultivate the ground, or even take the trouble of keeping flocks of sheep which have been offered them; or build houses & remain stationary. Never-the-less, they appear to me to stand some few degrees higher in civilization, or more correctly, a few lower in barbarism, than the Fuegians.

"It is very curious thus to see in the midst of a civilized people, a set of harmless savages wandering about without knowing where they will sleep, & gaining their livelihood by hunting in the woods. Their numbers have rapidly decreased; during my whole ride with the exception of some boys brought up in the houses, I saw only one other party. These were rather more numerous & not so well clothed. I should have mentioned that in addition to their state of independence of the Whites, the different tribes go to war. In an engagement which took place lately the parties, very singularly, chose the centre of the village of Bathhurst as the place of engagement; the conquered party took refuge in the Barracks. The decrease in numbers must be owing to the drinking of Spirits, the European diseases, even the milder ones of which such as the Measles, are very destructive, & the gradual extinction of the wild animals. It is said, that from the wandering life of these people, great numbers of their children die in very early infancy. When the difficulty in procuring food is increased, of course the population must be repressed in a manner almost instantaneous as compared to what takes place in civilized life, where the father may add to his labor without destroying his offspring."

Quoted in Howard E. Gruber, *Darwin on Man*. New York: E.P. Dutton, 1974, pp. 434–35.

DOCUMENT 2: DARWIN ON LOST CONTINENTS

The term "continental drift" did not exist in Darwin's day, for the field of plate tectonics, which has shown how the continents drift slowly across the earth's surface, was still unknown. Some of Darwin's colleagues suggested that ancient continents, such as the legendary Atlantis, or at least large extensions of the present continents, had once existed in the Atlantic, Pacific, and other oceans. In this June 25, 1856, letter to his friend Charles Lyell, the greatest geologist of his time, Darwin argues that the evidence for such lost continents is weak and that it is more likely that the present continents have remained more or less fixed for a long time.

MY DEAR LYELL,—I will have the following tremendous letter copied to make the reading easier, and as I want to keep a copy.

As you say you would like to hear my reasons for being most unwilling to believe in the continental extensions of late authors, I gladly write them, as, without I am convinced of my error, I shall have to give them condensed in my essay, when I discuss single and multiple creation; I shall therefore be particularly glad to have your general opinion on them. I may *quite likely* have persuaded myself in my wrath that there is more in them than there is. If there was much more reason to admit a continental extension in any one or two instances (as in Madeira) than in other cases, I should feel no difficulty whatever. But if on account of European plants, and littoral sea shells, it is thought necessary to join Madeira to the mainland, [botanist Joseph] Hooker is quite right to join New Holland to New Zealand, and Auckland Island (and Raoul Island to N.E.), and these to S. America and the Falklands, and these to Tristan d'Acunha, and these to Kerguelen Land; thus making, either strictly at the same time, or at different periods, but all within the life of recent beings, an almost circumpolar belt of land. So again Galapagos and Juan Fernandez must be joined to America; and if we trust to littoral sea shells, the Galapagos must have been joined to the Pacific Islands (2400 miles distant) as well as to America, and as Woodward seems to think all the islands in the Pacific into a magnificent continent; also the islands in the Southern Indian Ocean into another continent, with Madagascar and Africa, and perhaps India. In the North Atlantic, Europe will stretch half-way across the ocean to the Azores, and further north right across. In short, we must suppose probably, half the present ocean was land within the period of living organisms. The Globe within this period must have had a quite different aspect. Now the only way to test this, that I can see, is to consider whether the continents have undergone within this same period such wonderful permutations. In all North and South and Central America, we have both recent and miocene (or eocene) shells, quite distinct on the opposite sides, and hence I cannot doubt that *fundamentally* America has held its place since at least, the miocene period. In Africa almost all the living shells are distinct on the opposite sides of the inter-tropical regions, short as the distance is compared to the range of marine mollusca, in uninterrupted seas; hence I infer that Africa has existed since our present species were created. Even the isthmus of Suez and the Aralo-Caspian basin have had a great antiquity. So I imagine, from the tertiary deposits, has India. In Australia the great fauna of extinct marsupials shows that before the present mammals appeared, Australia was a separate continent. I do not for one second doubt that very large portions of all these continents have undergone *great* changes of level within this period, but yet I conclude that fundamentally they stood as barriers in the sea, where they now stand; and therefore I should require the weightiest evidence to make me believe in such immense changes within the period of living organisms in our oceans, where, moreover, from the great depths, the changes must have been vaster in a vertical sense.

Secondly. Submerge our present continents, leaving a few mountain peaks as islands, and what will the character of the islands be,—Consider that the Pyrenees, Sierra Nevada, Apennines, Alps, Carpathians, are non-volcanic, Etna and Caucasus, volcanic. In Asia, Altai and Himalaya, I believe non-volcanic. In North Africa the non-volcanic, as I imagine, Alps of Abyssinia and of the Atlas. In South Africa, the Snow Mountains, In Australia, the non-volcanic Alps. In North America, the White Mountains, Alleghenies and Rocky Mountains—some of the latter alone, I believe, volcanic. In South America to the east, the non-volcanic [Silla?] of Caracas, and Itacolumi of Brazil, further south the Sierra Ventanas, and in the

Cordilleras, many volcanic but not all. Now compare these peaks with the oceanic islands; as far as known all are volcanic, except St. Paul's (a strange bedevilled rock), and the Seychelles, if this latter can be called oceanic, in the line of Madagascar; the Falklands, only 500 miles off, are only a shallow bank; New Caledonia, hardly oceanic, is another exception. This argument has to me great weight. Compare on a Geographical map, islands which, we have *several* reasons to suppose, were connected with mainland, as Sardinia, and how different it appears. Believing, as I am inclined, that continents as continents, and oceans as oceans, are of immense antiquity—I should say that if any of the existing oceanic islands have any relation of any kind to continents, they are forming continents; and that by the time they could form a continent, the volcanoes would be denuded to their cores, leaving peaks of syenite, diorite, or porphyry. But have we nowhere any last wreck of a continent, in the midst of the ocean? St. Paul's Rock, and such old battered volcanic islands, as St. Helena, may be; but I think we can see some reason why we should have less evidence of sinking than of rising continents (if my view in my Coral volume has any truth in it, viz.: that volcanic outbursts accompany rising areas), for during subsidence there will be no compensating agent at work, in rising areas there will be the *additional* element of outpoured volcanic matter.

Thirdly. Considering the depth of the ocean, I was, before I got your letter, inclined vehemently to dispute the vast amount of subsidence, but I must strike my colours. With respect to coral reefs, I carefully guarded against its being supposed that a continent was indicated by the groups of atolls. It is difficult to guess, as it seems to me, the amount of subsidence indicated by coral reefs; but in such large areas as the Lowe Archipelago, the Marshall Archipelago, and Laccadive group, it would, judging, from the heights of existing oceanic archipelagoes, be odd, if some peaks of from 8000 to 10,000 feet had not been buried. Even after your letter a suspicion crossed me whether it would be fair to argue from subsidences in the middle of the greatest oceans to continents; but refreshing my memory by talking with Ramsay in regard to the probable thickness in one vertical line of the Silurian and carboniferous formation, it seems there must have been *at least* 10,000 feet of subsidence during these formations in Europe and North America, and therefore during the continuance of nearly the same set of organic beings. But even 12,000 feet would not be enough for the Azores, or for Hooker's continent; I believe Hooker does not infer a continuous continent, but approximate groups of islands, with, if we may judge from existing continents, not *profoundly* deep sea between them; but the argument from the volcanic nature of nearly every existing oceanic island tell against such supposed groups of islands,—for I presume he does not suppose a mere chain of volcanic islands belting the Southern hemisphere.

Fourthly. The supposed continental extensions do not seem to me, perfectly to account for all the phenomena of distribution on islands; as the absence of mammals and Batrachians; the absence of certain great groups of insects on Madeira, and of Acaciae and Banksias, &c., in New Zealand; the paucity of plants in some cases, &c. Not that those who believe in various accidental means of dispersal, can explain most of these cases; but they may at least say that these facts seem hardly compatible with former continuous land.

Finally. For these several reasons, and especially considering it certain (in which you will agree) that we are extremely ignorant of means of dispersal, I cannot avoid thinking that Forbes' 'Atlantis,' was an ill-service to science, as checking a close study of means of dissemination. I shall be really grateful to hear, as briefly as you like, whether these arguments have any weight with you, putting yourself in the position of an honest judge. I told Hooker that I was going to write to you on this subject; and I should like him to read this; but whether he or you will think it worth time and postage remains to be proved.

Yours most truly,
CHARLES DARWIN.

Francis Darwin, ed., *The Life and Letters of Charles Darwin.* 2 vols. New York: Basic Books, 1959, vol. 1, pp. 432–36.

DOCUMENT 5: DARWIN REMINISCES ABOUT HIS MASTERWORK

In this excerpt from his autobiography, mostly compiled in 1876, Darwin recalls his writing of The Origin of Species *in the late 1850s, as well as its translation into other languages, its many reviews, and information about specific topics and passages.*

I set to work by the strong advice of [Charles] Lyell and [Joseph] Hooker to prepare a volume on the transmutation of species, but was often interrupted by ill-health, and short visits to Dr. Lane's delightful hydropathic establishment at Moor Park. I abstracted the MS. begun on a much larger scale in 1856, and completed the volume on the same reduced scale. It cost me thirteen months and ten days' hard labour. It was published under the title of the *Origin of Species,* in November 1859. Though considerably added to and corrected in the later editions, it has remained substantially the same book.

It is no doubt the chief work of my life. It was from the first highly successful. The first small edition of 1250 copies was sold on the day of publication, and a second edition of 3000 copies soon afterwards. Sixteen thousand copies have now (1876) been sold in England; and considering how stiff [scholarly] a book it is, this is a large sale. It has been translated into almost every European tongue, even into such languages as Spanish, Bohemian, Polish, and Russian. It has also, according to Miss Bird, been translated into Japanese, and is there much studied. Even an essay in Hebrew has appeared on it, showing that the theory is contained in the Old Testament! The reviews were very numerous; for some time I collected all that appeared on the *Origin* and on my related books, and these amount (excluding newspaper reviews) to 265; but after a time I gave up the attempt in despair. Many separate essays and books on the subject have appeared; and in Germany a catalogue or bibliography on "Darwinismus" has appeared every year or two.

The success of the *Origin* may, I think, be attributed in large part to my having long before written two condensed sketches, and to my having finally abstracted a much larger manuscript, which was itself an abstract. By this means I was enabled to select the more striking facts and conclusions. I had, also, during many years, followed a golden rule, namely, that whenever a published fact, a new observation or thought came across me, which was opposed to my general results, to make a memorandum of it without fail and at once: for I had found by experience that such facts and thoughts were far more apt to escape from the memory than favourable ones. Owing to this habit, very few objections were raised against my views which I had not at least noticed and attempted to answer.

It has sometimes been said that the success of the *Origin* proved "that the subject was in the air," or "that men's minds were prepared for it." I do not think that this is strictly true, for I occasionally sounded not a few naturalists, and never happened to come across a single one who seemed to doubt about the permanence of species. Even Lyell and Hooker, though they would listen with interest to me, never seemed to agree. I tried once or twice to explain to able men what I meant by Natural selection, but signally failed. What I believe was strictly true is that innumerable well-observed facts were stored in the minds of naturalists ready to take their proper places as soon as any theory which would receive them was sufficiently explained. Another element in the success of the book was its moderate size; and this I owe to the appearance of Mr. [Alfred Russel] Wallace's essay; had I published on the scale in which I began to write in 1856, the book would have been four or five times as large as the *Origin*, and very few would have had the patience to read it.

I gained much by my delay in publishing from about 1839, when the theory was clearly conceived, to 1859; and I lost nothing by it, for I cared very little whether men attributed most originality to me or Wallace; and his essay no doubt aided in the reception of the theory. I was forestalled in only one important point, which my vanity has always made me regret, namely, the explanation by means of the Glacial period of the presence of the same species of plants and of some few animals on distant mountain summits and in the arctic regions. This view pleased me so much that I wrote it out *in extenso*, [at full length]. . . .

Hardly any point gave me so much satisfaction when I was at work on the *Origin*, as the explanation of the wide difference in many classes between the embryo and the adult animal, and of the close resemblance of the embryos within the same class. No notice of this point was taken, as far as I remember, in the early reviews of the *Origin*, and I recollect expressing my surprise on this head in a letter to [American botanist] Asa Gray. Within late years several reviewers have given the whole credit to [German scientists] Fritz Müller and [Ernst] Häckel, who undoubtedly have worked it out much more fully, and in some respects more correctly than I did. I had materials for a whole chapter on the subject, and I ought to have made the discussion longer; for it is clear that I failed to impress my readers; and he who succeeds in doing so deserves, in my opinion, all the credit.

This leads me to remark that I have almost always been treated honestly by my reviewers, passing over those without scientific knowledge as not worthy of notice. My views have often been grossly misrepresented, bitterly opposed and ridiculed, but this has been generally done, as I believe, in good faith. On the whole I do not doubt that my works have been over and over again greatly overpraised. I rejoice that I have avoided controversies, and this I owe to Lyell, who many years ago, in reference to my geological works, strongly advised me never to get entangled in a controversy, as it rarely did any good and caused a miserable loss of time and temper.

Autobiography and Selected Letters. Ed. Francis Darwin. New York: Dover Publications, 1958, pp. 44–46.

DOCUMENT 4: DARWIN ARGUES FOR AN ANCIENT EARTH

In this tract from his landmark The Origin of Species, *Darwin attempts to explain some of the overwhelming geological evidence for a very ancient earth, the surface of which has been repeatedly overlaid by sedimentary strata (layers of sediment). Note how, to support his views, he frequently cites the work of other noted scientists, including his friend Charles Lyell.*

On the Lapse of Time, as Inferred from the Rate of Deposition and Extent of Denudation

Independently of our not finding fossil remains of such infinitely numerous connecting links, it may be objected that time cannot have sufficed for so great an amount of organic change, all changes having been effected slowly. It is hardly possible for me to recall to the reader who is not a practical geologist, the facts leading the mind feebly to comprehend the lapse of time. He who can read Sir Charles Lyell's grand work on the Principles of Geology, which the future historian will recognise as having produced a revolution in natural science, and yet does not admit how vast have been the past periods of time, may at once close this volume. Not that it suffices to study the Principles of Geology, or to read special treatises by different observers on separate formations, and to mark how each author attempts to give an inadequate idea of the duration of each formation, or even of each stratum. We can best gain some idea of past time by knowing the agencies at work, and learning how deeply the surface of the land has been denuded, and how much sediment has been deposited. As Lyell has well remarked, the extent and thickness of our sedimentary formations are the result and the measure of the denudation which the earth's crust has elsewhere undergone. Therefore a man should examine for himself the great piles of superimposed strata, and watch the rivulets bringing down mud, and the waves wearing away the sea-cliffs, in order to comprehend something about the duration of past time, the monuments of which we see all around us.

It is good to wander along the coast, when formed of moderately hard rocks, and mark the process of degradation. The tides in most cases reach the cliffs only for a short time twice a day, and the waves eat into them only when they are charged with sand or pebbles; for there is good evidence that pure water effects nothing in wearing away rock. At last the base of the cliff is undermined, huge fragments fall down, and these, remaining fixed, have to be worn away atom by atom, until after being reduced in size they can be rolled about by the waves, and then they are more quickly ground into pebbles, sand, or mud. But how often do we see along the bases of retreating cliffs rounded boulders, all thickly clothed by marine productions, showing how little they are abraded and how seldom they are rolled about! Moreover, if we follow for a few miles any line of rocky cliff, which is undergoing degradation, we find that it is only here and there, along a short length or round a promontory, that the cliffs are at the present time suffering. The appearance of the surface and the vegetation show that elsewhere years have elapsed since the waters washed their base.

We have, however, recently learnt from the observations of Ramsay, in the van of many excellent observers—of Jukes, Geikie, Croll, and others, that subaerial degradation is a much more important agency than coast-action, or the power of the waves. The whole surface of the land is exposed to the chemical action of the air and of the rain-water with its dissolved carbonic acid, and in colder countries to frost; the disintegrated matter is carried down even gentle slopes during heavy rain, and to a greater extent than might be supposed, especially in arid districts, by the wind; it is then transported by the streams and rivers, which when rapid deepen their channels, and triturate the fragments. On a rainy day, even in a gently undulating country, we see the effects of subaerial degradation in the muddy rills which flow down every slope. Messrs. Ramsay and Whitaker have shown, and the observation is a most striking one, that the great lines of escarpment in the Wealden district and those ranging across England, which formerly were looked at as ancient sea-coasts, cannot have been thus formed, for each line is composed of one and the same formation, whilst our sea-cliffs are everywhere formed by the intersection of various formations. This being the case, we are compelled to admit that the escarpments owe their origin in chief part to the rocks of which they are composed having resisted subaerial denudation better than the surrounding surface; this surface consequently has been gradually lowered, with the lines of harder rock left projecting. Nothing impresses the mind with the vast duration of time, according to our ideas of time, more forcibly than the conviction thus gained that subaerial agencies which apparently have so little power, and which seem to work so slowly, have produced great results.

When thus impressed with the slow rate at which the land is worn away through subaerial and littoral action, it is good, in order to appreciate the past duration of time, to consider, on the one hand, the masses of rock which have been removed over many extensive areas, and on the other hand the thickness of our sedimentary formations. I remember having been much struck when viewing volcanic islands, which have been worn by the waves and pared all round into perpendicular cliffs of one or two thousand feet in height; for the gentle slope of the lava-streams, due to their formerly liquid state, showed at a glance how far the hard, rocky beds had once extended into the open ocean. The same story is told still more plainly by faults,—those great cracks along which the strata have been upheaved on one side, or thrown down on the other, to the height or depth of thousands of feet; for since the crust cracked, and it makes no great difference whether the upheaval was sudden, or, as most geologists now believe, was slow and effected by many starts, the surface of the land has been so completely planed down that no trace of these vast dislocations is externally visible. The Craven fault, for instance, extends for upwards of 30 miles, and along this line the vertical displacement of the strata varies from 600 to 3000 feet. Professor Ramsay has published an account of a downthrow in Anglesea of 2300 feet; and he informs me that he fully believes that there is one in Merionethshire of 12,000 feet; yet in these cases there is nothing on the surface of the land to show such prodigious movements; the pile of rocks on either side of the crack having been smoothly swept away.

On the other hand, in all parts of the world the piles of sedimentary strata are of wonderful thickness. In the Cordillera I estimated one mass of conglomerate at ten thousand feet; and although conglomerates have probably been accumulated at a quicker rate than finer sediments, yet from being formed of worn and rounded pebbles, each of which bears the stamp of time, they are good to show how slowly the mass must have been heaped together. Professor Ramsay has given me the maximum thickness, from actual measurement in most cases, of the successive formation in *different* parts of Great Britain; and this is the result:—

	Feet
Palaeozoic strata (not including igneous beds)	57,154
Secondary strata	13,190
Tertiary strata	2,240

—making altogether 72,584 feet; that is, very nearly thirteen and three-quarters British miles. Some of the formations, which are represented in England by thin beds, are thousands of feet in thickness on the Continent. Moreover, between each successive formation, we have, in the opinion of most geologists, blank periods of enormous length. So that the lofty pile of sedimentary rocks in Britain gives but an inadequate idea of the time which has elapsed during their accumulation. The consideration of these various facts impresses the mind almost in the same manner as does the vain endeavour to grapple with the idea of eternity.

Nevertheless this impression is partly false. Mr. Croll, in an interesting paper, remarks that we do not err "in forming too great a conception of the length of geological periods," but in estimating them by years. When geologists look at large and complicated phenomena, and then at the figures representing several million years, the two produce a totally different effect on the mind, and the figures are at once pronounced too small. In regard to subaerial denudation, Mr. Croll shows, by calculating the known amount of sediment annually brought down by certain rivers, relatively to their areas of drainage, that 1000 feet of solid rock, as it became gradually disintegrated, would thus be removed from the mean level of the whole area in the course of six million years. This seems an astonishing result, and some considerations lead to the suspicion that it may be too large, but even if halved or quartered it is still very surprising. Few of us, however, know what a million really means: Mr. Croll gives the following illustration: take a narrow strip of paper, 83 feet 4 inches in length, and stretch it along the wall of a large hall; then mark off at one end the tenth of an inch. This tenth of an inch will represent one hundred years, and the entire strip a million years. But let it be borne in mind, in relation to the subject of this work, what a hundred years implies, represented as it is by a measure utterly insignificant in a hall of the above dimensions. Several eminent breeders, during a single lifetime, have so largely modified some of the higher animals which propagate their kind much more slowly than most of the lower animals, that they have formed what well deserves to be called a new sub-breed. Few men have attended with due care to any one strain for more than half a century, so that a hundred years represents the work of two breeders in succession. It is not to be supposed that species in a state of nature ever change so quickly as domestic animals under the guidance of methodical selection. The comparison would be in every way fairer with the effects which follow from unconscious selection, that is the preservation of the most useful or beautiful animals, with no intention of modifying the breed; but by this process of unconscious selection, various breeds have been sensibly changed in the course of two or three centuries.

Species, however, probably change much more slowly, and within the same country only a few change at the same time. This slowness follows from all the inhabitants of the same country being already so well adapted to each other, that new places in the polity of nature do not occur until after long intervals, due to the occurrence of physical changes of some kind, or through the immigration of new forms. Moreover variations or individual differences of the right nature, by which some of the inhabitants might be better fitted to their new places under the altered circumstances would not always occur at once. Unfortunately we have no means of determining, according to the standards of years, how long a period it takes to modify a species; but to the subject of time we must return.

Charles Darwin, *The Origin of Species.* New York: New American Library, 1958, pp. 289–93.

DOCUMENT 5: DARWIN'S VIEWS OF GOD'S ROLE IN THE CREATION

This letter, written by Darwin to American scientist Asa Gray on May 22, 1860, a few months after the publication of The Origin of Species, *is one of the few written pieces of evidence for Darwin's personal religious views. As he explains, though he does not credit the creation of new species directly to God, he does suspect that nature's laws, including the process of evolution itself, were originally designed by some kind of greater intelligence.*

MY DEAR GRAY,—Again I have to thank you for one of your very pleasant letters of May 7th, enclosing a very pleasant remittance of £22. I am in simple truth astonished at all the kind trouble you have taken for me. . . . I am not at all surprised at the [book's] sale diminishing; my extreme surprise is at the greatness of the sale. No doubt the public has been *shamefully* imposed on! for they bought the book thinking it would be nice easy reading. I expect the sale to stop soon in England, yet [Charles] Lyell wrote to me the other day that calling at Murray's he heard that fifty copies had gone in the previous forty-eight hours. . . .

With respect to the theological view of the question. This is always painful to me. I am bewildered. I had no intention to write atheistically. But I own that I cannot see as plainly as others do, and as I should wish to do, evidence of design and beneficence on all sides of us. There seems to me too much misery in the world. I cannot persuade myself that a beneficent and omnipotent God would have designedly created the Ichneumonidæ with the express intention of their feeding within the living bodies of caterpillars, or that a cat should play with mice. Not believing this, I see no necessity in the belief that the eye was expressly designed. On the other hand, I cannot anyhow be contented to view this wonderful universe, and especially the nature of man, and to conclude that everything is the result of brute force. I am inclined to look at everything as resulting from designed laws, with the details, whether good or bad, left to the working out of what we may call chance. Not that this notion *at all* satisfies me. I feel most deeply that the whole subject is too profound for the human intellect. A dog might as well speculate on the mind of Newton. Let each man hope and believe what he can. Certainly I agree with you that my views are not at all necessarily atheistical. The lightning kills a man, whether a good one or bad one, owing to the excessively complex action of natural laws. A child (who may turn out an idiot) is born by the action of even more complex laws, and I can see no reason why a man, or other animal, may not have been aboriginally produced by other laws, and that all these laws may have been expressly designed by an omniscient Creator, who foresaw every future event in consequence. But the more I think the more bewildered I become; as indeed I have probably shown by this letter.

Most deeply do I feel your generous kindness and interest.

Yours sincerely and cordially.

Autobiography and Selected Letters. Ed. Francis Darwin. New York: Dover Publications, 1958, pp. 248–49.

DOCUMENT 6: THE QUESTION OF HUMAN DESCENT

This is a small part of the concluding chapter of Darwin's Descent of Man, *in which he sums up his argument that humans developed from more primitive creatures. Note that he deals with intellectual and moral, as well as physical, advances brought about by or during evolution.*

A brief summary will be sufficient to recall to the reader's mind the more salient points in this work. Many of the views which have been advanced are highly speculative, and some no doubt will prove erroneous; but I have in every case given the reasons which have led me to one view rather than to another. It seemed worth while to try how far the principle of evolution would throw light on some of the more complex problems in the natural history of man. False facts are highly injurious to the progress of science, for they often endure long; but false views, if supported by some evidence, do little harm, for every one takes a salutary pleasure in proving their falseness: and when this is done, one path towards error is closed and the road to truth is often at the same time opened.

The main conclusion here arrived at, and now held by many naturalists who are well competent to form a sound judgment is that man is descended from some less highly organised form. The grounds upon which this conclusion rests will never be shaken, for the close similarity between man and the lower animals in embryonic development, as well as in innumerable points of structure and constitution, both of high and of the most trifling importance,—the rudiments which he retains, and the abnormal reversions to which he is occasionally liable,—are facts which cannot be disputed. They have long been known, but until recently they told us nothing with respect to the origin of man. Now when viewed by the light of our knowledge of the whole organic world, their meaning is unmistakable. The great principle of evolution stands up clear and firm, when these groups or facts are considered in connection with others, such as the mutual affinities of the members of the same group, their geographical distribution in past and present times, and their geological succession. It is incredible that all these facts should speak falsely. He who is not content to look, like a savage, at the phenomena of nature as disconnected, cannot any longer believe that man is the work of a separate act of creation. He will be forced to admit that the close resemblance of the embryo of man to that, for instance, of a dog—the construction of his skull, limbs and whole frame on the same plan with that of other mammals, independently of the uses to which the parts may be put—the occasional reappearance of various structures, for instance of several muscles, which man does not normally possess, but which are common to the Quadrumana—and a crowd of analogous facts—all point in the plainest manner to the conclusion that man is the co-descendant with other mammals of a common progenitor.

We have seen that man incessantly presents individual differences in all parts of his body and in his mental faculties. These differences or variations seem to be induced by the same general causes, and to obey the same laws as with the lower animals. In both cases similar laws of inheritance prevail. Man tends to increase at a greater rate than his means of subsistence; consequently he is occasionally subjected to a severe struggle for existence, and natural selection will have effected whatever lies within its scope. A succession of strongly-marked variations of a similar nature is by no means requisite; slight fluctuating differences in the individual suffice for the work of natural selection; not that we have any reason to suppose that in the same species, all parts of the organisation tend to vary to the same degree. We may feel assured that the inherited effects of the long—continued use or disuse of parts will have done much in the same direction with natural selection. Modifications formerly of importance, though no longer of any special use, are long-inherited. When one part is modified, other parts change through the principle of correlation, of which we have instances in many curious cases of correlated monstrosities. Something may be attributed to the direct and definite action of the surrounding conditions of life, such as abundant food, heat or moisture; and lastly, many characters of slight physiological importance, some indeed of considerable importance, have been gained through sexual selection.

No doubt man, as well as every other animal, presents structures, which seem to our limited knowledge, not to be now of any service to him, nor to have been so formerly, either for the general conditions of life, or in the relations of one sex to the other. Such structures cannot be accounted for by any form of selection, or by the inherited effects of the use and disuse of parts. We know, however, that many strange and strongly-marked peculiarities of structure occasionally appear in our domesticated productions, and if their unknown causes were to act more uniformly, they would probably become common to all the individuals of the species. We may hope hereafter to understand something about the causes of such occasional modifications, especially through the study of monstrosities: hence the labours of experimentalists such as those of M. Camille Dareste, are full of promise for the future. In general we can only say that the cause of each slight variation and of each monstrosity lies much more in the constitution of the organism, than in the nature of the surrounding conditions; though new and changed conditions certainly play an important part in exciting organic changes of many kinds.

Through the means just specified, aided perhaps by others as yet undiscovered, man has been raised to his present state. But since he attained to the rank of manhood, he has diverged into distinct races, or as they may be more fitly called, sub-species. Some of these, such as the Negro and European, are so distinct that, if specimens had been brought to a naturalist without any further information, they would undoubtedly have been considered by him as good and true species. Nevertheless all the races agree in so many unimportant details of structure and in so many mental peculiarities that these can be accounted for only by inheritance from a common progenitor; and a progenitor thus characterised would probably deserve to rank as man.

It must not be supposed that the divergence of each race from the other races, and of all from a common stock, can be traced back to any one pair of progenitors. On the contrary, at every stage in the process of modification, all the individuals which were in any way better fitted for their conditions of life, though in different degrees, would have survived in greater numbers than the less well-fitted. The process would have been like that followed by man, when he does not intentionally select particular individuals, but breeds from all the superior individuals, and neglects the inferior. He thus slowly but surely modifies his stock, and unconsciously forms a new strain. So with respect to modifications acquired independently of selection, and due to variations arising from the nature of the organism and the action of the surrounding conditions, or from changed habits of life, no single pair will have been modified much more than the other pairs inhabiting the same country, for all will have been continually blended through free intercrossing. . . .

The high standard of our intellectual powers and moral disposition is the greatest difficulty which presents itself, after we have been driven to this conclusion on the origin of man. But every one who admits the principle of evolution, must see that the mental powers of the higher animals, which are the same in kind with those of man, though so different in degree, are capable of advancement. Thus the interval between the mental powers of one of the higher apes and of a fish, or between those of an ant and scale-insect, is immense; yet their development does not offer any special difficulty; for with our domesticated animals, the mental faculties are certainly variable, and the variations are inherited. No one doubts that they are of the utmost importance to animals in a state of nature. Therefore the conditions are favourable for their development through natural selection. The same conclusion may be extended to man; the intellect must have been all-important to him, even at a very remote period, as enabling him to invent and use language, to make weapons, tools, traps, &c., Whereby with the aid of his social habits, he long ago became the most dominant of all living creatures. . . .

The development of the moral qualities is a more interesting problem. The foundation lies in the social instincts, including under this term the family ties. These instincts are highly complex, and in the case of the lower animals give special tendencies towards certain definite actions; but the more important elements are love, and the distinct emotion of sympathy. Animals endowed with the social instincts take pleasure in one another's company, warn one another of danger, defend and aid one another in many ways. These instincts do not extend to all the individuals of the species, but only to those of the same community. As they are highly beneficial to the species, they have in all probability been acquired through natural selection.

A moral being is one who is capable of reflecting on his past actions and their motives—of approving of some and disapproving of others; and the fact that man is the one being who certainly deserves this designation, is the greatest of all distinctions between him and the lower animals. But in the fourth chapter I have endeavoured to shew that the moral sense follows, firstly, from the enduring and ever-present nature of the social instincts; secondly, from man's appreciation of the approbation and disapprobation of his fellows; and thirdly, from the high activity of his mental faculties, with past impressions extremely vivid; and in these latter respects he differs from the lower animals. Owing to this condition of mind, man cannot avoid looking both backwards and forwards, and comparing past impressions. Hence after some temporary desire or passion has mastered his social instincts, he reflects and compares the now weakened impression of such past impulses with the ever-present social instincts; and he then feels that sense of dissatisfaction which all unsatisfied instincts leave behind them, he therefore resolves to act differently for the future,—and this is conscience. Any instinct, permanently stronger or more enduring than another, gives rise to a feeling which we express by saying that it ought to be obeyed. A pointer dog, if able to reflect on his past conduct, would say to himself, I ought (as indeed we say of him) to have pointed at that hare and not have yielded to the passing temptation of hunting it.

Social animals are impelled partly by a wish to aid the members of their community in a general manner, but more commonly to perform certain definite actions. Man is impelled by the same general wish to aid his fellows; but has few or no special instincts. He differs also from the lower animals in the power of expressing his desires by words, which thus become a guide to the aid required and bestowed. The motive to give aid is likewise much modified in man: it no longer consists solely of a blind instinctive impulse, but is much influenced by the praise or blame of his fellows. The appreciation and the bestowal of praise and blame both rest on sympathy; and this emotion, as we have seen, is one of the most important elements of the social instincts. Sympathy, though gained as an instinct, is also much strengthened by exercise or habit. As all men desire their own happiness, praise or blame is bestowed on actions and motives, according as they lead to this end; and as happiness is an essential part of the general good, the greatest-happiness principle indirectly serves as a nearly safe standard of right and wrong. As the reasoning powers advance and experience is gained, the remoter effects of certain lines of conduct on the character of the individual, and on the general good, are perceived; and then the self-regarding virtues come within the scope of public opinion, and receive praise, and their opposites blame. But with the less civilised nations, reason often errs, and many bad customs and base superstitions come within the same scope, and are then esteemed as high virtues, and their breach as heavy crimes.

Charles Darwin, *The Descent of Man.* New York: Random House, n.d., pp. 909–13.

DOCUMENT 7: DARWIN ON INSECT-EATING PLANTS

This brief excerpt from Darwin's 1875 work, Insectivorous Plants, *illustrates the kind of studies to which he devoted himself in his last few years—mostly close observations of plants, insects, and worms. It also demonstrates his meticulous attention to detail.*

On the Manner in which Insects are caught.—We will now consider the action of the leaves when insects happen to touch one of the sensitive filaments. This often occurred in my greenhouse, but I do not know whether insects are attracted in any special way by the leaves. They are caught in large numbers by the plant in its native country. As soon as a filament is touched, both lobes close with astonishing quickness; and as they stand at less than a right angle to each other, they have a good chance of catching any intruder. The angle between the blade and footstalk does not change when the lobes close. The chief seat of movement is near the midrib, but is not confined to this part; for, as the lobes come together, each curves inwards across its whole breadth; the marginal spikes however, not becoming curved. This movement of the whole lobe was well seen in a leaf to which a large fly had been given, and from which a large portion had been cut off the end of one lobe; so that the opposite lobe, meeting with no resistance in this part, went on curving inwards much beyond the medial line. The whole of the lobe, from which a portion had been cut, was afterwards removed, and the opposite lobe now curled completely over, passing through an angle of from 120° to 130°, so as to occupy a position almost at right angles to that which it would have held had the opposite lobe been present.

From the curving inwards of the two lobes, as they move towards each other, the straight marginal spikes intercross by their tips at first, and ultimately by their bases. The leaf is then completely shut and encloses a shallow cavity. If it has been made to shut merely by one of the sensitive filaments having been touched, or if it includes an object not yielding soluble nitrogenous matter, the two lobes retain their inwardly concave form until they re-expand. The re-expansion under these circumstances—that is when no organic matter is enclosed—was observed in ten cases. In all of these, the leaves re-expanded to about two-thirds of the full extent in 24 hrs. from the time of closure. Even the leaf from which a portion of one lobe had been cut off opened to a slight degree within this same time. In one case a leaf re-expanded to about two-thirds of the full extent in 7 hrs., and completely in 32 hrs.; but one of its filaments had been touched merely with a hair just enough to cause the leaf to close. Of these ten leaves only a few re-expanded completely in less than two days, and two or three required even a little longer time. Before, however, they fully re-expand, they are ready to close instantly if their sensitive filaments are touched. How many times a leaf is capable of shutting and opening if no animal matter is left enclosed, I do not know; but one leaf was made to close four times, re-opening afterwards, within six days. On the last occasion it caught a fly, and then remained closed for many days.

This power of reopening quickly after the filaments have been accidentally touched by blades of grass, or by objects blown on the leaf by the wind, as occasionally happens in its native place, must be of some importance to the plant; for as long as a leaf remains closed, it cannot of course capture an insect.

Charles Darwin, *Insectivorous Plants*. New York: D. Appleton, 1897.

Chronology

B.C.

CA.495–435

Life of the Greek thinker Empedocles, who proposes an early version of the theory of evolution, including the idea that better-adapted life forms tend to replace less perfect forms, which then die out.

A.D.

1745–1751

French natural philosopher Pierre Maupertuis proposes the most complete and plausible pre-Darwinian theory of evolution.

1776

Britain's American colonies declare their independence, giving birth to the United States of America.

1789

The French Revolution begins.

1794–1796

Darwin's grandfather, Erasmus Darwin, publishes *Zoonomia,* in which he outlines his own version of evolution.

1798

British economist Thomas Malthus publishes his *Essay on Population,* which will later inspire both Darwin and another naturalist, Alfred Russel Wallace, to conceive of the principle of natural selection.

1804

Napoleon proclaims himself emperor of France.

1809

French scientist Jean Baptiste Lamarck introduces his version of evolution; Charles Darwin is born on February 12 in

Shrewsbury, in western England.

1812–1815

The War of 1812 is fought between the United States and Britain.

1815

Napoleon is defeated at Waterloo and goes into exile.

1818

English writer Mary Shelley publishes her most famous novel, *Frankenstein;* Darwin's father enrolls him in a local school run by Dr. Samuel Butler.

1825

Darwin begins attending Edinburgh University.

1831

In January, Darwin receives a degree in theology from Cambridge University; in December, he sails on the vessel *Beagle,* bound for an around-the-world voyage of exploration.

1833

The British end slavery throughout their empire.

1836

Mexican leader Santa Anna defeats a force of Texans defending the Alamo, the first of several armed confrontations destined to lead to war between the United States and Mexico; the *Beagle,* bearing Darwin, returns to England.

1837

Princess Victoria ascends the British throne, marking the beginning of a long reign that will come to be called the Victorian Age in her honor; Darwin publishes a journal of his adventures and discoveries on the *Beagle*'s voyage, and the volume soon proves a professional and financial success.

1838

Darwin reads Malthus's population essay and begins formulating the theory of natural selection.

1839

Darwin marries Emma Wedgwood.

1840

Britain passes the Act of Union, uniting Upper and Lower Canada.

1842

The Darwins move into Down House, in the countryside not far from London.

1843

English novelist Charles Dickens publishes *A Christmas Carol.*

1844

Darwin writes a 230-page outline of his theory and shows it to his friend, the noted botanist Joseph Hooker; an anonymous work titled *Vestiges of the Natural History of Creation* draws the attention of naturalists and other scientists, most of whom reject its proposals about evolution; Darwin publishes *Geological Observations of the Volcanic Islands.*

1846

The Mexican-American War begins; Darwin publishes *Geological Observations of South America.*

1848

German philosophers Karl Marx and Fredrich Engels write the *Communist Manifesto.*

1856

Darwin begins writing his masterwork, *The Origin of Species.*

1859

The Origin of Species is completed and published.

1860

Hooker and noted biologist Thomas H. Huxley successfully defend Darwin and his theory in a heated debate on evolution held at the prestigious Oxford University.

1861

The American Civil War erupts; Czar Alexander II frees millions of Russian serfs.

1865

The American Civil War ends; U.S. president Abraham Lincoln is assassinated by John Wilkes Booth.

1867

Russia sells Alaska to the United States; Darwin begins work on *The Descent of Man.*

1870

The German state of Prussia invades France.

1871

A devastating fire destroys large sections of the American city of Chicago; *The Descent of Man* is published.

1875

Darwin publishes *Insectivorous Plants* and *The Movements and Habits of Climbing Plants.*

1876

American novelist Mark Twain publishes *Tom Sawyer.*

1881

U.S. president John Garfield is assassinated by a disgruntled office-seeker.

1882

Darwin dies at Down House on April 19, at age seventy-three.

FOR FURTHER RESEARCH

BOOKS AND OTHER WRITINGS BY CHARLES DARWIN

Autobiography, in *Autobiography and Selected Letters.* Ed. Francis Darwin. New York: Dover Publications, 1958; and *The Autobiography of Charles Darwin: With the Original Omissions Restored.* Ed. Nora Barlow. New York: Krause, 1969.

The Descent of Man. New York: Random House, n.d.

Early Notebooks. Transcribed by Paul H. Barrett, in Howard E. Gruber, *Darwin on Man.* New York: E.P. Dutton, 1974.

Insectivorous Plants. New York: D. Appleton, 1897.

Journal of Researches into Geology and Natural History of the Various Countries Visited by H.M.S. Beagle. New York: AMS Press, 1972.

Letters, in Francis Darwin, ed., *The Life and Letters of Charles Darwin.* 2 vols. New York: Basic Books, 1959.

The Origin of Species. New York: New American Library, 1958.

Red Notebook, in Sandra Herbert, ed., *The Red Notebook of Charles Darwin.* Ithaca: Cornell University Press, 1979.

The Variation of Animals and Plants Under Domestication. 2 vols. New York: AMS Press, 1972.

BIOGRAPHIES AND STUDIES OF DARWIN

John Bowlby, *Charles Darwin: A New Life.* New York: W.W. Norton, 1990.

Ronald W. Clark, *The Survival of Charles Darwin: A Biography of a Man and an Idea.* New York: Random House, 1984.

Adrian Desmond and James Moore, *Darwin.* New York: Warner Books, 1992.

R.B. Freeman, *Charles Darwin: A Companion.* Folkstone: Dawson, Anchor Books, 1978.

Leonard Huxley, *Charles Darwin.* London: Watts, 1921.

William Irvine, *Apes, Angels, & Victorians: The Story of Darwin, Huxley, and Evolution.* New York: McGraw-Hill, 1955.

Walter Karp, *Charles Darwin and the Origin of the Species.* New York: American Heritage, 1968.

Alan Moorehead, *Darwin and the Beagle.* New York: Harper and Row, 1969.

Don Nardo, *Charles Darwin.* New York: Chelsea House, 1993.

Gerhard Wichler, *Charles Darwin: The Founder of the Theory of Evolution and Natural Selection.* New York: Pergamon Press, 1961.

HISTORICAL STUDIES AND PERSPECTIVES OF THE ERA IN WHICH DARWIN LIVED

George Fasel, *Europe in Upheaval: The Revolutions of 1848.* Chicago: Rand McNally, 1970.

Christopher Hibbert, *Daily Life in Victorian England.* New York: American Heritage, 1975.

———, *The Story of England.* London: Phaidon, 1992.

Kenneth O. Morgan, ed., *The Oxford Illustrated History of Britain.* New York: Oxford University Press, 1986.

Harold Perkin, *The Origins of Modern English Society, 1780–1880.* London: Routledge and Kegan Paul, 1973.

Lytton Strachey, *Queen Victoria.* New York: Harcourt, Brace and Company, 1921.

J.L. Talmon, *Romanticism and Revolt: Europe 1815–1848.* New York: Harcourt, Brace and World, 1967.

Philip A.M. Taylor, ed., *The Industrial Revolution in Britain: Triumph or Disaster?* Boston: D.C. Heath, 1958.

G.M. Young, *Portrait of an Age: Victorian England.* London: Oxford University Press, 1973.

STUDIES OF AND BY DARWIN'S PREDECESSORS, ASSOCIATES AND CONTEMPORARY CRITICS

Edward B. Bailey, *James Hutton: The Founder of Modern Geology.* New York: Elsevier Publishing, 1967.

George Basalla, *Victorian Science.* Garden City, NY: Doubleday, 1970.

Cyril Bibby, *T.H. Huxley: Scientist, Humanist, and Educator.* New York: Horizon Press, 1960.

John L. Brooks, *Just Before the Origin: Alfred Russel Wallace's Theory of Evolution.* New York: Columbia University Press, 1984.

Erasmus Darwin, *Zoonomia: Or the Laws of Organic Life.* 2 vols. New York: AMS Press, 1974.

Bentley Glass et al., eds., *Forerunners of Darwin: 1745–1859.* Baltimore: Johns Hopkins University Press, 1968.

Leonard Huxley, *Life and Letters of Thomas Henry Huxley.* 2 vols. New York: D. Appleton, 1900.

L.J. Jordanova, *Lamarck.* New York: Oxford University Press, 1984.

Desmond King-Hele, *Erasmus Darwin.* New York: Scribner's, 1963.

Edward Lurie, *Louis Agassiz: A Life in Science.* Chicago: University of Chicago Press, 1960.

Charles Lyell, *Principles of Geology.* New York: Straechert-Hafner, 1970.

Nocolaas A. Rupke, *Richard Owen: Victorian Naturalist.* New Haven: Yale University Press, 1994.

William B. Turrill, *Joseph Dalton Hooker: Botanist, Explorer and Administrator.* London: Scientific Book Guild, 1963.

Alfred Russel Wallace, *Darwinism: An Exposition of the Theory of Natural Selection.* New York: AMS Press, 1975.

——, *The Geographical Distribution of Animals.* 2 vols. New York: Hafner, 1962.

A. Williams-Ellis, *Darwin's Moon: A Biography of Alfred Russel Wallace.* London: Blackie, 1966.

MODERN WORKS EXPLAINING, DISCUSSING, OR CRITICIZING DARWIN'S IDEAS

Isaac Asimov, *The Wellsprings of Life.* New York: Abelard-Schuman, 1960.

J. Behe, *Darwin's Black Box: The Biochemical Challenge to Evolution.* New York: Free Press, 1996.

L. Sprague de Camp and Catherine Crook de Camp, *Darwin and His Great Discovery*. New York: Macmillan, 1972.

Daniel C. Dennett, *Darwin's Dangerous Idea: Evolution and the Meanings of Life*. New York: Simon and Schuster, 1995.

Michael Denton, *Evolution: A Theory in Crisis*. Bethesda, MD: Adler and Adler, 1985.

Duane T. Gish, *Evolution: The Fossils Say No!* San Diego: Creation-Life Publishers, 1978.

Howard E. Gruber, *Darwin on Man: A Psychological Study of Scientific Creativity*. New York: E.P. Dutton, 1974.

Robert M. Hazen and James Trefil, *Science Matters: Achieving Scientific Literacy*. New York: Doubleday, 1991.

Gertrude Himmelfarb, *Darwin and the Darwinian Revolution*. New York: W.W. Norton, 1959.

David L. Hull, *Darwin and His Critics: The Reception of Darwin's Theory of Evolution by the Scientific Community*. Cambridge, MA: Harvard University Press, 1973.

Phillip E. Johnson, *Darwin On Trial*. Washington, D.C.: Regnery Gateway, 1991.

Tom McGowen, *The Great Monkey Trial: Science vs. Fundamentalism in America*. New York: Franklin Watts, 1990.

Norman D. Newell, *Creation and Evolution: Myth or Reality?* New York: Columbia University Press, 1982.

Chet Raymo, *Skeptics and True Believers: The Exhilarating Connection Between Science and Religion*. New York: Walker and Company 1998.

Evan Shute, *Flaws in the Theory of Evolution*. Philadelphia: Presbyterian and Reformed Publishing, 1961.

MODERN STUDIES OF EVOLUTION
AND RELATED BIOLOGICAL TOPICS

Isaac Asimov, *In the Beginning*. London: New English Library, 1981.

J.H. Bennett, *Natural Selection, Heredity and Eugenics*. Oxford: Oxford University Press, 1983.

J.D. Bernal, *The Origin of Life*. Cleveland: World Publishing, 1967.

Peter J. Bowler, *Evolution: The History of an Idea.* Berkeley: University of California Press, 1989.

Richard Dawkins, *The Blind Watchmaker: Why the Evidence of Evolution Reveals a Universe Without Design.* New York: W.W. Norton, 1987.

Theodore H. Eaton, Jr., *Evolution.* New York: W.W. Norton, 1970.

Sydney W. Fox and Klaus Dose, *Molecular Evolution and the Origin of Life.* San Francisco: W.H. Freeman, 1972.

Stephen J. Gould, *Ever Since Darwin: Reflections of Natural History.* New York: W.W. Norton, 1977.

———, *The Panda's Thumb: More Reflections on Natural History.* New York: W.W. Norton, 1982.

Desmond Morris, *The Naked Ape: A Zoologist's Study of the Human Animal.* New York: Dell, 1967.

Carl Sagan, *The Dragons of Eden: Speculations on the Evolution of Human Intelligence.* New York: Ballantine Books, 1977.

Carl Sagan and Ann Druyan, *Shadows of Forgotten Ancestors: A Search for Who We Are.* New York: Random House, 1992.

George Gaylord Simpson, *The Meaning of Evolution.* New York: New American Library, 1951.

Steven M. Stanley, *Earth and Life Through Time.* New York: W.H. Freeman, 1986.

Robert Wesson, *Beyond Natural Selection.* Cambridge, MA: MIT Press, 1991.

INDEX